FROMMER'S

COMPREHENSIVE TRAVEL GUIDE

PARIS '91-'92

by Darwin Porter
Assisted by Danforth Prince

PRENTICE
HALL
PRESS

NEW YORK • LONDON • TORONTO • SYDNEY • TOKYO • SINGAPORE

FROMMER BOOKS
Published by Prentice Hall Press
A division of Simon & Schuster Inc.
15 Columbus Circle
New York, NY 10023

ISBN 0-13-326927-2
ISSN 0899-3203

Manufactured in the United States of America

CONTENTS

MAPS

A Disclaimer

Although every effort was made to ensure the accuracy of the prices and travel information appearing in this book, readers are advised that prices fluctuate in the course of time and travel information changes under the impact of the varied and volatile factors that affect the travel industry. The author and publisher cannot be held responsible for the experiences of the reader while traveling. Readers are invited to write the publisher with ideas, comments, and suggestions for future editions.

ÇA, C'EST PARIS!

Paris has been celebrated in such a torrent of songs, poems, stories, books, paintings, and movies that for millions of people it is an abstraction rather than a city.

To French people living in the provinces, Paris is the center of the universe, the place where laws and careers are made and broken, a giant magnet that draws the essence out of the country, a bubbling test tube eternally distilling new and alien ideas.

To North American tourists, it is still "Gay Paree," the fairy-tale town inviting you for a fling, the hub of everything "European," and the epitome of that nebulous attribute known as "chic." It remains the metropolis of pleasure, the picture postcard of blooming chestnut trees and young couples kissing by the Seine.

Say "Paris" to just about anyone and you produce an instant image of sidewalk cafés and strolling lovers beneath the Eiffel Tower. Mention its inhabitants and you conjure up a vision that is part Catherine Deneuve, part Yves Montand, part Simone de Beauvoir, part Albert Camus, part Toulouse-Lautrec . . .

Some of these images may be very dated, some more fantasy than fact. And yet through all the clichés threads an eternal reality, that special aura of enchantment that neither technical progress nor commercialization has been able to dispel.

To Hemingway, Paris was "a moveable feast," the city to which "there is never any ending."

To me, Paris is the glamour capital of the globe, by day a stone mosaic of delicate gray and green, by night a stunning, unforgettable sea of lights—white, red, and orange.

Broad, tree-lined boulevards open up before you, the mansions flanking them looming tall, ornate, and graceful. Everywhere you look are trees, squares, and monuments. Perhaps you'll come in spring when the trees lining the Esplanade are white with blossoms. In summer they turn a deep, lush green; in fall, golden russet.

Whether you see it for the first or fiftieth time, the effect always has a curiously personal note . . . this is Paris, beckoning to *me*. And the "me" is all humankind.

The discovery of the city and making it your own is and has always been the most compelling reason for coming to Paris. So many have come, and so many continue to come, that France has been called *le deuxième pays de tout le monde*—"everyone's second country."

HISTORY

A Case of Predestination

Paris owes its position to a river, its status to a revolution, and its beauty to a tyrant.

More than 2,000 years ago, a tribe of Gauls called the Parisii built a village on the larger of two islands rising out of the broad and navigable Seine. They couldn't have picked a better site. The island provided a stepping-stone for the communication route that ran from the cold European north to the sunny Mediterranean.

The Roman conquerors of Gaul found the place ideal for a fortified town, surrounded as it was by a natural moat. This island, now **Ile de la Cité,** was the egg from which modern Paris was hatched.

Gradually, as the city grew more populous, it spilled over onto both banks of the Seine, spreading farther and farther inland. From the air, the expansion of Paris can be seen as clearly as the age rings of a tree trunk. With Ile de la Cité at the core—looking curiously like an anchored battleship—the mass of houses pushes outward in concentric circles, each ring representing a former boundary line overrun by the swelling metropolis.

Most cities become national capitals by accident. With Paris, it was predestination as soon as there was such a country as France. Standing at the meeting point of the Teutonic North and the Latin South, it was the logical seat of government for whichever faction would dominate the nation.

Nothing could alter its position as the first city of the land—not even 20 years of occupation by the English and their Burgundian allies, who held the area until driven out in 1437 by the army, spurred on by Joan of Arc.

Barricades and Boulevards

But until the thunderbolt year of 1789, Paris was no more than merely the brightest bauble in the crowns of its various monarchs, a piece of real estate to be trimmed or decorated as it pleased the royal whim.

Louis XIV, the "Sun King" and most absolute of all absolute monarchs, decided that he didn't like Paris, and he transferred his seat of government to Versailles. There he turned a hunting lodge into the most fabulous palace the world had ever seen, staffed it with 6,000 officials and servants, and left Paris as a capital in name only.

The city's revenge for this slight had to wait until the Revolution, and Louis XVI. One of the first acts of the Paris mob was to march out to Versailles, slaughter the Swiss palace guards, and drag the absentee king, and thus the government, *back* to Paris.

Today, you'll find few visible traces of the Revolution in Paris. The **Bastille** was totally leveled; the square that saw the "National Razor" shave off cartloads of heads is today the dazzling **place de la Concorde,** and the old **Hôtel de Ville,** from which Danton and Robespierre conducted the Terror, burned down more than 80 years ago.

But the spiritual heritage of the Revolution lingers on. It gives the city its jauntily independent swagger, its sardonic contempt for "provincials," the knowledge that its wishes are commands to the powers that be.

Which they are. Unlike, say, the administrations of Washington, D.C., every French government has had to cock a sharp ear to the murmurs of its capital. The stark fear of those terrible mobs and their barricades is unbroken to this day. Even the great Bonaparte never bothered to hide his concern about "What will Paris say?"

The Revolution gained Paris a power it never relinquished. All authority in France radiates from here; all roads lead here. Paris houses a quarter of all the nation's civil servants and more than a third of all university students.

It took a buffoonish demagogue, however, to bestow upon Paris the beauty that made it the envy of the civilized world. He was Napoléon III, nephew of the Corsican, who made himself first president, then emperor of France. Victor Hugo dubbed him "Napoleon the Little"—and had to spend years in exile for that crack.

The "other" Bonaparte may have been a terrible general and a dismal politician, but he had an inspired touch when it came to city planning. Together with Baron Haussmann, the prefect of Paris, he gave the capital the most lavishly magnificent facelift any municipality has ever received.

Between 1860 and 1870 the maze of winding cobblestone streets in the ancient quarters of the city were penetrated by superb boulevards—wide, rule-straight, flanked by palatial buildings and shaded by some 250,000 chestnut and plum trees. Their names became architectural legends: the **boulevards St-Michel, St-Germain, Haussmann, Malesherbes, Sébastopol, Magenta, Voltaire,** and **Strasbourg.**

Haussmann cleared Ile de la Cité of its medieval brickwork and stench and transformed it into a showcase for **Notre-Dame.** He created the **avenue de l'Opéra** (as well as the **Opéra**) and the 12 avenues that radiate star-like from the **Arc de Triomphe** and gave the square its name of **place de l'Etoile** (renamed **place Charles de Gaulle** following the general's death, although the change met with great resistance). Finally, he laid out the two elegant parks on the western and southeastern fringes of the city: **Bois de Boulogne** and **Bois de Vincennes.**

When Napoléon III, his face heavily rouged to hide the agony caused by bladder stones, rode into Prussian captivity in 1871, he left behind him a defeated nation and a shattered army. But he also bequeathed to it the most stunning capital on earth.

GETTING TO KNOW PARIS

The beauty of Paris is more than skin-deep; it goes in three layers right down to the city's bones. The first layer is thrust upon you immediately; the second permeates you slowly; the third you have to go out and discover.

The top layer consists of the spectacle presented by, for in-

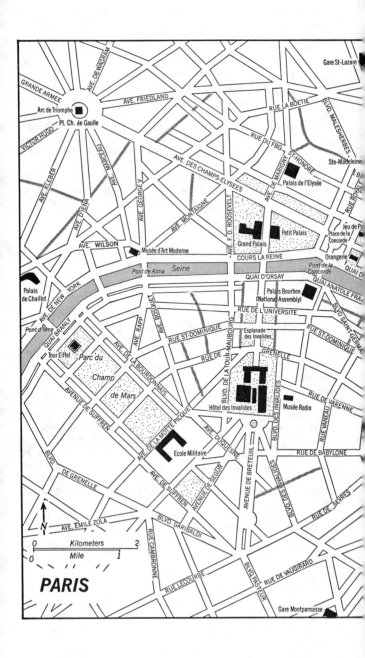

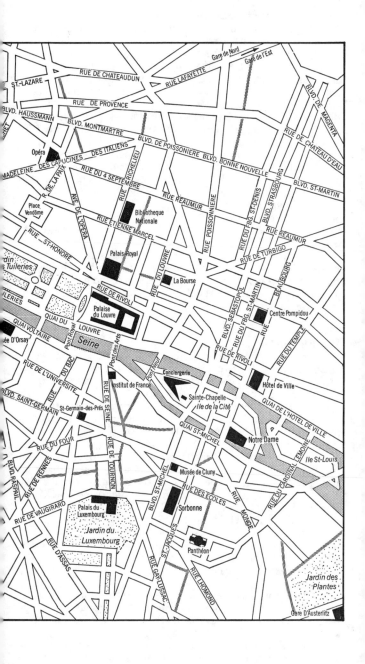

stance, the sweep of the **Champs-Elysées** at night, with the floodlit **Arc de Triomphe** in the distance, or the fountain-sprayed **Trocadéro** by the **Eiffel Tower.**

The second stage offers less flamboyance and more intimacy, like the old stone **Seine bridges** at twilight, or the dreamy quiet of **place des Vosges.** The mood prevails at any one of a hundred sidewalk cafés in the early afternoon, the sun throwing patterns on the tables through the lacework of overhead leaves.

The third layer—and perhaps the finest—is reserved for explorers, those who take time to nose through narrow alleys and poke into half-hidden courtyards or climb hills instead of riding up. A sudden glimpse so utterly enchanting that one is at a loss even to snap a picture. It may be a small Renaissance figure carved into a moss-covered church wall. Or a secret garden patch behind a Gothic archway. Or a totally unexpected view of the gleaming white dome of **Sacré-Coeur** high up on **Montmartre.** Or the jewel-box charm of the tiny, silent **place Fürstenberg,** with its four trees and single streetlight, just one step away from the bustle of **boulevard St-Germain.**

Only when you've penetrated this triple layer can you appreciate the gem that is Paris. But there's danger in this knowledge . . . you may find yourself hooked on the city for life and become one of the thousands of travelers who discover that they can't really be happy anywhere else.

The Parisians

If the more than two million or so Parisians share one characteristic, it is their big-city spirit, the somewhat aggressive, novelty-addicted, extremely cynical metropolitanism that makes "provincial" the worst insult in their dictionary.

Tolerance, gentleness, and patience are not their strongest points. They don't suffer fools gladly (although they adore eccentrics), and the gravest crime a public figure can commit in their eyes is to make himself ridiculous.

Their wit has been dreaded for centuries. It is totally lacking in cockney good humor or American folksiness, and can cut like a razor. A fairly typical sample would be the bon mot coined at the expense of a sadly disappointing prime minister named M. Marie. The Parisians promptly called him "The Immaculate Deception."

The Parisians' behavior pattern is produced by their environment. Paris, for all its matchless splendor, is a hard place in which to scramble for a living. Working hours are long, competition murderous, the traffic nerve-grinding, accommodations crowded and difficult to get, the pace hectic, and the cost of everything the highest in the country.

Add to this the generally low rates of pay, the mocking showcases of a thousand unattainable luxuries, and the jungle of red tape planted by an archaic bureaucracy, and you'll comprehend the reason for the Parisians' notorious astringency.

But this hard-boiled shell often protects a soft center. There is a startling contrast between the face Parisians show to passing strangers and their manner toward anyone with whom they share even the slightest personal rapport.

Compliment a surly bistro owner on his or her cuisine and—nine times out of ten—he or she will melt before your eyes. Admire a Parisian's car or dog and you'll find you have a loquaciously knowledgeable companion for the next five minutes. Ask about the correct pronunciation of a French word (before you mispronounce it), and you'll instantly have a language teacher.

For Parisians, some kind of personalized, individual contact seems necessary to display their best qualities: their famed charm, their savoir-faire, the delightful courtesy that marks their social life.

"Les Américains"

At 35 rue de Picpus, a few blocks from the place de la Nation, there is a spot over which the Stars and Stripes has flown for more than 150 years. It lies in a small secluded cemetery and marks the grave of the **Marquis de Lafayette**—the man who forged the chain during the American Revolution that has linked the two countries ever since.

It was here that Col. Charles E. Stanton (*not* General Pershing) uttered the famous words, *Lafayette, nous voilà!* ("Lafayette, we are here!") to announce the arrival of the Doughboys on the soil of America's hard-pressed old ally during World War I.

Politicans may blow hot and cold, but Paris remains studded with tokens of a deep friendship that hopefully will endure as long as this city stands. Our similar revolutions made for a strong common bond.

At **Pont de Grenelle,** at Passy, you'll find the original model of the Statue of Liberty, which France presented to the people of the United States. One of the most impressive paintings in the **Musée de l'Armée** shows the battle of Yorktown, which—however you learned it at school—was a combined Franco-American victory. And throughout the city, you'll keep coming across statues, monuments, streets, squares, and plaques commemorating George Washington, Benjamin Franklin, Presidents Wilson and Roosevelt, Generals Pershing and Eisenhower, and scores of lesser names that have carved themselves into the heart of France's capital.

Some of the carvings are invisible. They linger in the spirit of the Left Bank, the writers' and artists' quarter around **St-Germain-des-Prés.** The names are those of Ernest Hemingway and F. Scott Fitzgerald, of John Dos Passos and Gertrude Stein, of Mary McCarthy and Henry Miller . . . the legion of American literary greats who worked here and left their signatures indelibly printed on the very bricks of the district.

Nobody knows the exact number of Americans still living in Paris. Not quite as many as during the Roaring Twenties perhaps, but still thousands. You'll find them studying at the Sorbonne, playing in a string of jazz clubs, working in business offices, design centers, and art studios, lecturing to students, and—yes—still toiling away in Left Bank writers' garrets or their current equivalents, the no-star hotels.

An International City

The metropolis is so packed with minority groups that the true natives ironically refer to themselves as the "Parisians of Paris."

There are the Russians—descendants of the flood of White Russian refugees who poured into Paris after the Bolshevik Revolution—the Poles, English, Belgians, Italians, and Spaniards. Here, too, are vast colonies of Vietnamese, Algerians, Moroccans, Lebanese, and West Africans, all of them mingling with less friction than anyone who's ever heard a UN debate would have believed possible.

The Parisians have always been "color-blind," in the best meaning of the term. Whatever their prejudices and quirks—and they have plenty—the hue of a person's skin or the shape of his or her eyes has never struck them as being of any consequence.

In return, they have gained a city that is free of ghettos and their poisons, where you can stroll anywhere, anytime, without feeling displaced. This is a city that can absorb every alien current without losing its identity.

II

PARIS FAST FACTS

Before you check into your hotel, you've got to reach it, and therefore coping with the Parisian transport system suddenly becomes all-important if the capital is your gateway. Of course, people walk and search in Paris, but chances are you'll need a more practical method of transport than your feet.

The concierge of your hotel, incidentally, is a usually reliable dispenser of information, offering advice about everything. If he or she fails you, the following summary of pertinent survival facts may prove useful.

AIRPORTS: Chances are, you'll land at one of the two major international airports: Orly, 8½ miles from Paris, or Charles de Gaulle, 14¼ miles from the city.

At **Charles de Gaulle Airport** (tel. 47-58-20-18 for transportation information, 48-62-12-12 for flight information), there are two terminals—Aérogare 1 for foreign carriers and Aérogare 2 for Air France. From Aérogare 1, you take a moving walkway to the passport checkpoint and the Customs area. Both terminals are linked by a shuttle bus *(navette)*.

A taxi, of course, is the most luxurious and expensive way to go from the airport into the city center. Depending on traffic, fares range from 150F ($22.65) to 200F ($30.20). At night (from 8pm to 7am), fares more than double in price.

The shuttle bus connecting Aérogare 1 with Aérogare 2 also transports passengers to the Roissy rail station and a direct RER train. The RER leaves every 15 minutes on a high-speed run to such Métro stations as Gare du Nord, Châtelet, Luxembourg, Port-Royal, and Denfert-Rochereau. A typical fare—say, from Roissy to Porte-Maillot Métro station—is 36F ($5.45). You can also take an Air France shuttle bus. A ride to the Arc de Triomphe is 38F ($5.75) and, depending on traffic, usually takes less than 45 minutes.

Returning to Charles de Gaulle Airport, Air France buses leave for Aérogare 1 every 20 minutes, for Aérogare 2 every 15 minutes. You board at the bus terminal in the basement of the Palais des Congrès at Porte Maillot. The trip normally takes about 30 minutes, but during rush hours it's advisable to allow another half hour.

Orly Airport (tel. 45-50-32-30 for transportation information, 48-67-12-34 for flight information) also has two terminals—Orly Sud (South) and Orly Ouest (West)—that are linked by a shuttle bus. Air France buses leave the de Gaulle airport for the Orly terminals and return every half hour. The ride takes 50 to 75 minutes. At Orly, board this bus at exit B.

Orly's west terminal is for domestic flights; all others use Orly Sud, where passport and Customs checkpoints are on the first floor. Air France buses leave Orly Sud every 12 minutes from exit I, heading for Gare des Invalides. At exit D, you can board bus 215 for place Denfert-Rochereau in the south of Paris. Don't take a freelance taxi from Orly Sud. It's much safer and surer to get a metered cab from the line, which is under the scrutiny of a policeman.

A taxi from Orly to the center of Paris costs about 130F ($19.65), even more at night. A trip from Orly to, say, l'Opéra will take about 45 minutes.

A shuttle bus leaves Orly about every quarter of an hour, heading for the RER rail terminus, Pont-de-Rungis/Aéroport-d'Orly. There you can catch an RER train for the 30-minute trip into the center of Paris. An RER trip to Invalides, for example, costs 29F ($4.35).

To return to Orly Airport, you can get an Air France bus at the Invalides terminal to either Orly Sud or Orly Ouest every 15 minutes, for about a 30-minute run.

AMERICAN EXPRESS: For many a pipeline or lifeline to the United States, these offices are at 11 rue Scribe, 9e (tel. 42-66-09-99), which is close to the Opéra (also the Métro stop). Hours are 9am to 5pm Monday through Friday. The bank window is open on Saturday from 9am to 5pm, but you can't pick up mail until Monday.

BABYSITTERS: There are several agencies you can call. It might be a good idea to verify that the sitter and your child speak the same language before you commit yourself. **Institut Catholique,** 21 rue d'Assas, 6e (tel. 45-48-31-70), runs a service from among its students. The price is 26F ($3.90) an hour. The main office is open from 9am to noon and 2 to 6pm Monday to Saturday only.

BANKS: The above-mentioned **American Express** may be able to service most of your banking needs. If not, most banks in Paris are open from 9am to 4:30pm Monday through Friday. A few are open on Saturday. Ask at your hotel for the location of the bank nearest to you. Shops and most hotels will cash your traveler's checks, but not at the advantageous rate a bank or foreign exchange office will give you. So make sure you've allowed enough funds for *le weekend.*

BUSINESS HOURS: In general, these are Monday to Saturday from 9am to 6pm, with a long time-out for lunch. (Some shops are closed on Saturday, others may take Monday off.)

CIGARETTES: Bring in as many as Customs will allow if you're addicted to a particular brand, as American cigarettes are very expensive in France. A possible solution is to learn to smoke French cigarettes. Don't expect them to taste anything like your familiar brand, but you may acquire a liking for the exotic. One of the most popular French cigarettes is called Gauloise Bleu.

CLIMATE: Paris has an uncommonly long springtime, lasting through April, May, and June, and an equally extended fall, from September through November. The climate is temperate throughout the year, without those extremes so common in New York and Chicago. The coldest months are December and January, when the average high reaches 42°F. There's occasional snow during these months. The warmest months are July and August, when the daily averages range between 55° and 76°F. Sunshine is plentiful in summer; rainfall is moderate but heavier in winter.

CONSULATES AND EMBASSIES: If you lose a passport or have some such emergency, the consulate or embassy will usually handle your individual needs. Hours and offices of the various foreign consulates and embassies are as follows:

United States: 2 av. Gabriel, 75008 Paris (tel. 42-96-12-02), open Monday to Friday from 9am to 4pm. Passports are issued at its annex at 2 rue St-Florentin (tel. 42-96-12-02, ext. 2613), which lies off the northeast section of the place de la Concorde. To get a passport replaced costs about $42. Métro: Concorde.

Canada: 35 av. Montaigne, 75008 Paris (tel. 47-23-01-01), open Monday to Friday from 9 to 11:30am and 2 to 4pm. The Canadian Consulate is around the corner at 16 rue d'Anjou (same phone). New passports are issued at the latter address. Métro: F. D. Roosevelt or Alma-Marceau.

Great Britain: 35 rue du Faubourg St-Honoré, 75008 Paris (tel. 42-96-12-02), open from 9:30am to 1pm and 2:30 to 5:30pm. Métro: Concorde or Madeleine.

Australia: 4 rue Jean-Rey, 75015 Paris (tel. 40-59-33-00), open Monday to Friday from 9:15am to 12:15pm and 2 to 4:30pm. Métro: Bir-Hakeim.

New Zealand: 7 bis rue Léonard-de-Vinci, 75016 Paris (tel. 45-00-24-11), open Monday to Friday from 9am to 1pm and 2:30 to 6pm. Métro: Victor-Hugo.

CURRENCY: See Chapter III, "Getting to Know Paris," for details on the French franc.

CUSTOMS: As a general rule, people arriving in France via airports stand less chance of being inspected than those arriving by train or automobile. In any case, a visitor more than 15 years of age coming from a non-European country may import duty free 200 cigarettes or 50 cigars. You are allowed two liter bottles of wine and one of alcoholic spirits. In addition, you may bring in two still cameras of different makes with ten rolls of film for each, plus a motion-picture camera with ten reels of film. Aside from hunting guns, the government strictly forbids the importation of guns and ammunition.

DENTISTS: If a toothache strikes you at night or in the early hours of the morning (and doesn't it always?), telephone 43-37-51-00 anytime between 8pm and 8am Monday through Friday. On Saturday, Sunday, and holidays, you can call this number day or night. You can also call on the **American Hospital,** 63 bd. Victor-Hugo, Neuilly (tel. 46-41-25-25). A bilingual (English-French) dental clinic is on the premises, open 24 hours a day. Métro: Pont de Levallois or Pont de Neuilly.

DOCTORS: Some large hotels have a doctor attached to their staff. If yours doesn't, I'd recommend the **American Hospital,** 63 bd. Victor-Hugo, Neuilly (tel. 46-41-25-25). An emergency service is open 24 hours daily, including 43 outpatient or inpatient specialties housed under one roof. Métro: Pont de Levallois or Pont de Neuilly.

DOCUMENTS REQUIRED: In recent years Americans and Canadians traveling to France were required to obtain a visa in advance. However, since July 1989 only special groups, such as journalists on assignment and students enrolling in French schools, must still obtain visas. For tourism or business visits of less than 90 days, all you need now is a valid passport.

With today's ever-changing political climate, it's always a good idea to confirm the situation. Contact the **French Embassy** (4101 Reservoir Rd. NW, Washington, DC 20007; tel. 202/944-6000), or the **French Consulate** (935 Fifth Ave., New York, NY 10021; tel. 212/606-3653).

DRUGSTORES: If you need one during off-hours, have your concierge get in touch with the nearest Commissariat de Police. An agent there will have the address of a nearby pharmacy open 24 hours a day. French law requires that the pharmacies in any given neighborhood designate which one will remain open all night. The address of the one that will stay open for that particular week will be prominently displayed in the windows of all other drugstores.

One of the most centrally located all-night pharmacies is **Pharmacy Dhéry,** 84 av. des Champs-Elysées, 8e (tel. 45-62-02-41). Métro: George-V.

ELECTRICAL APPLIANCES: In the main, expect 200 volts, 50 cycles, although you'll encounter 110 and 115 volts in some older establishments. Adapters are needed to fit sockets. Many hotels have two-pin (in some cases, three-pin) sockets for electric razors. It's best to ask at your hotel before plugging in any electrical appliance.

EMERGENCY: If you need an ambulance on an SOS call, there are several things you can do. Many hotels rely on the Paris fire department, which rushes cases to the nearest emergency room. Its number is 45-78-74-52. An independently operated, privately owned ambulance company is S.A.M.U. (tel. 45-67-50-50). Otherwise, a roving band of vehicle-borne doctors, each with a car-radio connection, can be contacted at S.O.S. Médecin (tel. 47-07-77-77).

You can reach the police at 9 bd. du Palais, 4e (tel. 42-60-33-22). Métro: Cité. In an emergency, call 17. To report a fire, dial 18.

HOLIDAYS: In France, they are known as *jours fériés*. Shops and banks are closed, as well as many (but not all) restaurants and museums. Major holidays include January 1, Easter Sunday, Ascension Day (40 days after Easter), Pentecost (seventh Sunday after Easter), May 1, May 8 (V-E Day in Europe), July 14 (Bastille Day), August 15 (Assumption of the Virgin Mary), November 1 (All Saints' Day), November 11 (Armistice Day), and December 25 (Christmas).

INFORMATION: You can get in touch with the **official tourist office** in Paris at 127 av. des Champs-Elysées, 72008 Paris (tel. 47-23-61-72). Hours are daily 9am to 8pm in summer and daily 9am to 6pm in winter. Métro: Charles de Gaulle (Etoile).

Before leaving for Paris, you can gather information at the **French Tourist Office,** 628 Fifth Ave., New York, NY 10020; 645 N. Michigan Ave., Chicago, IL 60601; 9401 Wilshire Blvd., Beverly Hills, CA 90212; and Suite 500, 1 Hallidie Plaza, San Francisco, CA 94102. To request brochures or travel information via telephone, call the "France on Call" hotline (tel. 900/420-2003; 50¢ per minute).

LANGUAGE: In the wake of two World Wars and many shared experiences, not to mention the influence of English movies, TV, and records, the English language has made major inroads. It is almost a second language in some parts of Paris. An American trying to speak French might even be understood.

LAUNDRY: Many hotels provide this service, and if they do, it's likely to be expensive. To cut costs, I recommend that you search the Paris phone directory for a *laverie automatique* and find one near your hotel. Watch out for Sunday and Monday closings.

LIQUOR: One of the joys of visiting Paris is to savor French champagnes, brandies, and wines. They have no equal in the world, in my opinion. The national beverage is wine, and it's consumed at every meal except breakfast (and sometimes even then). Scotch whisky is so very expensive that I recommend that while in France you avoid imports and stick to the local products.

MAIL: Post offices abound in Paris, as many as three or four per arrondissement. Some offices remain open late, including those in railway stations. Otherwise, regular hours Monday through Friday are 8am to 7pm, 8am to noon on Saturday. The central post office, Paris Louvre RP, 52 rue du Louvre, 75001 Paris (tel. 40-28-20-00; Métro: Louvre), is open daily 24 hours.

Stamps can be purchased not only at post offices, but also at your hotel reception desk (usually) and at *café-tabacs* (tobacconists). At present, it costs 4.25F (65¢) to send an airmail letter to the United States, providing it doesn't weigh more than five grams. Mail sent to Paris *poste restante*—that is, General Delivery—can be picked up here, but only if you have your passport.

NEWSPAPERS: English-language newspapers are available at nearly every kiosk (newsstand) in Paris. Published Monday through Saturday, the *International Herald-Tribune* is the most popular paper read by visiting Americans and Canadians. Kiosks are generally open daily from 8am to 9pm.

PETS: If you have certificates from a vet and proof of antirabies vaccination, you can bring most house pets into France.

POLITICS: France, as everybody knows, is a republic. Its Parliament, chosen through free elections, consists of the National Assembly and the Senate. An average visitor can tour in all parts of the country without any government interference if he or she doesn't run afoul of the law.

RAILROAD INFORMATION: Paris is served by seven principal rail stations. The average tourist will pass through **Gare des Invalides,** where trains depart for Orly Airport, or **Gare du Nord,** where trains leave not only for Charles de Gaulle Airport but for points in the north of the country as well as Holland and Belgium. Trains for the northwest leave from **Gare St-Lazare;** for the west, from **Gare Montparnasse;** for eastern France and Germany, from **Gare de l'Est;** and for the southwest (the Pyrenées) from **Gare d'Austerlitz.** For general information about departures, call 45-82-50-50.

RELIGIOUS SERVICES: France is a Roman Catholic country, and churches of this denomination are found in every city and hamlet of the land. In addition, many churches in Paris conduct services in English. The **American Church,** 65 quai d'Orsay, 7e (tel. 47-05-07-99; Métro: Invalides), is nondenominational. The **First Church of Christ Scientist** is at 36 bd. St-Jacques, 14e (tel. 47-07-26-60; Métro: Glacière); **Second Church of Christ Scientist,** 58 bd. Flandrin, 16e (tel. 45-04-37-74; Métro: Dauphine); and the **Third Church of Christ Scientist,** 45 rue La Boétie, 8e (tel. 45-62-19-85;

Métro: St-Augustin). The **Great Synagogue** is at 44 rue de la Victoire, 9e (tel. 42-85-71-09; Métro: La Peletier). A Roman Catholic church where English is spoken is **St. Joseph's,** 50 av. Hoche, 8e (tel. 45-63-21-61; Métro: Charles de Gaulle). Another similar Catholic church is **Mission Anglophone,** 22 rue Claude-Lorrain, 16e (tel. 45-27-05-09; Métro: Exelmans).

REST ROOMS: Those French in dire need duck into a café or brasserie, as these can be found on almost every city block in Paris. It's customary to make a small purchase. Métro stations and underground garages usually contain public bathrooms, but cleanliness varies.

SAFETY: Whenever you're traveling in an unfamiliar city or country, stay alert. Be aware of your immediate surroundings. Wear a moneybelt and don't sling your camera or purse over your shoulder; wear the strap diagonally across your body. This will minimize the possibility of your becoming a victim of a crime. Every society has its criminals. It's your responsibility to be aware and alert even in the most heavily touristed areas.

Be aware of child pickpockets. They roam the French capital, preying on tourists around sights such as the Louvre, Eiffel Tower, and Notre-Dame, and they especially like to pick your pockets in the Métro, sometimes blocking you off the escalator. A band of these young thieves can clean your pockets even while you try to fend them off. Their method is to get very close to a target, ask for a handout (sometimes), and deftly help themselves to your money, passport, whatever.

TAXES: Watch it: you could get burned. As a member of the European Common Market, France routinely imposes a value-added tax **(VAT)** on many goods and services—currently 18.6%. However, for so-called luxury items—and these range from caviar to motorcycles—the tax is 33.3%.

TELEGRAMS: Telegrams may be sent from any Paris post office during the day (see "Mail," above) and anytime during the day or night at a 24-hour post office. In telegrams to the United States, the address is counted. There is no special rate for a certain number of words. There are, however, night telegrams sent during the slack hours that cost less. If you're in Paris and wish to send a telegram in English, dial 42-33-21-11.

TELEPHONE/TELEX: No longer an international joke, the French telephone system has been vastly upgraded in recent years. Public phone booths are found in cafés, restaurants, Métro stations, post offices, airports, train stations, and, occasionally, on the streets. Some of these booths work with tokens called *jetons,* which can be purchased at the post office or at any café from the cashier. (It's customary to give a small tip if you buy them at a café.) Phone booths accept coins of 50 centimes, 1F, and 5F. Generally, you pick up the receiver and insert the *jeton,* then dial when you hear the tone, pushing the button when there is an answer. On modernized public phones that take coins instead of slugs it's possible to make long-distance calls, including transatlantic ones. The French also use a *télécarte,* a telephone debit card, which can be purchased at rail stations, post offices, and other places. Sold in two versions, it allows callers to use from 50 to 120 charge units by inserting the card in a phone. They cost 40F ($6.05) and 96F ($14.50), respectively.

If possible, avoid making calls from your hotel, as some French establishments double or triple the charges on you. When you're calling long distance within France (say, to Versailles), dial 16, wait for the dial tone, and then dial the eight numbers of the person you are calling. To call the United States, first dial 19, then after the tone, dial 1 (the same for Canada), then slowly dial the area code and the seven-digit number. Calls to the United States and Canada can be made fairly rapidly, depending on the time of day and period of the year.

For information dial 12.

If you want to send a **telex,** chances are that your hotel will send one for you.

TIME: French summer time lasts from around April to September, and runs one hour ahead of French winter time. Depending on the time of year, France is six or seven hours ahead of Eastern Standard Time in the United States.

TIPPING: This is practiced with flourish and style in France, and, as a visitor, you're expected to play the game. All bills, as required by law, show *service compris,* which means the tip is included.

Waiters: In restaurants, cafés, and nightclubs, service is included. However, it is the custom to leave something extra, especially in first-class and deluxe establishments, where 10% to 12% extra is often the rule. In inexpensive places, 8% to 10% will suffice.

Porters: Usually a fixed fee is assessed, about 5F (75¢) to 10F ($1.50) per piece of luggage. You're not obligated to give more; however, many French people do, ranging from 50 centimes (10¢) to 2F (30¢).

Theater ushers: Give at least 2F (30¢) for seating up to two persons.

Hairdressers: The service charge is most often included; otherwise, tip at least 15%, more in swankier places.

Guides: In museums, guides expect 5F (75¢) to 10F ($1.50).

Cloakroom attendants: Often the price is posted; if not, give at least 2F (30¢) to 5F (75¢).

Hotels: The service charge is added, but tip the bellboy extra—from 6F (90¢) to 20F ($3) for three bags (more in deluxe and first-class hotels). A lot depends on how much luggage he has carried and the class of the establishment. Tip the concierge based entirely on how many requests you've made of him or her. Give the maid about 20F ($3) if you've stayed for three or more days. The doorman who summons a cab expects another 5F (75¢), likewise your room-service waiter, even though you've already been hit for 15% service. Incidentally, most small services around the hotel should be rewarded with a 5F (75¢) tip.

III

GETTING TO KNOW PARIS

1. ORIENTATION
2. GETTING AROUND

Paris isn't such a big city—as world population centers go. It occupies 432 square miles of land—only six more than the "Paris of the West," San Francisco. It's far more populous, containing some 2 million people in the city itself, 8½ million including the environs. But it's compact, and the majority of tourist attractions are so concentrated that it's a sheer joy to navigate.

The city is bisected by the wide arc of the **Seine.** The northern part is called the **Right Bank** (*Rive Droite*), and the southern part the **Left Bank** (*Rive Gauche*). The unusual designations make sense when you stand on a bridge facing downstream and watch the waters flow out toward the sea—to your right is the north bank; the south is on your left.

Thirty-two bridges link the Right and Left banks—as well as the two small islands at the center of the Seine, the **Ile de la Cité,** out of which contemporary Paris grew, site of the imposing Notre-Dame, and the **Ile Saint-Louis,** a moat-guarded oasis of sober 17th-century mansions. These islands can cause some confusion to walkers who think they've just crossed a bridge from one bank to the other, only to find themselves caught up in an almost medieval maze of old buildings and courtyard greenery.

The best way to orient yourself to Paris is to climb to a high point on a clear day and simply look around. The best places for this: either the **Eiffel Tower** or the **Arc de Triomphe.** From the top of the Eiffel Tower, you can see all of Paris in one giant sweep. The view from the Arc de Triomphe is more detailed. From the place de l'Etoile (renamed place Charles de Gaulle) beneath you 12 avenues radiate, sweeping majestically across the minor city streets, like giant wheel spokes; you see the place de la Concorde down the Champs-

Elysées, the green lawns of the Bois de Boulogne, the stately white buildings of the Palais de Chaillot, and the honky-tonk joints of Pigalle. The city crowds around, condensed and intimate like a scale model, and you feel you could reach out and pick up a bridge to examine it or pluck some sugar off the birthday-cake peaks of Sacré-Coeur.

After taking in the overall view, take a boat ride up the Seine (for details, see Chapter VI, "What to See and Do in Paris"). Choose a sunny day when the breeze is warm and you can sit outside on deck. Tune out the gabble around you and the recorded guide in four languages. Specific buildings aren't the point—and anyway you can hardly mistake the luminous towers of Notre-Dame. Sit and absorb Paris, letting its sights and sounds seep into you.

You'll see the shadowy quay where Voltaire worked and died. Gargoyles will gape down at you with the irritability of old age. Golden horses will take flight overhead from the stanchions of Pont Alexandre III. Barge women will be exchanging confidences over family clotheslines. Students—curled up in puppy clusters on the banks—will tease your boatload as it glides past, with hoots and guitar fanfares. Not all these, of course, are remarkable sights, but each is an essential piece of the Parisian landscape.

---

1. Orientation

CITY LAYOUT

The city is divided into 20 municipal wards called "arrondissements," each with its own mayor, city hall, police station, and central post office. Some even have remnants of market squares left over from those independent days before the city burst its boundaries and engulfed the surrounding towns. Most city maps are outlined by arrondissement, and all addresses include the arrondissement number (written in Roman or Arabic numerals and followed by "e" or "er"). Paris also has its own version of a zip code. And thus the proper mailing address for a hotel is written as, say, 75014 Paris. The last two numbers, 14, indicate that the address is in the Fourteenth Arrondissement, in this case, Montparnasse.

Not all arrondissements concern the visitor—"tourist" Paris is only a minute proportion of the city as a whole—but a passing acquaintance with the more relevant districts can help you get your bearings.

When people speak of the Right Bank, they are usually referring to that traditionally monied area on the north side of the Seine comprising the **First, Second,** and **Eighth** arrondissements. Here are houses of fashion, the Stock Exchange, luxury trades such as the perfume industry, the most elegant hotels, expensive restaurants, smartest shops, and the most fashionably attired women and men. Along the river, in the First, are the classically precise Tuileries Gardens and the Louvre. The Second is a business district, with many offices and shops, and together with the Ninth forms the Opéra quarter. The Eighth includes the vast showplace of the Champs-Elysées, linking the mighty Arc de Triomphe with the delicate Obélisque on the place de la Concorde.

The **Third** Arrondissement embraces one of the most historic and increasingly fashionable districts of Paris, the Marais, with architectural interest centering around its old mansions and the place des Vosges, called the Palais Royal in the days of Henri IV. Its main attraction today is the Picasso Museum.

The **Fourth** Arrondissement encompasses both small islands in the Seine. Cross the river to the south and you reach the **Fifth** Arrondissement and next to it, the **Sixth,** what people mean when they speak of the Left Bank—that part of the city dedicated to art and scholarship. The Fifth is the Latin Quarter, center of Paris University and site of the Sorbonne. Students, cafés, and cheap restaurants abound. The adjoining Sixth, heartland of the publishing industry, is the most colorful quarter of the city, an exciting, Greenwich Village–like area, where the School of Fine Arts sends out waves of earnest would-be artists. This is also the finest area for finding a good budget-priced hotel or meal.

Neighboring the Seine is the **Seventh** Arrondissement, which is primarily smart and residential, with embassies and government ministries operating out of what once were the fabulous mansions of French aristocracy. At the western river edge stands the Eiffel Tower. In the center is Napoleon's Tomb and the Invalides Army Museum (beside this is the city air terminal).

Look at a city map and you will see that these arrondissements, One to Eight, form a circular core in the center of the city. Other districts have their attractions, of course. The famed **Sixteenth,** which shades out from the Seine to the vast park of the Bois de Boulogne, has the classiest living quarters, as well as the museums in the Palais de Chaillot. The part of the **Seventeenth** closest to l'Etoile is equally smart and riddled with executive-priced apartments. The delightful hill of Montmartre, crowned by Sacré-Coeur, is in the **Eighteenth.** But you could easily confine yourself to that magic inner circle and take in almost everything you came to Paris to see.

If you are staying more than two or three days, consider investing in one of the inexpensive pocket-size books that include the *plan de Paris* by arrondissements, available at all major newsstands and bookstores. Most of these guides provide you with a Métro map, a fold-out map of the city, and indexed maps of each arrondissement, with all the streets listed and keyed.

WHEN TO COME

April in Paris is as magical as promised. Autumn is even better. In August, Parisians traditionally evacuate for their annual holiday and put the city on a skeleton staff to serve visitors. Now, too, July has become a popular vacation month, with many a restaurateur shuttering up for a month-long respite.

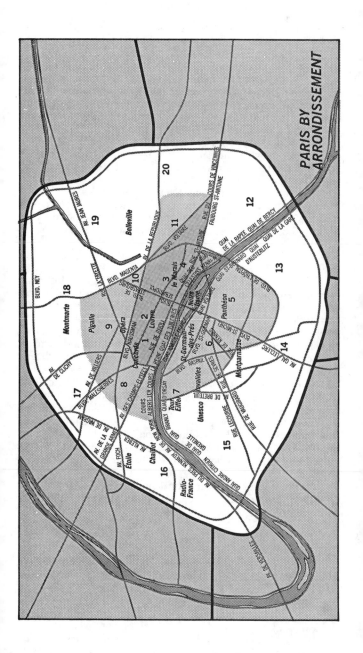

PARIS BY ARRONDISSEMENT

Paris's Average Daytime Temperature and Rainfall

	Jan	Feb	Mar	Apr	May	June	July	Aug	Sept	Oct	Nov	Dec
Temp °F	38	39	46	51	58	64	66	66	61	53	45	40
Rainfall "	3.2	2.9	2.4	2.7	3.2	3.5	3.3	3.7	3.3	3.0	3.5	3.1

From May through September, the city is swamped with tourists, and you must write well in advance for hotel reservations. Avoid the first two weeks in October, when the annual motor show draws thousands of boy-at-heart enthusiasts.

The best time to come to Paris is off-season, in the early spring or late autumn, when the tourist trade has trickled to a manageable flow and everything is easier to come by—hotel rooms, Métro seats, even good-tempered waiters.

Paris has an uncommonly long springtime, lasting through April, May, and June, and an equally extended fall, from September through November. The climate is temperate throughout the year, without those extremes so common to New York and Chicago.

WHAT TO WEAR

Parisians are both stylish *and* conservative. Big-city clothes are in order here, the kind of thing you might wear to visit San Francisco or when walking along Fifth Avenue in New York. If it suits Miami Beach or Malibu, it won't look good on the rue de Rivoli. Men will feel at ease in suits or sports jackets of a weight appropriate to the season. Women will fit in wearing suits, skirts and sweaters, simple dresses, and good pants. Unlike the British, the French tend to dress down rather than up. But always with style. Parisian women go to work, restaurants, or the theater wearing beautifully cut and tailored pants suits. You can follow their lead; you won't be turned away at the door by some disapproving manager. While ties for men are advisable in the poshest places, they are seldom required in more moderate restaurants. Even churches don't insist that women wear head coverings, although that, of course, is your option. The only special precaution is a travel umbrella to take with you on your rounds.

Not that you can't wear your designer jeans—you just can't wear them everywhere. In a student café on the Left Bank they're hardly out of place.

THE CURRENCY

French currency is based on the **franc (F)**, which consists of 100 **centimes (c)**. Coins come in units of 5, 10, 20, and 50 centimes; and 1, 2, 5, and 10 francs. Notes come in denominations of 10, 20, 50, 100, 200, and 500 francs. Around 1960 the French issued new coins and notes which are current today and known as "new francs."

All banks are equipped with foreign-exchange prices, and you will find exchange offices in the airports and airline terminals. Banks are open from 9am to noon and 2 to 4pm Monday through Friday. Major bank branches also open their exchange departments on Saturday between 9am and noon.

The Franc and the Dollar

At this writing $1 = approximately 6.65F (or 1F = 15¢), and this was the rate of exchange used to calculate the dollar values given in this book (rounded to the nearest nickel). This rate fluctuates from time to time and may not be the same when you travel to France.

As for the prices quoted in francs throughout these pages, they are accurate at press time, but, inflation being what it is worldwide, they cannot be guaranteed. The wise traveler will allow for increases in the prices given, particularly in the second year (1992) of this edition's lifetime. Therefore the following table should be used only as a guide:

Francs	Dollars	Francs	Dollars
1	.15	30	4.53
2	.30	35	5.29
3	.45	40	6.04
4	.60	45	6.80
5	.76	50	7.55
6	.91	75	11.33
7	1.06	100	15.10
8	1.21	110	16.61
9	1.36	120	18.12
10	1.51	130	19.63
11	1.66	140	21.14
12	1.81	150	22.65
13	1.96	175	26.43
14	2.11	200	30.20
15	2.27	250	37.75
20	3.02	500	75.50
25	3.78	750	113.25

NETWORKS AND RESOURCES

For Students

Armed with a student identification card in Paris, you can enjoy many bonuses, including savings of up to 40% on transportation and 50% off admission to many museums. You'll need proof of student status, best obtained by requesting an **International Student Identity Card** ($10) from the **Council on International Education Exchange,** 205 E. 42nd St., New York, NY 10017. Write first for the *Student Travel Catalog* containing the application form that, properly filled out and submitted with payment and required documentation, will expedite receiving your

ISIC. Allow three to four weeks for delivery during the busiest travel seasons.

A good base for students is the **Maison d'Etudiants J. de Rufz de Lavison,** 18 rue Jean-Jacques-Rousseau, 75001 Paris (tel. 45-08-02-10), which receives both male and female students from May through October, charging them 89F ($13.45) per person daily, including a continental breakfast, taxes, and service, as well as showers. A three-day minimum stay is required. Métro: Louvre.

Year-round temporary housing (60 beds) for students, male and female, ages 18 to 30, is available at the **Association des Etudiants Protestants de Paris,** 46 rue de Vaugirard, 75006 Paris (tel. 43-54-31-49), on the Left Bank. They have a library and various cultural activities. Rates, including a continental breakfast and showers, are 58F ($8.75) daily in a dormitory (four to six beds), or 70F ($10.55) per person in a double. Métro: Luxembourg, St-Germain, or Odéon.

For Senior Citizens

For those who reach what the French call "the third age," there are a number of discounts. At any railway station in the country, a senior citizen (that means *hommes* or *femmes* 60 years old or older) can obtain a **Carte Vermeil** (Vermilion Card), for a cost of 125F ($18.20). With this card, a person gets a reduction of 50% on train fares in both first- and second-class compartments, but not during peak periods. Further discounts include a 10% reduction on all rail excursions.

The French domestic airline, Air Inter, honors "third agers" by giving them 25% to 50% reductions on its regular, nonexcursion tariffs. Again, certain flights are not included. Carte Vermeil allows reduced prices on certain regional bus lines as well as on theater tickets in Paris. Reductions are available on about 20 Air France flights a week to Nice. Finally, half-price admission to state-owned museums is yet another concession the French make to the aging.

The Vermilion Card is valid for one year and can be purchased at any major railway station in France. For more information, get in touch with the **French National Railroads,** 610 Fifth Ave., New York, NY 10020 (tel. 212/582-2110).

For Everyone

You need never be totally alone in Paris. There's always someone who speaks your language standing ready to dispense aid, give you information, and help you solve problems. **Welcome Offices** in the center of town will give you free maps, informative booklets, and "Paris Monthly Information," an English-language listing of all current shows, concerts, and theater. At 127 Champs-Elysées, 8e (tel. 47-23-61-72), you can get information regarding both Paris and the provinces. The office is open in summer daily from 9am to 8pm, in winter daily from 9am to 6pm.

2. Getting Around

Paris is a city for walkers, for strollers-about whose greatest joy in life is rambling through unexpected alleyways and squares, sniffing out a city's innermost secrets. Whatever your specific intention when you come, one long, free, exhilarating saunter will be enough to convince you that you don't *want* to spend your Parisian days charging from art-book exhibition to history-book monument. Given a choice of conveyance, make it your own two feet every possible time. Only when you're dead tired and can't walk another step, or in a roaring hurry to reach an exact destination, should you consider the following swift and prosaic means of urban transport.

BY METRO

If the Paris subway system, the Métropolitain, had an English slogan, it would be: "So simple a child can work it." That would be no overstatement. The Métro is so brilliantly organized, so efficient, and so well signposted that if you do get lost, don't mention it to your Parisian friends. They'll have too good a laugh at your expense.

One run of the course is all you need to get the details down pat. Walk to any Métro station and look at the huge map posted outside. Decide on the station you want to reach. Now put your finger on the station where you are standing (it will be circled in red) and trace the quickest route. In some of the larger stations, such as the Opéra, there are automatic light-up maps to do this for you. You may have to change from one line to another. Interchange stations are circled in black.

Now run your finger to the end of the line you wish to take. The name of the last stop is the "Direction" you are going toward. Cling to this name with the tenacity of mother love. It will guide you through the station maze of ticket takers, swinging metal gates, narrow stairwells, moving platforms, even lead you from the elevated line out into the open air and underground again, eventually to deposit you safely on the guaranteed correct coach.

Enter the station and buy a ticket. You only have to specify first or second class. One fare covers every station on the urban lines. On the Sceaux line, as well as on the Boissy-Saint-Léger and the Saint-Germain-en-Laye lines, which serve the suburbs, fares are charged according to the distance covered.

First Class may be cozier, but second class is cheaper—only 5F (75¢) per ticket in contrast to 7.40F ($1.10) in first class. Your best buy is a *carnet* (a ticket book), which contains ten individual second-class tickets for only 31.20F ($4.70), 47F ($7) in first class.

Or you can purchase **Paris Visite,** which allows you to ride the Métro (and buses) anywhere you want to go. A one-day pass costs $5; a three-day pass, $15; and a five-day pass, $25. It's avail-

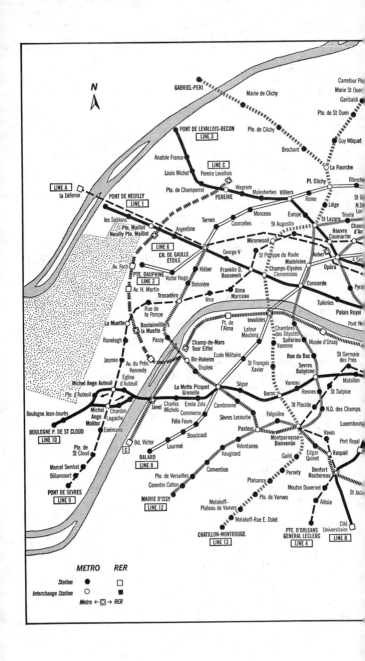

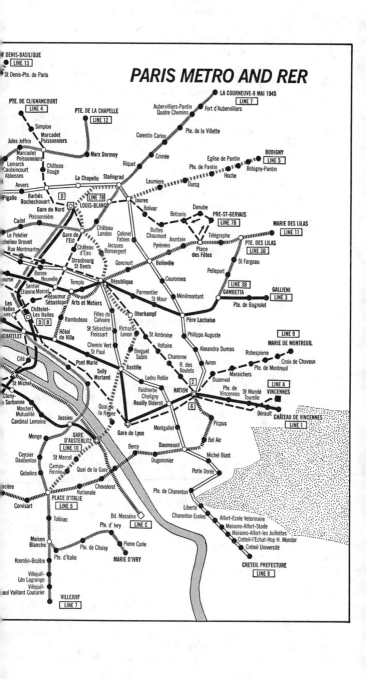

PARIS METRO AND RER

able from **Marketing Challenges International,** 10 East 21st St., New York, NY 10010 (tel. 212/529-8484). The price is subject to change, of course, but probably not by much.

Hold on to your ticket now, until you've finished your journey. There are occasional ticket checks in first-class or second-class compartments, and on the station platforms and corridors. Locate your "Direction" and start walking. Maps and station lists on the walls will reassure you as you go.

The tickets are checked at the entrances by automated turnstiles, a labor-saving device that saves the Métro a lot of money and eliminates all that confetti. Insert your ticket in the machine and pass through the turnstile.

If you are changing trains, get out at the interchange station, determine the "Direction" of the next line you want to take, and follow the bright-orange "Correspondance" signs until you reach the proper platform. Don't be tricked out into the open by a "Sortie" sign, which means "Exit." If you are, you'll have to pay another fare and start all over again.

The Métro starts running in the morning at 5:30, and the cars pull into their barns for the night around 1:15am. *Remember:* Take precautions against pickpockets.

BY BUS

This is a more slapdash, less efficient way to get where you want to go, but marvelous for seeing Paris in the close-up, ticking off famous buildings and peeking into people's windows. Use the ticket books purchased at Métro stations or else Métro tickets, which can be used in buses, giving you an average ride of about two to three miles. You can also buy tickets at bus terminal kiosks, in café-tabac stores, and in other various retail shops bearing a red circular RATP sign. Bus journeys are divided into stages, and you are charged according to the distance you are going.

Within the city limits, charges never exceed two tickets. If you stay a few days, you can buy a special "Go as you please" tourist ticket valid on all RATP networks for three or five days, at a cost of 70F ($10.55) to 115F ($17.35), respectively. These can be purchased at major Métro stations, such as Etoile.

If you plan to stay in Paris for more than a few days, consider a **Carte Orange,** which is issued in two different varieties: *coupon mensuel* (monthly), and *coupon hebdomadaire* (weekly). These coupons allow unlimited travel on the Métro and buses. Bring an ID photograph with you to apply for the card; you can purchase one at a Métro ticket counter. The cost of the monthly pass is 173F ($26.10) in second class, 260F ($39.25) in first class. The weekly pass is 49F ($7.40) in second class, 74F ($11.15) in first class.

If you intend to do any serious bus riding, pick up an RATP bus map at the office on place de la Madeleine, 8e, or at the tourist offices at RATP headquarters, 53 bis quai des Grands Augustins, 75006 Paris. You can also write to the RATP to obtain maps of the transportation systems operated by this authority and other information and pamphlets on the networks. When in Paris, you can also telephone the enquiry center (tel. 43-46-14-14) to get precise details on the fares, routes, and schedules concerning buses as well as the Métro.

Learn bus-stop customs. Wait for a bus at a bus stop, and wave to the driver to stop the bus. On each stop post, the route numbers are displayed as well as the name of the place served. When waiting at a bus stop, get in line and board in order. You are entitled to defend your place in line with your life. *No* tactic is considered unmannerly. There are 55 bus lines in Paris, many running out to the near suburbs. The majority operate only between 7am and 8:30pm. A few run as late as 12:30am. And even fewer maintain service on Sunday and holidays.

You may also want to use the bus system for excursions outside Paris. Many different trips are offered from Easter to the beginning of October during the weekends at reasonable prices to off-the-beaten-path places. You can, of course, go to such standard attractions as Chartres, Amiens, Beauvais, Chantilly, Compiègne, Epernay en Champagne, Fontainebleau, Orléans, Vaux-le-Vicomte, even Mont-Saint-Michel. Also, you can visit various châteaux in the Loire Valley. To get more details on the prices and on the sightseeing tours, you can write to the RATP at its headquarters (address above). When in Paris, you can also get the details and book space by going to the office at the place de la Madeleine. It is open Monday to Friday from 7:30am to 6:45pm, on Saturday, Sunday, and holidays from 6:30am to 6pm.

BY TAXI

This is not the cheapest means of propulsion, but it's nothing to get paranoiac about, either. Paris's cab drivers are decent enough chaps—with amazingly placid dispositions considering the insanity of their working conditions—and they seldom try to gouge you too much. Most of those surcharges they like to tack on are legal anyway.

To begin with, all legitimate taxis have meters. (If yours doesn't, get out and find one that does.) The flag drops at 9.50F ($1.45), and from that moment on it's 2.58F (40¢) per kilometer. If your trip should take you outside any of the boundaries of the 20 arrondissements, you'll pay 4.02F (60¢) per kilometer. At night, expect to pay 5.30F (80¢) per kilometer.

You're not required to pay for the driver's empty return ride between airports and the center of the city, but you are assessed 4.20F (65¢) extra to be delivered to railroad stations.

You are allowed several small pieces of luggage free if they're transported inside and do not weigh more than five kilograms. Any suitcases weighing more are carried in the trunk at a cost of 3.50F (55¢) per piece of luggage. On top of the fare, tip from 12% to 15% —the latter usually elicits a *merci*.

Beware of those no-meter cabs that await tipsy patrons outside nightclubs—or settle the tab in advance. Regular cabs can be hailed on the street when their signs read "Libre." Taxi stands are frequently found near Métro stations.

BY CAR

Don't even consider driving a car in Paris. You don't have the requisite nerve, skill, and above all, ruthlessness of the humblest Parisian driver. Parking is impossible, and so many of the inner streets survive from the days when the hand-carted litter was the common mode of transportation that two cars and a pedestrian are all that's needed these days for a traffic jam. Add to this the Parisians' glee in irritating their fondest neighbor, and you can see why you don't want to get involved.

If you insist on ignoring my well-meant advice, then here are a few tips: Get an excellent street map and ride with a co-pilot, because there's no time to think at intersections. Wherever you see "Zone Bleue," it means that you can't park without a parking disc, which you attach to your windshield, setting the disc's clock to show the time of arrival. Between 9am and noon you may park for one hour, from noon to 2:30pm you get 2½ hours, and thereafter to 5pm it's back to one hour. These discs are available at garages, police stations, and hotels. The rules are suspended on Sunday and holidays.

But don't even consider exploring the French countryside without a car, unless you intend to see the bigger cities only. There are few pleasures more magnificent than cruising through the back lanes of the provinces, stopping for a memorable lunch at country hotels.

Rules for Driving

Everyone in the car, in both the front and the back seats, must wear seatbelts. Children under 10 years old are required to ride in the backseat. Drivers are supposed to yield to the car on their right, except where signs indicate otherwise, as at traffic circles.

Other Tips

Watch for the gendarmes who consistently countermand the lights and aren't patient fellows. Horn-blowing is absolutely forbidden in Paris except for dire emergencies. Parisians have a proclivity for dire emergencies, however.

Car-Rental Agencies

All the major car-rental companies don't have the same price arrangement. Of the major worldwide competitors, the cheapest weekly arrangements, as of this writing and subject to change, are offered by Budget Rent-a-Car, followed by National/Europcar and Hertz. Among the four companies, Avis is the most expensive. In most cases, the best deal is a weekly rental with unlimited mileage.

Renting a car is easy. You'll need to present a valid driver's license and be at least 23 years old for the cheaper models and at least 25 for the more expensive vehicles. Renters must also present a passport and a credit card unless payment is arranged in North America before leaving home. It usually isn't obligatory, but certain companies, perhaps the smaller ones, have at times asked for the presentation of an international driver's license.

Budget Rent-a-Car (tel. toll free 800/527-0700 in the United States and Canada) has 21 locations inside Paris as well as at the airports. Cars can usually be picked up in one city and dropped off in another city with no additional charge if you warn Budget in advance when you make a reservation; otherwise, there's an extra charge of 700F ($105.70).

The least expensive car will probably be a two-door Opel Corsa with manual transmission and very few frills. Prices vary with the season, but Budget usually falls at the less expensive end of the spectrum compared to many of its competitors. Discounts are usually granted for rentals of two weeks or more. Automatic transmissions are regarded as a luxury item in Europe, so if you need one, you'll sometimes pay dearly for it. At all of the car-rental companies you'll pay an additional 25% government tax on top of the cumulative price of your rental.

Clients who want to protect themselves against international currency-exchange fluctuations can ask Budget to "lock" the exchange rate in effect at the time of booking. In such cases, a reservation must be made and paid for in North America at least 14 days before the anticipated pickup of the car.

It's very wise to ask the appropriate questions about insurance before you drive away. Budget, along with its competitors, will offer you an additional insurance policy known as a collision damage waiver (CDW). Some insurance is already automatically built into most contracts, but many renters (including myself) usually consider it inadequate for newcomers driving on unfamiliar roads in unfamiliar traffic patterns. A CDW, if you decide to accept it for between $10 and $21 extra per day, depending on the value of the car, will eliminate most (or all, depending on the company) of your financial responsibility in the event of theft or accidental damage to your car. It's a very good idea to take it—I always do.

National Car Rental is represented in Paris through its European affiliate, **Europcar**, 145 av. Malakoff, 75016 Paris (tel. 45-00-08-06, toll free 800/227-3876 in the United States). It maintains branches at the airports, as well as at about another 15 locations within the city. Its headquarters can rent you a car on the spot, but to qualify for the cheaper weekly rental you must reserve at least one day in advance while you're still in North America.

Hertz, 27 rue St-Ferdinand, 75017 Paris (tel. 45-74-97-39, toll free 800/654-3001 in the United States), is well represented in Paris, with 17 locations as well as offices at Orly and Charles de Gaulle airports. Most visitors opt for the cheaper weekly rental, which must be reserved at least two days in advance.

Avis, 5 rue Bixio, 75007 Paris (tel. 45-50-32-31, toll free 800/

331-1084 in the United States), has offices in Paris at both Orly and Charles de Gaulle. Prices vary with the season, but the most favorable rates are given to drivers who reserve a car at least two business days in advance.

PARIS ACCOMMODATIONS

Paris supports more than 1,400 hotels—among which only a handful at the top are world-famous. Of course, if you're willing to pay the tab at the top hotels, you can rent some of the finest rooms in Europe. But many modestly run hotels also provide top value. Their only drawback is that they are known among shrewd travelers and are likely to be booked, especially in summer. I've surveyed some of the best of them. Therefore, I suggest reserving rooms a full month in advance at *any* time of the year and as far as six weeks ahead during the tourist-jammed months from early May through mid-October. You may want to send a one-night deposit just to be sure.

The majority of Parisian hotels share a problem—noise. It's strange how Paris traffic sounds seem to magnify in the narrow streets, echoing and reechoing through the chimney-topped canyons. Add in late-night revelers and early-morning markets, and I'd heartily recommend that light sleepers request rooms at the back.

Hotel breakfasts are fairly uniform and include your choice of coffee, tea, or chocolate, a freshly baked croissant and roll, plus limited quantities of butter and jam or jelly. It's nowhere near as massive as the English or American breakfast, but it has the advantage of being quick to prepare, is at your door moments after you call down for it, and can be served at almost any hour requested.

If they were so inclined, the French could ask a riddle going something like "When is a hotel not a hotel?" The answer is when it's another kind of building. The word *hôtel* in French has several meanings. It means a lodging house for transients, of course. But it also means a large mansion or town house, such as the Hôtel des Invalides, once a home for disabled soldiers, now the most important military museum in the world. Hôtel de Ville means town hall;

Hôtel des Postes refers to the general post office; and Hôtel-Dieu is a hospital. So watch that word.

Now, having cleared away the background information, let's get down to specifics on where *you* are going to be staying.

1. Very Expensive Hotels

DELUXE

Deluxe hotels are rated by the government as "four-star luxury," meaning that these hotels, very simply put, are among the finest in the world. High prices and supreme facilities go hand in hand here.

On the Right Bank

If you crave smartness in your surroundings, choose a Right Bank hotel. That puts you central to all the most elegant shops—Dior, Cardin, St. Laurent—and within walking distance of such important sights as the Arc de Triomphe, the place de la Concorde, the Tuileries Gardens, and the Louvre. The Opéra is in this area, and its attendant attraction, the American Express office. And for relaxing after sightseeing during the day or for an apéritif at night, you have all the glittering cafés along the Champs-Elysées.

The Right Bank is noted for "hotel-palaces" internationally celebrated. They're also among the most expensive deluxe citadels in the world.

Le Bristol, 112 Faubourg St-Honoré, 75008 Paris (tel. 42-66-91-45). The decoration is sumptuous, the art of museum caliber, the service impeccable. This is one of the top two or three hotels not only in Paris, but in all of Europe. Naturally, its clientele is among the international upper crust, with particular appeal to the diplomatic corps.

Founded in 1924 by Hippolyte Jammet, Le Bristol is a true palace. It's on the famous shopping street of Paris, near many of the capital's most elegant boutiques. Nearby is the Palais de l'Elysée, the official residence of the French president. The hotel is not large enough to be a monument, as is Le Ritz; instead, it's just the right size for a guest to receive individualized old-world attention.

The façade is in the classic 18th-century Parisian style, characterized by an entrance of glass and wrought iron. The furnishings are of the highest caliber. For example, signed Louis XV and Louis XVI pieces abound. In the writing room and study are gilt clocks, crystal chandeliers, even an 18th-century tapestry. In yet another salon hangs an F. H. Drouhais portrait of Marie Antoinette. Her husband, Louis XVI, is represented in a marble bust by Pajou. Some of the salons open onto a formal patio, landscaped with potted plants and shrubbery.

The management has seen to it that all 152 bedrooms and

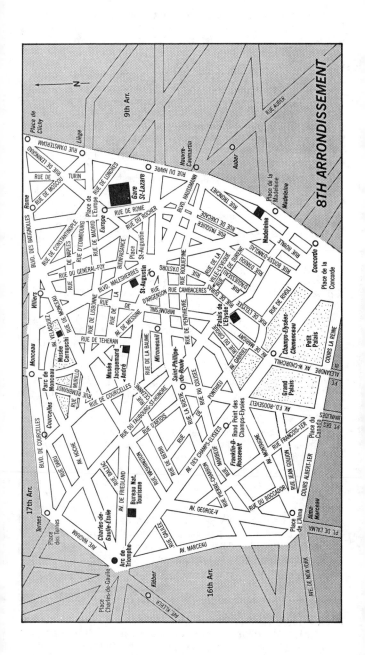

8TH ARRONDISSEMENT

suites are furnished opulently and luxuriously. Original oil paintings, Oriental carpets, antiques and skillfully made reproductions, inlaid woods, and the mandatory bronze and crystal have been used extensively. Depending on the size of the room, its view and location, the prices are 1,735F ($262) to 2,400F ($362.40) for a single, 2,400F ($362.40) to 3,500F ($528.50) for a double (twin beds).

The hotel's Restaurant d'Eté is open April to the end of October, and its Restaurant d'Hiver is open November to the end of March. Tea and drinks are served in a large, quiet garden in summer. The hotel has a heated indoor pool with sauna and solarium on the rooftop, with a view of Sacré-Coeur. It's open from 7am to 10pm for the exclusive use of hotel guests. Métro: St-Philippe-du-Roule.

Le Ritz, 15 place Vendôme, 75001 Paris (tel. 42-60-38-30), is a legend. Many critics have called it "the greatest hotel in the world," and with its $25-million facelift it aims to keep that reputation. You're assured that you'll be in "close proximity to the most important French and foreign banks." In 1898 César Ritz, the self-proclaimed "little shepherd boy from Niederwald," converted Le Ritz into a hotel that would soon make the word "ritzy" part of the language. Here he welcomed Edward VII and lesser royalty. The luxurious suites were occupied by the Rothschilds, the Goulds, the Vanderbilts, and the Astors. In the 1920s the hotel was host to such famous stars as Mary Pickford and Charlie Chaplin. Fitzgerald loved the bar more than Hemingway did. Marcel Proust wrote of the Ritz. Everybody from Greta Garbo to Rose Kennedy to, regrettably, Herman Göring has strolled down its long shopping corridor, called "Temptation Walk," with showcases representing the wares of some of the most prestigious shops in Paris.

The 143-room hotel startled Paris by providing a private bath with every room. When corpulent King Edward VII got stuck in a regular tub with one of his lovely young bathing companions, the king-size tub was invented.

The bedrooms are probably the most fastidiously maintained in the entire French capital. Antique chests, bronze hardware, marble baths, mellow woods, crystal lights—everything is well chosen and tastefully coordinated both in style and color.

The hotel, actually two town houses, opens onto one of the most historic squares of Paris, the place Vendôme. The town houses were joined together, their union creating the various courtyards and gardens. The public rooms are furnished with gilt and mirrors, Louis XV–and Louis XVI–style furniture, as well as tapestries and stately bronze torchères. Diners can take meals in the grill room or the Espadon. The hotel has installed a fitness club with a swimming pool that is an architectural masterpiece, a symbol of Ritz luxury. The Ritz Club is composed of a bar, salon with fireplace, restaurant, and dance floor.

Singles range in price from 2,300F ($347.30) to 2,800F ($422.80); doubles run 2,800F ($422.80) to 3,500F ($528.50), tax included. Métro: Opéra.

Hôtel de Crillon, 10 place de la Concorde, 75008 Paris (tel. 42-65-24-24), offers the most dramatic setting in Paris. It overlooks the place de la Concorde, the square on which the guillotine

claimed the lives of such celebrated victims as Louis XVI, Marie Antoinette, Madame du Barry, Madame Roland, and Charlotte
Corday. Designed by the famed Gabriel, the building was the former home of the duke of Crillon. Although more than 200 years
old, it has only been a hotel since 1909. As such, it sheltered
Woodrow Wilson during his stay in Paris following World War I.

The colonnaded exterior is so discreet you won't think this is a
hotel at first—rather, it seems the headquarters of a minister of government. The hotel envelops a large, formal courtyard, which is one
of the ideal places in Paris for those of refined taste to order afternoon tea. The formal 18th-century courtyard is surrounded by
flowers and plants.

Massively restored, the hotel still evokes the 18th century, with
parquet floors, crystal chandeliers, sculpture, 17th- and 18th-
century tapestries, gilt moldings, antiques, and paneled walls. If
you get a front room, you'll be treated to a view of what has been
called one of the most beautiful city plazas in the world. Tranquility
seekers should ask for a chamber opening onto an inner courtyard.
The rooms, for the most part, are generous in size and classically
furnished. All the bathrooms are fresh and well maintained, lined
with travertine or pink marble.

The Crillon's two restaurants, the elegant Les Ambassadeurs
and the more informal L'Obelisque, both serve high-quality meals.
Expect to spend at least 250F ($37.60) at Les Ambassadeurs for a
fixed-price menu, including wine and service. At L'Obelisque, you
can dine for 180F ($27.05) and up.

The hotel is now owned by Jean Taittinger of the Taittinger
champagne family, and, naturally, the bars of this hotel are stocked
with the family's product.

Singles rent for 1,650F ($248.10) to 2,000F ($300.75); doubles, 2,050F ($308.25) to 3,000F ($451.10). Métro: Concorde.

Marriott Prince de Galles, 33 av. George-V, 75008 Paris (tel.
47-23-55-11). When it was constructed in 1927, the cognoscenti of
the era's stratospheric social life adopted its art deco/neo-Byzantine
courtyard as their preferred rendezvous point. Later in the 1950s
diarist and composer Ned Rorem recorded the trysts and trials of
the "unapproachable innermost snob-life of Paris" that transpired
within the hotel walls. Eras change but the allure of the "Prince of
Wales" remains. Marriott's adoption (and meticulous restoration)
of this palace maintained the impeccable standards for which it was
known, perhaps subtly imbuing it with doses of American efficiency, but basically leaving it as a very Parisian monument to the good
life.

The hotel occupies a platinum location only a short promenade
from the Champs-Elysées, the Arc de Triomphe, and the glamorous
boutiques of the avenue Montaigne. Guests are greeted at the door
with a smile by a team of uniformed attendants, who quickly ar-
range for cars to be parked and baggage sent to one of the plushly
upholstered, very spacious accommodations. A cluster of French
sofas and armchairs is grouped around bouquets of flowers, comple-
menting the Regency detailing of the six-sided lobby. The paneled
bar, with its leather-upholstered copies of 18th-century armchairs, is

one of the great hotel bars of Paris. Many guests enhance their sybaritic fling with a meal in the paneled dining room, which even Madame de Sévigné might have been tempted to write about. Both the dining room and the quietest bedrooms look out over the famous courtyard, sides of which are covered with elaborate mosaics whose glistening surfaces might resemble the background of a painting by Gustav Klimt.

Each of the high-ceilinged accommodations contains an ultra-comfortable bathroom whose surfaces repeat the Edwardian/art deco tilework that works so successfully on the hotel's façade. The 171 elegantly furnished, air-conditioned bedrooms all contain color TVs with in-house movies, direct-dial phones, radios, and lots of sunflooded space. A well-trained staff seems eager to respond to queries and requests, and to safeguard the complete privacy that many of this hotel's well-heeled guests demand.

Singles cost 1,900F ($285.70) to 2,200F ($330.85); doubles, 2,100F ($315.80) to 2,400F ($360.90), taxes and service included. Métro: George-V.

Plaza Athénée, 23-27 av. Montaigne, 75008 Paris (tel. 47-23-78-33), was known to Mata Hari. It's also been known to about half of all the visiting celebrities of Paris. It is pure gilded luxury set in the midst of the foreign embassies (the rich ones) and the temples of haute couture, from which it draws many of its guests. It is said that there are two employees per each guest in the 220-room citadel dedicated to the good life. Between the Seine and the Champs-Elysées, it is a veritable palace. Arched windows and ornate balconies evoke the pre–World War I style. A liveried attendant stands under a glass shelter waiting to help you out of your taxi. When you check in, the reception staff seats you at a Louis XVI marquetry desk that faces an antique Flemish painting.

The style of the hotel is exemplified by the Montaigne Salon, with its mellow wood-grain paneling and marble fireplace. In the courtyard, tables are sheltered by parasols, and climbing vines and borders of flowers add a touch of gaiety. The more preferred air-conditioned bedrooms overlook this courtyard. The well-maintained units each have a private tile bath that is especially large and fine, with double basins and shower included. Other amenities such as a small refrigerator, ample closet space, and taffeta draperies make the rooms elegant, comfortable places to stay.

Meals are an occasion, as the food is superb. The preferred choice for dining is La Régence-Plaza, a room of handsome hand-carved oak paneling, its large curvy-topped windows fronting the Avenue Montaigne. It is known for its lobster soufflé. With its bright colors and decoration, the Grill Relais Plaza is the meeting place of "tout Paris," especially at lunch, drawing dress designers and personalities from the world of publishing, cinema, and art. The Bar Anglais is a favorite spot for a late-night drink (it's open until 1:30am).

Standard singles start at 2,500F ($375); doubles, at 2,700F ($406) and up. Métro: Alma-Marceau.

George V, 31 av. George-V, 75008 Paris (tel. 47-23-54-00), is affectionately called "George Sank" by the bustling expenseaccounters who crowd its ornate lobby. Midway between the Champs-Elysées and the Seine, it is sheer luxury. (Reportedly, the management keeps a "black file" on the mysterious "whims and preferences" of its habitués.) The George V is often referred to as "the French Waldorf-Astoria." The service is excellent, beginning with registration at the Empire reception desk. From here on, just press a buzzer and servants will attend to your whim and fancy.

The public lounges are adorned with tapestries and 100- and 200-year-old paintings. Inlaid marble walls in the Pompeian style add the right touch of staid dignity. The preferred rooms overlook the courtyard, and those that boast terrace balconies as well are the height of perfection. In fair weather, you can have lunch in the courtyard.

The 292-room hotel is better than ever, a far cry from the way it was when in 1944 General Eisenhower made it his headquarters during the Liberation. A complete refurbishing program is under way, and the hotel rooms are fully air-conditioned.

A single with bath is priced from 1,820F ($123.31) to 1,930F ($139.85); a double with bath from 2,470F ($371.45) to 2,580F ($387.95), taxes and service included. Métro: George-V.

Meurice, 228 rue de Rivoli, 75001 Paris (tel. 42-60-38-60), is one of the great palaces of Paris. When he was in Paris, that self-proclaimed "mad genius," Salvador Dalí, made his headquarters at the Meurice, staying in suite no. 108, which used to shelter Alfonso XIII, the former king of Spain who was forced into exile.

Massively renovated and overhauled, the 152-room Meurice has retained a decidedly 18th-century aura, with gilt-edged paneled walls, Flemish and French tapestries, Louis XVI–style furniture, and the ubiquitous crystal chandeliers. The bedrooms, redecorated, air-conditioned, and soundproof, are well furnished and most comfortably equipped, although not with antiques.

The Meurice Restaurant is just what you'd expect in the world's dining capital, the home of the true French haute cuisine. The Pompadour cocktail lounge is a gracious rendezvous for cocktails and tea, and the elegant Meurice Bar offers drinks in the warm atmosphere of its renovated décor.

One person pays 2100F ($315.80); two people pay from 2,700F ($406.00). Métro: Tuileries or Concorde.

Paris Inter-Continental, 3 rue de Castiglione, 75001 Paris (tel. 42-60-37-80), has been called the largest and most glamorous deluxe hotel in Paris. Back in the 19th century when it was known as the Continental, it was the epitome of the "grand luxe" hotel, reigning as the "queen of the rue de Rivoli." Now massively and meticulously restored, it has found new life in this century. Across from the Tuileries Gardens, it was originally opened in 1878. By 1883 it was entertaining such illustrious guests as Victor Hugo. Over the years it sheltered such tenants as Jean Giraudoux, Omar Bradley, and Lyndon Johnson.

At the colonnaded front entrance note the pair of bronze candelabra—they were purchased from a palace in Leningrad. The main lounge, with its rich Persian carpeting, is furnished with period pieces. The 424 bedrooms have been handsomely and tastefully outfitted in the classic French idiom, with many reproductions of Louis XVI pieces. Paneled walls and color-coordinated draperies and bedspreads create the effect of an intimate salon. All the rooms are air-conditioned and have direct-dial phone, color TVs with in-house movies, radios, and minibars. There is 24-hour room service.

Instead of the old-fashioned grand dining room, the hotel prefers the more modern way of having several intimate "character" rooms. One of the more favored is the Terrasse Fleurie, a restaurant in the interior courtyard landscaped to depict the four seasons. Estrela is a disco open from 10pm to dawn. Café Tuileries is a typical French restaurant and bar in the Belle Epoque style, serving breakfasts, snacks, light meals, informal suppers, cocktails, and French pastries (open till 11:30pm for food, 2am for the bar). Singles cost 1,700F ($255.64) to 2,000F ($300.75); twins, 2,000F ($300.75) to 2,300F ($345.86). Métro: Concorde.

Hôtel Lancaster, 7 rue de Berri, 75008 Paris (tel. 43-59-90-43), was once an exquisite private house off the Champs-Elysées, with an open forecourt and stables. When the house was opened to "paying guests," the salon became known among artists and writers. There is an assortment of fine antiques and pictures. Since its inception, the 66-room Lancaster has maintained much of the feeling of a private club and is perhaps the most British-influenced hotel in Paris. Nowadays it is likely to attract movie stars, everybody from Gregory Peck to Peter Ustinov.

The average bedchamber is richly furnished in a traditional manner, containing paneled walls, brocaded Louis XVI furniture, gilt mirrors, and tasteful accessories. The baths are commodious, each having its own special style. The more expensive rooms are larger and better positioned, mostly opening onto a quiet courtyard.

The stables of the original house were transformed into an almost regal dining room, where you can enjoy fine food after before-dinner drinks in the Grand Salon. In good weather, drinks and meals are served in the garden.

A single is priced from 1,500F ($226.50) to 1,690F ($255.20); a double, 1,955F ($295.20) to 2,300F ($347.30). Métro: George-V.

Royal Monceau, 35-39 av. Hoche, 75008 Paris (tel. 45-61-98-00), completed in 1925, has through the years been host to a wide social and political spectrum of guests, ranging from occupying Nazi officers to Golda Meir, from King Farouk to Ho Chi Minh. Today the 219-room hotel combines the best of French restraint with true Gallic flair. In an upper-class neighborhood, it is within the sight lines of the nearby Arc de Triomphe.

From the moment guests pass beneath the translucent art nouveau canopy of the intricately carved façade, an attentive staff is there to serve them. The airy lobby radiates the kind of lavish spaciousness you'd expect to find in the wings of a 19th-century museum. In its center, an oval-shaped dome covered with murals of cerulean skies and fluffy clouds creates a canopy over huge bouquets of flowers.

The accommodations are filled with Directoire furniture and

all the plush upholstery and electronics you'd expect. Each is air-conditioned and has a marble-covered bathroom.

The establishment's sophisticated designers transformed a courtyard into an attractive restaurant, Le Jardin, by building a glassed-in gazebo whose rounded walls combine space-age construction with French neoclassicism. Views of the double tiers of plants, including a 20-foot magnolia and dozens of flowering shrubs, are visible through lattice windows. Two other restaurants and a piano bar provide an ample dining choice. In the hotel's basement, a health club combines the equipment of a state-of-the-art gym with elements from the baths of a Roman emperor.

Singles cost 1,550F ($234.05) to 2,150F ($324.65); doubles, 2,150F ($324.65) to 2,650F ($400.15), taxes and service included. Métro: Charles de Gaulle (Etoile).

Raphaël, 17 av. Kléber, 75116 Paris (tel. 45-02-16-00), enjoys special patronage from the Italian-American movie world, plus a host of world celebrities. Right near the Arc de Triomphe, the hotel is a tranquil oasis of stately dignity.

When you pay your bill you can admire an original Turner, the orange-and-gold painting to the right of the cashier. The tone of the hotel is set by the main hallway, with its dark-paneled walnut walls, oil paintings framed in gilt, and lavish bronze torchères. The rich wood-paneling theme continues into the music salon, with its opera-red carpeting and marble fireplace.

The 89 bedrooms are impressive, furnished in a luxuriously conventional way, with brass-trimmed chests, tables of inlaid wood, armoires, and silk draperies.

If you're staying here, you'll surely want to have a meal in the formal dining room, with its gold-and-red carpeting, its paneled walls of white, and arched windows with rich draperies, or enjoy your favorite drink in the wood-paneled English bar.

Prices depend on where the rooms face. A single costs 1,400F ($211.40) to 1,900F ($286.90); a large room for two people goes for 2,300F ($347.30) to 2,800F ($422.80), including taxes. Métro: Kléber.

Hôtel Lotti, 7-9 rue Castiglione, 75001 Paris (tel. 42-60-37-34), just off the historic place Vendôme, is known as a "junior Ritz." Inside its doors unfolds an elegant French world of marble and gilt, tapestries and crystal. The 133 air-conditioned bedrooms turn to the 19th century for their inspiration, using reproductions of the furnishings of that era. Rosewood and mahogany, gilt and silk damask, even tambour desks, re-create the ambience of an elegant town-house bedroom. Some of the upper-story rooms were probably used at one time by servants of wealthy clients; each has its own particular, garretlike style.

Singles cost 1,250F ($188.75) to 1,850F ($279.35); doubles are 1,600F ($241.60) to 2,100F ($317.10). Métro: Opéra.

On the Left Bank

The Right Bank has the monopoly on luxury hotels, but not exclusively. The Hilton astonished Paris in 1966 when it became the first deluxe hotel to open on the Left Bank, invading the 15th Arrondissement in the vicinity of the Eiffel Tower. Hotel Meridien Montparnasse stands in the Fourteenth Arrondissement, an area that is rapidly undergoing massive restoration.

Hilton International Paris, 18 av. Suffren, 75015 Paris (tel. 42-73-92-00). On a tract of land only a short distance away from the Eiffel Tower, Hilton built one of the city's most impressive modern hotels, shattering the Right Bank's monopoly on grand hotels. Today, 25 years later, it has become a focal point of social life in this part of the city.

Built in the Hilton format of maximum comfort, with strong doses of Parisian flavor and virtually every convenience and efficiency a hotel could hope for, this 11-story, completely air-conditioned hotel is designed around window walls of glass, streamlined throughout with contemporary gadgets, and backed up by a professional staff along with computer-age security system.

Each of the well-furnished bedrooms has a generous bathroom covered with an appealingly tinted series of marble slabs, an oversize sink, and dozens of square yards of towels, terrycloth bathrobes, and lots of sweetly scented toilet articles. The emphasis throughout the hotel is on personal service and amenities such as readily available ice cubes, a minibar, baby-sitting service, a nearby underground garage (most valuable in Paris), and same-day laundry and cleaning services, a representative of a major airline and a major car-rental company, a beauty parlor, and several chic boutiques.

The 456 rooms are soundproof.

The breakfast buffet served on La Terrasse is one of the best in Paris. Also on the premises of this top-notch hotel are three bars and Le Western, a steakhouse with a cowboy theme and a definite sense of humor. Singles rent from 1,250F ($188.75) to 1,750F ($264.25); doubles, 1,500F ($226.50) to 1,925F ($290.70). RER: Champs de Mars.

Hôtel Méridien Montparnasse, 19 rue du Commandant-Mouchotte, 75014 Paris (tel. 43-20-15-51), is the largest hotel on the Left Bank, its skyscraper tower dominating Montparnasse. In the 25-story tower are 950 rooms, including 33 suites and apartments. Rooms are soundproof and color-coordinated, all with views of the city. They are equipped with direct-dial phones, color TVs with cable, minibars, alarm clocks, and air conditioning.

The hotel offers three restaurants. Montparnasse '25 serves a high-level French cuisine and takes its look from the 1920s, with black lacquered furniture, gold-leaf sculptures, and reproductions of works by Modigliani and Van Dongen. The glass-enclosed Restaurant Justine overlooking the gardens has both a buffet and à la carte specialties. An adjoining place for before-dinner drinks is the Platinum Bar with its gray, black, and pearl hues. There is also the Café Atlantic in the lobby.

Singles cost 1,100F ($166.10), doubles go from 1,250F ($188.75) to 1,500F ($226.50), tax included. Métro: Montparnasse-Bienvenue.

MODERN, FOUR STARS

These hotels are one notch below the four-star luxury rating and are less expensive. They don't have the spectacular lobbies and the vast array of amenities common to the deluxe landmarks, but they are top rate in every other way.

On the Right Bank

Hôtel Balzac, 6 rue Balzac, 75008 Paris (tel. 45-61-97-22), possibly the most successful renovation in this part of Paris, opened late in 1985 in a neighborhood well acquainted with 19th-century grandeur. The gilding on the wrought-iron balustrades was barely dry before the hotel was adopted by cognoscenti as one of the most refreshing hotels Paris has seen in this price category in a long time.

When they created it, a team of French and Lebanese designers added well-studied touches of the best décors of England, Italy, and France to a sophisticated series of public rooms that include elements of art deco, Palladian revival, and neo-Byzantine. A recessed alcove in the lobby is covered with hand-painted tendrils and vines, which seem to grow into the glistening white marble of a sun-flooded atrium. Kilim carpets, plum-colored upholstery, burnished paneling, and antique oil portraits add to the allure. The hotel restaurant, Le Sallambier, is recommended separately.

Accommodations are accessible via a glass-walled elevator that glides silently upstairs past acres of Turkish-patterned carpeting. Each of the 56 bedrooms is outfitted with glistening marble bathrooms, thick upholstery, and tastefully monochromatic décors of blue-gray or spice. Each contains a minibar, radio, phone, and color TV with half a dozen channels. A few suites lie on the uppermost floor. Singles are 1, 280F ($193.30) to 1,460F ($220.45); doubles are 1,680F ($253.70). Là Bas, a private club, is accessible to hotel guests. Métro: George-V.

Hôtel Le Warwick, 5 rue de Berri, 75008 Paris (tel. 45-63-14-11), which opened in 1981, occupies a desirable location near a corner at the upper end of the Champs-Elysées. It is a bastion of comfort and convenience. The décor is elegant and contemporary. Perhaps because it is owned by a group of investors from Hong Kong, many of the lacquered accents in the public rooms are of deep Chinese red, alternating with mirrors and lots of plants. Even the young staff is attired, as is the establishment's façade, in shades of maroon.

About 30% of the 148 bedrooms have evergreen-covered terraces looking out at views of the Eiffel Tower and the 18th-century buildings across the street. Businesspeople from across North and South America, along with such celebrities as Boy George and Grace Jones, appreciate the soundproof windows, the opulent marble-covered baths, the bronze and peach accents, the 24-hour video on the color TVs, and the attractively concealed minibars. All units are air-conditioned, and there is a parking garage.

The ground floor contains the Swann Bar, in remembrance of

If Oscar Wilde Could See It Now

L'Hôtel, 13 rue des Beaux-Arts, 75006 Paris (tel. 43-25-27-22), was a 19th-century "fleabag." It was called the Hôtel d'Alsace, and its major distinction was that Oscar Wilde, broke and down and out, died here. In one of the upstairs rooms he wrote to Frank Harris, the Victorian author, to send "the money you owe me." However, today's clients aren't exactly on poverty row. Through the lobby of what is known only as L'Hôtel march a lot of show business and fashion personalities.

On the Left Bank, the 25-room l'Hotel is the love-hobby creation of French actor Guy-Louis Duboucheron. He's responsible for establishing this intimate atmosphere of super-sophistication, a hotel that's been called a "jewel box." A Texas architect, Robin Westbrook, was hired to gut the core of d'Alsace, making a circular courtyard and an interior evocative of the Tower of Pisa.

You'll feel like a movie star yourself when you take a bath in your tub of rosy-pink imported Italian marble. At the edge of your tub will be a delicate vase holding a single rose. Throughout the building antiques are used with discretion, an eclectic collection that includes Louis XV and Louis XVI, as well as Empire and Directoire.

For nostalgia buffs, the ideal rooms and the re-creation of Wilde's original bedchamber and that of Mistinguette, the legendary star of the French stage. In the latter room, the star's original furniture—designed by Jean-Gabriel Domergue—has been installed. Celebrities from Katharine Hepburn to Mick Jagger have enjoyed these rooms.

Breakfast is served in a stone cellar, which in the evening becomes a tavern for intimate dinners. The Winter Garden is a luxurious piano bar/restaurant.

For all this pampering, however, you must pay the piper. The smallest rooms for two go from 950F ($143.45) to 1,800F ($271.80). Larger doubles (two have fireplaces) opening onto the garden begin at 2,000F ($302). Métro: St-Germain-des-Prés.

Marcel Proust, with live piano music and views into the hotel's elegant restaurant, recommended separately.

Accommodations cost from 1,600F ($241.60) for a single, 2,300F ($347.30) for a double. Children under 12 stay free in their parents' room. Métro: George-V.

Le Méridien Paris Etoile, 81 bd. Gouvion-St-Cyr, 75017 Paris (tel. 40-68-34-34), is the largest hotel in France. Under Air France's aegis, the 1,027-room, air-conditioned hotel is a first of its kind in Paris. It caters to groups as well as to individuals. The location is opposite the air terminal at the Porte-Maillot Métro stop on the Neuilly-Vincennes line. The setting of the hotel is contemporary French, and the overscale lobby chandelier is an eye-catcher.

Bedrooms are designed to provide convenience and comfort, and often you get a good view as well. In the rooms you'll find TV, direct-dial phones, and partitioned baths.

There are four restaurants, featuring everything from traditional French cuisine (Le Clos Longchamp) to Japanese specialties. At Le Méridien you can enjoy music, from a musical apéritif hour at 6pm to a 10pm jazz session at the Lionel Hampton Jazz Club.

Singles or doubles rent from 1,250F ($188.75) to 1,700F ($256.70), including service and tax. Métro: Porte Maillot.

On the Left Bank

Pullman St-Jacques, 17 bd. St-Jacques, 75014 Paris (tel. 45-89-89-80), affiliated with Pullman International Hotels, is an 800-room, 14-story glass-and-steel hotel, refreshingly stylish and very French. The main lobby has been upgraded, with a marble fountain in the middle. Not only are the public rooms attention-getting, but the bedrooms have color-coordinated textures and fabrics. They come complete with refrigerators, direct-dial phones, TVs, radios, and air conditioning. Tile bathrooms have both showers and tubs, plus a separate toilet area. The most winning of the public rooms is a bistro called Le Français, a re-creation of a turn-of-the-century brasserie, with bentwood chairs, 1890s posters, potted palms, and Belle Epoque lighting fixtures. A meal here costs from 225F ($34).

Singles go for 1,055F ($159.30), with doubles costing 1,180F ($178.20), including tax and a continental breakfast. Métro: St-Jacques.

FIRST CLASS

These hotels are rated three stars by the government, which means they have very large bathrooms, dining facilites, and 24-hour desk personnel. What they don't have are grand prices and celestial reputations.

On the Right Bank

Hôtel Westminster, 13 rue de la Paix, 75002 Paris (tel. 42-61-57-46), lies between the Opéra and the place Vendôme. Its sister hotel in Paris is the contemporary Le Warwick in the Eighth Arrondissement. The Westminster is traditional but, following a massive renovation, it has all the modern comforts as well.

The hotel was originally built during Baron Haussmann's reorganization of Paris in 1846 and incorporated an old convent. By 1907 it has been declared a national monument and is today a landmark. At the turn of the century the hotel was purchased by Monsieur Bruchon, who renovated it and began a famous collection of clocks, which today is one of the characteristics of the hotel. In 1981 it was acquired by Warwick International Hotels, which completely renovated it.

Attracting both visitors and the business traveler, it offers 102 guest rooms, each individually decorated (no two are alike). Of these, 23 are singles, 61 are doubles, and 18 are suites. Pastel color schemes blend with the rich paneling, molded ceilings, and marble-topped fireplaces. Many antiques, mainly from the Louis XIV era, are found in both the public and private guest rooms. Each accommodation has its own luxurious private bath, as well as minibar, color TV, radio, direct-dial phone, and air conditioning.

This comfortable, cozy hotel also offers 24-hour room service and an atmospheric bar and gourmet restaurant, Le Celadon.

Singles begin at 1,620F ($244.60), doubles or twins at 2,000F ($302). Métro: Opéra.

Hôtel San Régis, 12 rue Jean-Goujon, 75008 Paris (tel. 43-59-41-90), until 1922 a fashionable town house, stands in the midst of embassies and exclusive boutiques (Christian Dior is across the street), enjoying in a quiet and modest way its position as one of the best hotels in Paris in its price bracket. It is right off the Champs-Elysées, only a short walk from the Seine. Many guests here find it much like a private club. There is a small and attentive staff who quickly learn your whims and fancies and make you feel at home.

Each of the 33 accommodations is unique and decorated with discretion and taste. All units have a private bath, color TV, music, and air conditioning. A few have a separate sitting room, and many overlook a side garden. The hotel has a lounge and a bar and restaurant.

The price for a single ranges from 1,150F ($173.65) to 1,325F ($200.10), doubles from 1,750F ($264.25) to 2,000F ($302). Métro: F. D. Roosevelt.

La Résidence du Bois, 16 rue Chalgrin, 75116 Paris (tel. 45-00-50-59), is an exquisite 19-room villa, all shiny white with a mansard roof, tucked away in a shady lane off the parklike avenue Foch, only two minutes from the Arc de Triomphe. Go here only if you like quiet luxury, Relais & Châteaux–style. Monsieur and Madame Desponts bought this 300-year-old mansion from the Comte de Bomeau in 1964 and turned it into a retreat for discriminating guests. When they finished their careful restoration, they brought in their vast collection of antiques (mostly Louis XVI), gilt-framed paintings, crystal chandeliers, bronzes, sculpture, and brocaded silk draperies—making each room a charming world.

Although the rooms evoke the 17th and 18th centuries with classic patterns of silk fabrics on the walls, the bathrooms are modern.

A favorite spot in cooler months is an intimate drinking lounge, with huge armchairs positioned around a fireplace. In the cellar is a historic room where the mansion's first owner, an eminent physician, performed operations. A small front garden is screened from the lane by a stone wall and a wrought-iron fence, a few aged trees lending it a country feeling. In the rear garden are tables for breakfast.

Double rooms range in price from 1,050F ($158.55) to 1,550F ($234.05). Métro: Argentine.

Novotel Paris Les Halles, place Marguerite-de-Navarre, 75001

Paris (tel. 42-21-31-31). Set alongside the edge of the beaux arts lattices of the place des Halles, this hotel is considered one of the best Novotels in its worldwide network. Its cubist-inspired mirror-sheathed façade and sloping skylights mimic the most daring of the Beauborg neighborhood's futuristic architecture. Built in 1986, the hotel contains a lobby flooded with sunlight from overhead windows and a small-scale copy of the Statue of Liberty along with an alluring and stylish bar on a dais above the ground floor. A greenhouse-inspired restaurant, Les Jardins de St. Eustache, honors the ancient church on the opposite side of the square.

Each of the 285 rooms contains a no-nonsense but comfortable and efficient décor, with one double bed and one single (which serves as a couch or a bed), as well as a minibar, color TV with video movies, and a streamlined private bath. All units offer the same floor plan and furnishings, but the most sought-after ones overlook Les Halles with its fountains, shrubbery, and carousel. With tax and service, singles cost 700F ($105.70); doubles, 740F ($111.75). A public parking lot lies a few steps from the hotel's entrance. Métro: Les Halles.

Résidence Foch, 10 rue Marberau, 75016 Paris (tel. 45-00-46-50), is a gracious and artistic 25-room hotel run by Monsieur and Madame Schneider. Off avenue Foch, it's only a few minutes from the Arc de Triomphe and a short walk from the Bois de Boulogne. Popular with the diplomatic corps, the hotel is well decorated. All rooms contain private bath, direct-dial phone, radio, TV, and clock. Singles are 560F ($84.55); doubles are 660F ($99.65). Prices quoted include tax, service, and a continental breakfast. Guests drop in for afternoon drinks in the front bar/lounge, enjoying its warm, quiet atmosphere. Métro: Porte Dauphine or Porte Maillot.

Château Frontenac, 54 rue Pierre-Charron, 75008 Paris (tel. 47-23-55-85), has broken imaginatively from its past. The hotel is in a classic Parisian building, but it has been totally revamped. Stylish baths have been added and the décor turned contemporary, with low, modern furniture. All rooms are equipped with self-dial telephone, minibar, TV, radio, and private bath. Between the Champs-Elysées and avenue George-V, the 100-room "château" also has a restaurant and bar. A single room with bath costs 520F ($78.50) to 720F ($108.70); twins, 800F ($120.80) to 920F ($138.90). Métro: F. D. Roosevelt.

Hôtel de France et Choiseul, 239-241 rue St-Honoré, 75001 Paris (tel. 42-61-54-60), is a remake of a gracious 1720 town house, just off the glamorous place Vendôme. Actually, it's been a hotel since the 1870s, and became a fashionable oasis in fin-de-siècle Paris. Now, more than a century later, it has been completely remodeled. The 120 bedrooms—most of which open onto the inner courtyard —were entirely gutted, then turned into bandbox-size accommodations that are, nevertheless, attractively decorated. All sorts of conveniences are offered as compensation for the lost Belle Epoque glamour: a refrigerator, television, radio, a dressing table, plus a decorative tile bath with all the latest gadgets. All are color-coordinated, and every room has its token Louis XVI–style chair "to set the right tone." A few minisuites have been installed on the top floor under the mansard roof, with a rustic staircase leading up to twin beds on a balcony. There is a charming restaurant, La Lafayette, opening onto the inner courtyard and consisting of the historic salon where Lafayette received the subsidies to participate in the American War of Independence. Singles are 950F ($143.45); doubles and twins, 1,400F ($211.40), peaking at 2,000F ($302) in a deluxe unit. Taxes and service are included. Métro: Concorde, Tuileries, Opéra, or Madeleine.

Le Grand Hôtel, 2 rue Scribe, 75009 Paris (tel. 42-68-12-13), is a good example of a successful renovation of an old hotel, under the aegis of Inter-Continental Hotels. Parts of the Grand were created by Charles Garnier, the architect of the Opéra, and these are retained in their original splendor. The hotel was inaugurated by the Empress Eugénie. Now with its new lease on life, it is once again one of the leading first-class Parisian hotels.

On its five floors the triangular building contains 515 refurbished, fully equipped guest rooms, each decorated with a tasteful color scheme. All are air-conditioned and have private baths, color TVs, and minibars. Many overlook the inner courtyards of the building.

The Grand Hôtel is also the home of the world-famous Café de la Paix, where every visitor sooner or later is bound to spend some time watching Paris go by.

A single room costs 1,460F ($220.45) to 1,700F ($256.70); a double, 1,660F ($250.65) to 1,890F ($285.40), tax included. Métro: Opéra.

Keep It a Secret

Relais Saint-Germain, 9 carrefour de l'Odéon, 75006 Paris (tel. 43-29-12-05), is an oasis of charm and comfort. But keep it a secret, as it rents only nine bedrooms, with private bath or shower. A tall, slender hotel adapted from a 17th-century building, its décor is a happy medley of traditional and modern. Of course, all the necessary amenities were tucked in under the beams as well, including air conditioning, soundproofing, video, minibar, direct-dial phone, private safe, and hairdryer.

Rates are 950F ($143.45) to 1,050F ($158.55) single, 1,200F ($181.20) double or twin, including breakfast, service, and taxes. Métro: Odéon.

Régina, 2 place des Pyramides, 192 rue de Rivoli, 75001 Paris (tel. 42-60-31-10). The place Vendôme, the Opéra, the *Mona Lisa*, the Tuileries—all are virtually at your doorstep. But everything inside the 120-room Regina is peaceful and relaxing, starting with the flagstone courtyard, with its dolphin fountain and urns of flowers. Antiques, some of which would have been familiar to Madame de Pompadour and Marie Antoinette, are used wisely to create an old-fashioned, French big-city hotel. Bronze statuary, inlaid desks, and private salons for that cozy tête-à-tête, create the ambience.

All rooms contain private baths and cost 950F ($143.45) single, 1,160F ($175.15) to 1,400F ($211.40) double. Métro: Pyramides, Tuileries, or Louvre.

On the Left Bank

Mapotel Pont-Royal, 7 rue de Montalembert, 75007 Paris (tel. 45-44-38-27), stands on a comparatively calm corner between the boulevard St-Germain and the Seine, a handy spot that gives you quick access to the Right Bank (and the Louvre) across the bridge, the artists' quarter a few blocks to the east, and the air terminal a short walk to the west. It is also convenient to the Musée d'Orsay. The 80-room hotel has long been a favorite with French writers who meet in the bar with their publishers, as well as art-gallery owners from the dozens of shops nearby. They are often seen in the hotel's fine restaurant, Les Antiquaires, with a terrace on the street and a menu gastronomique. Rooms are done in a traditional style, often with beds either of ornate brass or inlaid wood, and there are gilt mirrors, regency chests and desks, plus such conveniences as TVs, radios, and refrigerators stocked with drinks.

Including a continental breakfast with orange juice, rates in a single range from 800F ($120.80) to 940F ($141.95); in a double, 1,150F ($173.65) to 1,500F ($226.50). Taxes and service are also included. Métro: rue du Bac.

OTHER CHOICES

On the Right Bank

Alexander, 102 av. Victor-Hugo, 75016 Paris (tel. 45-53-64-65), is a 60-room hotel with a fine sense of French taste and flair. The bedrooms feature color-coordinated spreads and draperies balanced by patterned walls. An open courtyard with a small garden is an attractive feature, and the lounge invites a cozy tête-à-tête.

Singles start at 720F ($108.70), doubles at 950F ($143.45). These prices include taxes and service. English is spoken. Métro: Victor-Hugo.

Royal-Alma, 35 rue Jean-Goujon, 75008 Paris (tel. 42-25-83-30), is near the Seine and about an eight-minute walk from the Champs-Elysées. Completely renovated in 1985, the 83-room hotel is in the heart of some of the most expensive real estate in Paris. There's a bar leading off the main lobby into the restaurant, carpeting throughout eight floors, and comfortably appointed but simple, compact bedrooms, all with private baths, TVs, radios, phones, hairdryers, and access to nearby parking. From the windows of the seventh and eighth floors, you have a view of the Seine and the Eiffel Tower.

Singles or doubles are priced at 900F ($135.90), with triples at 1,260F ($190.25). Métro: Alma-Marceau.

Le Pavillon de la Reine, 28 place des Vosges, 75003 Paris (tel. 42-77-96-40). Lovers of Le Marais have long lamented the lack of a hotel on this square where Victor Hugo lived. However, the inauguration of this hotel in 1986 changed that oversight. The entrance is through a tunnel leading under the northern border of the square. At the end of the tunnel, flanked with vine-covered lattices and a small formal garden, is a cream-colored villa whose simplified neoclassical façade blends perfectly into the neighborhood. The hotel of the Bertrand-Chevalier family is relatively new, but it fits into the landscape so perfectly you can't tell.

Inside, the Louis XIII décor evokes the era when the place des Vosges was in its heyday. Wing chairs with flame-stitched upholstery, coupled with iron-banded Spanish antiques, create a feeling of hospitable rusticity. Each of the 30 bedrooms is uniquely different; some are duplexes with sleeping lofts set above a cozy salon. Each contains weathered beams from older buildings, reproductions of famous oil paintings, a marble-sheathed bathroom, color TV, minibar, and phone. Motorists appreciate the 25 underground parking spaces.

Accommodations for one or two guests start at 950F ($143.45). Métro: Bastille.

Résidence Lord Byron, 5 rue de Chateaubriand, 75008 Paris (tel. 43-59-89-89), lies just off the Champs-Elysées on a curving street of handsome buildings. Inside this 31-room hotel are fine antique reproductions and framed prints of butterflies and of scenes in France. The bathrooms are as functional as they are attractively decorated. If you choose to have breakfast here, you can order it in the petit salon or in a shaded inner garden.

A large bedroom for two with a private bath rents for 800F ($120.80). A few suites with two beds and baths are also available, costing 1,000F ($151). Métro: George-V.

Hôtel Pierre, 25 rue Théodore-de-Banville, 75017 Paris (tel. 47-63-76-69), was given its name as a facetious counterpoint to the owner's favorite North American hotel, the Pierre in New York. To create it, the owners combined a trio of 19th-century buildings into a clean and modern hotel with art deco styling. Opened in 1986, it sits at the end of a residential street a short walk from the Arc de Triomphe.

Each of the 50 stylish accommodations contains a TV set with video movies, a minibar, a safe with a combination lock, and a phone. Each is outfitted with monochromatically restful shades of blue and gray. Hôtel Pierre is a member of the Best Western reservations system. The rates are 610F ($92.10) in a single, 650F ($98.15) in a double. Métro: Ternes.

On Ile Saint-Louis

Hôtel des Deux-Iles, 59 rue St-Louis-en-l'Ile, 75004 Paris (tel. 43-26-13-35), is a restored 17th-century mansion on this most charming of Seine islands. The interior decorator, Roland Buffat, was so successful with his two other hotels on the same street (Hôtel de Lutèce and Hôtel Saint-Louis) that he decided to open his most elaborate hotel to date. The tropical garden of plants and flowers sets the tone, suggesting the charm and taste level provided by this highly recommended 17-room hotel. Bamboo and reed are used extensively in both the public and private rooms. Monsieur Buffat suggests a touch of whimsy by his use of a cage of white doves. The favorite meeting place is the rustic-style tavern on a lower level, where guests in cool weather gather around the open fireplace. A single with shower costs 550F ($83.05), rising to 650F ($98.15) in a double with complete private bath. Métro: Pont-Marie.

Hôtel de Lutèce, 65 rue St-Louis-en-l'Ile, 75004 Paris (tel. 43-26-23-52), is like a drink of sparkling champagne. This winning little hotel is on the historic Ile St. Louis, where everybody seemingly wants to live, although there just isn't enough room. You pass through the glass entrance doors into what appears to be the attractive and inviting living room of a Breton country house. All this is the creation of interior designer Roland Buffat. The all-purpose reception salon and lounge focuses on a stone fireplace surrounded by soft downy couches and armchairs. Tall plants and modern paintings add the new look, while antique tables and crude tile floors pay homage to the traditional. Each of the 23 bedrooms is uniquely decorated, many with antiques interspersed with tasteful reproductions, and all have private bath. The duke and duchess of Bedford have been known to treat the Lutèce as if it were their Paris town house.

The rates start at 680F ($102.70) for either a single or double, taxes and service included. Métro: Pont-Marie.

On the Left Bank

Lutétia, 45 bd. Raspail, 75006 Paris (tel. 45-44-38-10), is one of the largest hotels on the Left Bank, returned to its beautiful traditional art deco 1910 style after a major renovation in the spring of 1984. With 289 rooms, it always seems to tuck you in somewhere —even when every hotel accommodation in the city is seemingly occupied. Businesspeople are especially fond of the Lutétia, as it has facilities appropriate to a large city hotel. Amenities include the elegantly decorated Brasserie Lutétia, a bar, ten large reception lounges and ten small ones, and that indispensable porter who produces theater tickets.

Most of the bedrooms are fully renovated. Some guests, however, preferring the untouched vintage accommodations, choose the old-fashioned but very comfortable rooms of traditional style. Each room, modern or ancient, has its own radio, TV, direct-dial telephone, and minibar.

The cost for a double room with a private bath is from 1,200F ($181.20) to 1,700F ($256.70), dropping to 1,100F ($166.10) to 1,600F ($241.60) for a single with bath. Service charge and taxes are included; breakfast is extra. Métro: Sèvres-Babylone.

Grand Hôtel Littré, 9 rue Littré, 75006 Paris (tel. 45-44-38-68), is a total remake of an old hotel. Some of the accommodations

A Former Cloister

Relais Christine, 3 rue Christine, 75006 Paris (tel. 43-26-71-80), welcomes a sophisticated international clientele into what used to be a 16th-century Augustinian cloister. This is really one of the most unusual hotels in this part of town. You enter from a narrow cobblestone street first into a symmetrical courtyard and then an elegant reception area dotted with baroque sculpture, plush upholsteries, and a scattering of Renaissance antiques. The Auvergne-based Bertrand family converted the building from a warehouse for a nearby publishing company into this elegant hotel in 1979.

Just off the reception area is a paneled sitting room and bar area ringed with 19th-century portraits and comfortable leather chairs. You won't have experienced the hotel, however, until you go down into the vaulted breakfast room on the lower level, whose ancient well is spotlit from within and whose massive central stone column witnessed all the activity in what used to be the cloister's kitchen.

Each of the 51 bedrooms is individually decorated with antiques or antique reproductions and lots of flair. Accessories might include massively beamed ceilings and plush wall-to-wall carpeting. Double rooms range from 1,100F ($166.10) to 2,000F ($302). Métro: St-Michel.

are done in a stylized Italian marble. Its location in the heart of Montparnasse on a quiet street makes it ideal for those requiring peace in noisy Paris.

All the furnishings are reproductions of traditional French pieces, 100 bedrooms employing adaptations of Louis XVI items, using a liberal dose of bold colors. Every room contains a private bath, phone, and radio. You can dine in the lower-level restaurant, or entertain guests within a pair of moderately formal salons. One of them has wood paneling and Doric columns and a collection of antique chests.

The rates are kept simple: 620F ($93.60) in a single, 770F ($116.25) in a double. Métro: Montparnasse.

2. Moderately Priced Hotels

ON THE RIGHT BANK

Hôtel Mayfair, 3 rue Rouget-de-Lisle, 75001 Paris (tel. 42-60-38-14), is considered a snug, safe oasis in the vicinity of the Tuileries, lying between chic place Vendôme and the traffic of the place de la Concorde off the rue de Rivoli. Paneling and velvet are key-notes of the public rooms, each elegantly furnished in a refined taste. A personalized welcome awaits you in one of the 53 well-furnished bedrooms, each with Louis XVI décor and private bath or shower, minibar, and TV.

The rate in a single room is 715F ($107.95); in a double, 1,025F ($154.80).

Hôtel de Castille, 37 rue Cambon, 75001 Paris (tel. 42-61-55-20), is a renovated hotel near the headquarters of Chanel and across the street from the "back door" of the Ritz. A series of beige marble panels and big mirrors, wall sconces, and a black-trimmed elevator bank grace the lobby area.

The 62 sunny rooms are painted in a variety of pastel colors and outfitted in a streamlined art deco, featuring clean white baths with gray marble sinks, minibars, and TVs with in-house movies.

Quiet for a hotel so close to major shops, museums, and busy boulevards, it is only a few minutes' walk from place Vendôme, place de la Concorde, or place de la Madeleine. On the premises is a restaurant, Le Relais Castille, done in colors of flame and rust. Lunch and dinner are served in the inside garden court.

Including a continental breakfast, service, and taxes, rates are 1,185F ($179) single, 1,480F ($223.50) double. However, during fashion shows prices rise and the hotel fills up quickly. Métro: Madeleine.

Hôtel de la Bretonnerie, 22 rue Ste-Croix-de-la-Bretonnerie, 75004 Paris (tel. 48-87-77-63), is a bit of old Paris updated. In Le Marais, a short walk from the Pompidou Center, this 17th-century mansion, once occupied by French aristocrats, was modernized successfully in 1987 with a healthy respect for tradition, as reflected by the freestone walls, the exposed beams, Louis XIII–style furniture, and mezzanines and rooms under the eaves. In a cozy, intimate atmosphere, Monsieur and Madame Sagot offer a total of 31 comfortable bedrooms, most with private bathtubs and all the rest with shower. In a single or double, rates begin at 450F ($67.95), rising to 700F ($105.70). Breakfast is served. Métro: Hôtel-de-Ville.

Tivoli-Etoile, 7 rue Brey, 75017 Paris (tel. 43-80-31-22), is the best and most up-to-date hotel on this street of accommodations, right near place de l'Etoile. Lying right off the Champs-Elysées, the 30-room hotel is only 150 feet from the Etoile (Charles de Gaulle) Métro station. It has been completely redecorated; each room contains a private bath, radio, TV, direct-dial phone, and up-to-date furnishings. For this midcity location, the charge is 585F ($88.35) for a single, 610F ($92.10) for two people, including continental breakfast. The hotel opens onto an inner patio. If you're a motorist, you'll find a parking lot nearby.

In the same neighborhood, the management also runs the **Hôtel Plaza Etoile,** 21 av. Wagram, 75017 Paris (tel. 43-80-42-24). Its 40 up-to-date rooms are well cared for, and are furnished in modern pieces, containing color TV, radio, hair dryers, safe, and either a complete bath or a shower with toilet. Best of all, breakfast

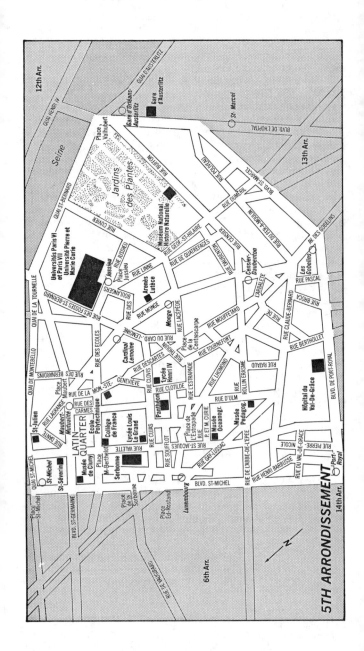

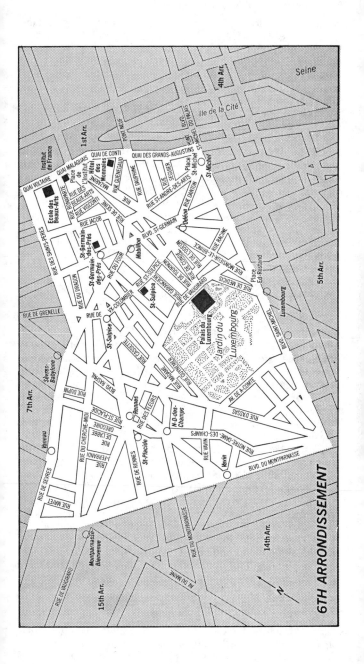

6TH ARRONDISSEMENT

is served on a lovely terrace overlooking avenue Wagram, and there is a pleasant bar, Le Tiffany. The rate is 650F ($98.15) double, including continental breakfast. Métro: Charles de Gaulle (Etoile).

ON THE LEFT BANK

Odéon Hôtel, 3 rue de l'Odéon, 75006 Paris (tel. 43-25-90-67), where some now-famous American artists stayed in the 1930s and 1940s, has been transformed to resemble a colorful Normandy inn. The renovation uncovered old beams, rough stone walls, and high, crooked ceilings. After new plumbing was installed, rooms were designed and furnished, each with a character of its own. Furnishings have successfully blended the old with the modern, ranging from oak and bookbinder wallpaper to bright contemporary fabrics. The 34 rooms are equipped with either private bath or shower. The guest lounge is dominated by an old Parisian tapestry, an amusingly beamed and mirrored ceiling, and black leather furnishings. The hotel is one minute from the Odéon Théâtre and boulevard St-Germain.

Singles range from 550F ($83.05) to 600F ($90.60); doubles from 600F ($90.60) to 700F ($105.70), tax and service included. Métro: Odéon.

Hôtel de Fleurie, 32 rue Grégoire-de-Tours, 75006 Paris (tel. 43-29-59-81), just about 70 feet off the boulevard St-Germain on this colorful little Left Bank street, is one of the best of the "new" old hotels. Restored to its former glory in 1988, the façade is studded with statuary that is spotlit by night, recapturing its 17th-century elegance. The stone walls have been exposed in the reception salon, with its refectory desk where guests check in. It has latticework, and an exposed beamed ceiling. An elevator takes you to the 29 well-furnished, modern bedrooms; a spiral staircase leads down to a breakfast room.

A double with complete bath rents for 600F ($90.60), the price rising to 850F ($128.35) in a twin-bedded room with bath. Singles cost 550F ($83.05). Métro: Odéon.

La Villa, 29 rue Jacob, 75006 Paris (tel. 43-26-60-00), is a four-star choice (formerly the Hôtel d'Isly) on the corner of a street where Richard Wagner lived from 1841 to 1842. The 30 bedrooms and five suites of La Villa were designed by Marie-Christine Dorner, one of the best decorators in the field. All the rooms are soundproof and air-conditioned, containing private baths.

The cost is 700F ($105.70) in a single, 900F ($135.90) to 1,300F ($196.30) in a double. Suites are more expensive, of course. Métro: St-Germain-des-Prés.

Hôtel St-Germain-des-Prés, 36 rue Bonaparte, 75006 Paris (tel. 43-26-00-19). Much of this 30-room hotel's allure comes from its enviable location in the Latin Quarter—behind a narrow façade on a well-known Left Bank street near many shops. Janet Flanner, the legendary correspondent for *The New Yorker* in the 1920s, lived here for a while. Each of the bedrooms is small and charming, often with exposed old ceiling beams. Floral patterns abound in the sitting rooms, and the public rooms often have 18th-century-inspired paneling and wall niches. Each of the bedrooms contains a private bath, minibar, TV, and phone.

Rates are 650F ($97.75) in a single, 700F ($105.25) in a double. Métro: St-Germain-des-Prés.

Hôtel Le Saint-Grégoire, 43 rue de l'Abbe-Grégoire, 75006 Paris (tel. 45-48-23-23), is a 21-room sparkler that opened in 1989. A restored town house–style structure, the well-run hotel is rated three stars. All of its handsomely furnished bedrooms have private bath or shower, each with separate toilets, direct-dial phone, color TV, and many modern conveniences. Some of the rooms have private terraces as well. Lighting is subtle in the vaulted breakfast room where the only meal of the day is served. In winter, there's a cozy fire in the sitting room.

Two people pay from 740F ($111.20) to 1,000F ($150.40), the latter price for a junior suite facing the garden. Métro: St-Placide.

Hôtel Le Sainte-Beuve, 9 rue Ste-Beuve, 75006 Paris (tel. 45-48-20-07), is the answer to your dreams: a small, tastefully restored hotel in Montparnasse, with its many memories of long gone but still fabled personalities. Situated around the corner from Rodin's famous statue of Balzac, Sainte-Beuve is a 23-room charmer. Its décor was conceived by the celebrated decorator David Hicks, and that means a warm, cozy atmosphere, all aglow with rose-colored chintz. Breakfast can be served in bed, and you can also enjoy an intimate lobby bar with a fireplace. The hotel is decorated mainly with provincial pieces. Each accommodation has a private bath with a separate toilet, TV, direct-dial phone, and individual safe, as well as a minibar.

Double-bedded and twin rooms cost from 630F ($95.15) to 1,000F ($151), with a suite and apartment going for even more. Tax and service are included. Métro: Vavin.

Hôtel Le Colbert, 7 rue de l'Hôtel-Colbert, 75005 Paris (tel. 43-25-85-65). How can you miss by staying at this little centuries-old 38-room inn? It's not only on the Left Bank, a minute from the Seine, but it provides a fine view of Notre-Dame from many of its rooms. There's even a small courtyard, setting the hotel apart from the bustle of Left Bank life.

You enter a tastefully decorated lobby area, with marble floors, red cut-velvet wallpaper, and a view of the wrought-iron spear-topped fence separating the evergreen trees of the courtyard from the narrow street outside. A sunny bar area is filled with gilt-accented French furniture. The rooms are well designed and tailored, furnished for the most part with good pieces. Most of them provide comfortable chairs and space for a breakfast area. The baths (one for every room) have been recently renovated; the beds are inviting, and units include such amenities as a phone, plenty of towels, and efficient maid service. Singles cost 505F ($76.25); doubles, 625F ($94.40) to 790F ($119.30). Métro: Maubert-Mutualité or St-Michel.

A 300-Year-Old Town House

Hôtel de l'Université, 22 rue de l'Université, 75007 Paris (tel. 42-61-09-39), has rapidly become the favorite little hotel for those who want to stay in a St-Germain-des-Prés atmosphere. Unusually fine antiques furnish this 300-year-old, 27-room converted town house. It's the love child of Madame Bergmann, who has a flair for restoring old places and a collector's nose for assembling antiques. She's renovated l'Université completely, giving each bedroom a private bath.

A favorite room is no. 54, all in shades of Gainsborough blue, with a rattan bed and period pieces as well as a marble bath. No. 35, opening onto the courtyard, is another charmer—there's a fireplace and a large provincial armoire decorated in shades of orange. A small breakfast room, in the bistro style, opens onto a tiny courtyard with a fountain. Everything is personal—and reservations are imperative.

The prices depend on the plumbing, with singles in the 500F ($75.50) bracket, and doubles for 650F ($98.15). A suite for two costs 1,000F ($151). Tariffs include tax and service. It's not terribly cheap, but it's well worth the money if you desire a glamorous setting. Métro: St-Germain-des-Prés.

Hôtel du Pas-de-Calais, 59 rue des Saints-Pères, 75006 Paris (tel. 45-48-78-74), is a historic building with literary connections that has been smartly updated. The five-story structure was built in the 17th century by the Lavalette family and inhabited by Chateaubriand from 1811 to 1814. Possibly its most famous guest was Jean-Paul Sartre, who struggled away with the play *Dirty Hands* in room no. 41 during the hotel's prerestoration days.

Today the hotel retains its elegant façade, complete with its massive wooden doors. Its 41 modern rooms have large baths, color TV, safety box, and hair dryer. The inner rooms surround a modest courtyard, with two garden tables and several green trellises. Off the somewhat sterile lobby is a comfortable, carpeted sitting room with TV.

Two guests in a room with private bath pay 650F ($98.15); singles in similar accommodations are charged 530F ($80.05). Continental breakfast is included. Métro: St-Germain-des-Prés.

Aviatic, 105 rue de Vaugirard, 75006 Paris (tel. 45-44-38-21), is a bit of old Paris, with a modest inner courtyard and a vine-covered lattice on the walls. It's been a 25-room, family-run hotel of character and elegance for a century. The reception lounge, with its marble columns, brass chandeliers, antiques, and petit salon, provides an attractive traditional setting. Completely remodeled, the hotel lies in an interesting center of Montparnasse, with its cafés frequented by artists, writers, and jazz musicians. Each comfortably furnished room has a private bath, direct-dial phone, minibar, and color TV.

Singles are 580F ($87.60), doubles 650F ($98.15), including tax, service, and a continental breakfast. The staff speaks English. Métro: Montparnasse-Bienvenue.

Hôtel de Bourgogne et Montana, 3 rue de Bourgogne, 75007 Paris (tel. 45-51-20-22), is the perfect selection for those who want a central hotel with a quiet, almost sedate ambience. A six-story, 35-room, middle-aged structure, the Bourgogne fits inconspicuously into the aristocratic place du Palais-Bourbon, opposite the mansion that houses the president of the National Assembly. Two blocks equidistant from the Seine and the air terminal, it is directly across the river from the place de la Concorde.

Everything about this hotel is relaxing and intimate. The staff is a personable lot, quick with helpful attentions. The guest rooms are provided with deep-cushioned easy chairs. A tiny, two-person elevator carries you up to your room. On the ground floor is a circular writing room with columned walls and a cozy lounge. Meals are served daily in the homey dining room.

Singles range from 430F ($64.95) to 650F ($98.15). Doubles begin at 650F ($98.15) and go up to 850F ($128.35). Breakfast, service, and taxes are included. Métro: Invalides or Chambre-des-Députés.

---

3. Great-Value Choices

ON THE RIGHT BANK

Family Hôtel, 35 rue Cambon, 75001 Paris (tel. 42-61-54-84). How such a pleasant, family-operated hotel can exist in such a swank neighborhood is still a mystery to first-time visitors to Paris. It stands near the House of Chanel, diagonally across the street from the Ritz. This 25-room hotel has witnessed decade after decade of improvements and popularity. The bedroom furnishings vary in origin from the 19th century to the late 1960s, making for a comfortable atmosphere.

Singles with bath start at 425F ($64.20); doubles with bath, 520F ($78.50). Breakfast is extra. Métro: Concorde.

Hôtel de Neuville, 3 place Verniquet, 75017 Paris (tel. 43-80-26-30), lies within a prosperous neighborhood, about a 10-minute walk from the Arc de Triomphe. Originally built in the 19th century as a private house, it has a symmetrical façade embellished with evenly spaced wrought-iron balconies; in summer, potted plants are sometimes arranged along them. Inside, Ionic columns add warm tones and textures to the lobby. Each of the 28 bedrooms, although small, contains a pink-beige color scheme and several modern conveniences, including a private bath. The owner, Monsieur Bigeard, was formerly a chef at France's diplomatic headquarters, quai d'Orsay. Today his talents are exhibited at his own restaurant in the hotel, Les Tartines.

Singles are 510F ($77), with doubles costing 600F ($90). Métro: Pereire.

Hôtel Brighton, 218 rue de Rivoli, 75001 Paris (tel. 42-60-30-03), in spite of its English-sounding name, is a very French hotel, and a good one at that. You're in the heart of one of the major shopping streets of Paris, right across from the Louvre. In fact, if you're lucky enough to snare a room at the front, you'll look out not only upon this world-famous art museum but on the Tuileries as well. A scattering of accommodations open onto tiny balconies; on a clear day, you can see the Seine and the Eiffel Tower in the distance. Each of the 68 clean, comfortable rooms contains a private bath or shower. They are furnished in a traditional style, often with brass beds.

Rates are 375F ($56.65) in a single, 595F ($89.85) in a double, including a continental breakfast. Métro: Louvre.

Hôtel Opal, 19 rue Tronchet, 75008 Paris (tel. 42-65-77-97), is a real find. In the heart of Paris, in back of the Madeleine Church and within an easy walk of the Opéra, this is a rejuvenated hotel. Decorated with style and taste, it offers 36 entirely renovated but small bedrooms, each with private bath or shower, minibar, color TV, and direct-dial phone. Some readers may want to ask for one of the closet-size bedrooms on the top floor, reached by a narrow staircase. These are really attic rooms, but some have skylights opening onto the rooftops of Paris. A single with bath ranges from 400F ($60.40) to 450F ($67.95); a double goes for 500F ($75.50). Métro: Madeleine.

Hôtel Bastille Speria, 1 rue de la Bastille, 75004 Paris (tel. 42-72-04-01), occupies a seven-story cream-colored building set on a street corner near the Bastille, the Bastille Opera, and the Marais. Its completely renovated interior is far more modern than its mansard exterior implies, thanks to a complete overhaul of the building in the late 1980s. Each of the 42 bedrooms contains an acoustical ceiling, simple but comfortable furniture, a private bath, TV, minibar, and direct-dial phone. Singles cost from 350F ($52.65) to 370F ($55.65), doubles from 370F ($55.65) to 430F ($64.65). Métro: Bastille.

Hôtel Volney Opéra, 11 rue Volney, 75002 Paris (tel. 42-61-85-24), is a comfortable and attractive place to stay near the Opéra and the place Vendôme. The 31 bedrooms are large, with baths or showers, TVs, direct-dial phones, and minibars. Some have balconies. Singles are between 490F ($74) and 510F ($77), doubles from 520F ($78.50) to 540F ($81.55), depending on whether there is a tub or shower in the bathroom. Métro: Opéra.

Madeleine-Plaza, 33 place de la Madeleine, 75008 Paris (tel. 42-65-20-63), is a delight. It has a prime Right Bank position, at the center of all the best shopping districts and within equal walking distance of both the Tuileries and the Opéra. There's a striking view of the Madeleine Church from its front windows.

The 55 rooms are contemporary enough to please the most motel-jaded. Headboards and breakfast tables are of shiny brown

Formica. Black leather easy chairs provide comfortable resting places. The bedrooms are not overly spacious, but all have color TVs, showers or baths, and minibars. For those who don't want their breakfast in bed (at whom the manager can only express wonder), there is a sunlit breakfast room overlooking the church. Doubles with shower start at 380F ($57.40), increasing to 450F ($67.95) and 570F ($86.10) with bath. All rates include service and tax. Métro: Madeleine and also Auber for the express tube.

Les Trois Couronnes, 30 rue de l'Arc de Triomphe, 75017 Paris (tel. 43-80-46-81). Jean-Louis and Paule Lafont renovated an older hotel near the Etoile in 1983. Today their creation combines a décor that embraces both art deco and art nouveau. They used personal objects they had collected for many years, including a 19th-century carved oak mantelpiece flanked with bearded statues (it's been turned into a reception desk) and a narrow marble fireplace that came from a private house in Versailles.

The colors used throughout the 20 bedrooms are cheerfully appropriate and blend well with the elmwood trim. On the premises are a vaulted breakfast room, which you can reach via an elevator, a winding staircase with a light forged-iron balustrade, and an up-to-date security system. Each of the rooms comfortably houses one or two people, and is equipped with private bath, TV, and minibar. Each rents for 495F ($74.75). Métro: Charles de Gaulle (Etoile).

La Régence Etoile, 24 av. Carnot, 75017 Paris (tel. 43-80-75-60), is an especially good buy in the district surrounding the Arc de Triomphe. Many of its 38 rooms are particularly well furnished, some with reproductions of French antiques. And most important, all rooms come equipped with a tile bath as well as direct-dial phones and color TVs. Singles rent from 380F ($57.40) to 500F ($75.50); rooms for two with double beds cost 520F ($78.50) to 580F ($87.60). There's a garage nearby. Métro: Charles de Gaulle (Etoile).

Etoile-Maillot, 10 rue de Bois-de-Boulogne, 75016 Paris (tel. 45-00-42-60). You pay a moderate price for prestigious living in this 28-room hotel, which is on a shady street halfway between the Arc de Triomphe and the Bois de Boulogne. Although it offers only a minimum of public rooms, its bedrooms, all with phone, TVs, baths, and minibars, are decorated with an unusually fine collection of antiques: bulging bombé chests with marble tops, Louis XV and Louis XVI tapestry-covered chairs, Oriental rugs, gilt and inlaid marquetry beds. Rates are 560F ($92.10) single, 590F ($89.10) double. Breakfast is included. English is spoken. Métro: Argentine or Charles de Gaulle (Etoile).

Prince Albert, 5 rue St-Hyacinthe, 75001 Paris (tel. 42-61-58-36), is a 32-room hotel that looks as if it had been transplanted panel by panel from some English country town. The wood-walled lobby and lounge set the atmosphere, with more paneling leading back to a miniature bar with a mixture of English and French furniture.

But there the similarity to an English inn ends, for despite the fact that the Prince Albert does a seam-bursting business in British clients, it is a distinctly French hotel when it comes to comfort, meaning that the central heating is turned up full blast in winter, and the drafts are programmed *out*, not in.

All units contain private baths or showers and have color TVs, minibars, and electronic safes. A single with shower costs 325F ($49.10); a single with complete bath is 425F ($64.20); a double with bath rents for 475F ($71.75). Rates include taxes and service. Métro: Tuileries.

Hôtel Henri IV, 25 place Dauphine, 75001 Paris (tel. 43-54-44-53). Four hundred years ago the printing presses for the edicts of Henri IV filled this narrow building. Today the orderly rows of trees in the square outside contribute to one of the loveliest locations in Paris. A sojourn here lures a loyal clientele of budget-conscious academicians, journalists, and francophiles. The low-ceilinged lobby, one flight above street level, is cramped and a bit bleak. But that is dispelled by the friendliness of Monsieur and Madame Maurice Balitrand. The 20 bedrooms, reached via a winding stairwell, saw better days under Clemenceau, but many devotees consider them romantically threadbare. None contains its own bath, shower, or toilet, but each has a sink.

The real allure of this place, aside from its dramatic location, is the prices. Singles go for 90F ($13.60); doubles, 120F ($18.10) to 150F ($22.65); and triples, 190F ($28.70). All include breakfast. Métro: Pont-Neuf.

Hôtel de Sèze, 16 rue de Sèze, 75009 Paris (tel. 47-42-69-12). Off the avenue de l'Opéra, this hotel is small but exceptional. Its public rooms sport some Louis XVI–type furnishings. The 25 bedrooms, however, provide pot luck: some are graceful with antiques, others somewhat sterile with contemporary pieces.

Rates are based on whether the room has a shower or bath. The singles and doubles range from 285F ($43.05) to 325F ($49.10). Some triples are rented for 385F ($58.15). Taxes and service are included, and English is spoken. Métro: Madeleine.

Hôtel du Nil, 10 rue du Helder, 75009 Paris (tel. 47-70-80-24), has to be valued for its location and price, not its lounge and entryway. Although it resembles many small hotels of Paris, its situation is prime, right near the Opéra and just a short walk from the boulevards Haussmann and des Italiens. There are no salons, but you can always meet a friend at the nearby Café de la Paix for a coffee and croissant.

All rooms contain phones, TVs, and minibars. The plumbing varies; some rooms have only showers, others have complete baths. Rates are 238F ($35.95) to 296F ($44.70) single, 254F ($38.35) to 337F ($50.90) double, depending on the plumbing; 378F ($57.10) triple, 414F ($62.50) quad, with complete bath. All tariffs include breakfast, service, and taxes. The hotel also operates a restaurant at the same address. Métro: Opéra.

Hôtel du Grand Turenne, 6 rue de Turenne, 75004 Paris (tel. 42-78-43-25), is for those who want to live in what was once the heart of aristocratic Paris, an increasingly chic thing to do these days. Le Marais is still a bastion of inexpensive hotels. The entrance of the Grand Turenne has a canopy with potted plants placed about. Inside this little two-star hotel you'll find unqualified respectability. It's one of the more expensive hotels in the Marais, as it has been considerably upgraded in recent years, with many comforts and modern conveniences added. The public rooms are warmly cluttered. All have bath or shower. Singles are 300F ($45.30), doubles are 320F ($48.30). Métro: St-Paul-le-Marais.

ON ILE SAINT-LOUIS

Hôtel Saint-Louis, 75 rue St-Louis-en-l'Ile, 75004 Paris (tel. 46-34-04-80), is a small hotel fashionably and romantically positioned on the historic Ile Saint-Louis. Guy Record discovered this hotel and did a good job of converting its 21 rooms. Along with his wife, Andrée, he maintains a charming family-type atmosphere that is becoming harder and harder to find in Paris. Many of the upper-level accommodations reached by elevator offer views over the rooftops of Paris. I prefer the rooms on the fifth floor, which have the most atmosphere and are decorated with old wood and selections of attractive furniture. Pleasant accessories decorate the rooms, and there are antiques in the small reception lounge. All rooms are equipped with baths or showers, and toilets. The breakfast room lies in the cellar near a tiny residents' lounge beneath stone vaulting dating from the 14th century.

A double ranges in price from 460F ($69.45) to 560F ($84.55). Métro: Pont-Marie.

ON THE LEFT BANK

Hôtel Jardin des Plantes, 5 rue Linné, 75005 Paris (tel. 47-07-06-20), opened in 1986 in a location near the Panthéon and just across from the Jardin des Plantes. The 33 rooms all have bathrooms, TVs, direct-dial phone, minibars, hair dryers, and double-glazed windows.

The hotel has a vaulted lounge in the basement, a sauna, a place for ironing, and an elevator. The neighborhood is the haunt of students and poets, the setting for the University of Paris and some of its oldest and finest schools.

Rates are based on whether the room has a shower or bathtub. Singles cost 340F ($51.35) to 540F ($81.55); doubles, 380F ($57.40) to 580F ($87.60). The higher prices are for rooms on the fifth floor with access to a flowered terrace. Métro: Jussieu.

Hôtel du Quai Voltaire, 19 quai Voltaire, 75007 Paris (tel. 42-61-50-91), is an inn with a past and one of the most magnificent views in all Paris. The hotel occupies a prime site on the Left Bank quays of the Seine, halfway between the pont Royal and the gracefully arched pont du Carrousel. Twenty-nine of its 33 rooms—many of them renovated—gaze at the Louvre, directly across the tree-shaded river.

Nor can the Voltaire be easily matched for famed guests. Living here through the years have been: Charles Baudelaire, Jean Sibelius, Richard Wagner, and Oscar Wilde. Photos of Wagner and Baudelaire are enshrined in the small, plush sitting room inside the main door.

The rooms are pleasantly appointed. But the focal point of every front room is that view—seen through floor-to-ceiling double French windows. The rooms are equipped with modern baths or showers. Singles range from 350F ($52.85) to 430F ($64.95); doubles, 480F ($72.50) to 540F ($81.55). Métro: rue du Bac.

Hôtel de l'Académie, 32 rue des Saints-Pères, 75007 Paris (tel. 45-48-36-22). The exterior walls and the old ceiling beams are all that remain of the 17th-century residence for the private guards of the duc de Rohan. In 1983 it was completely renovated to include an elegant marble and light-grained oak reception area, Second Empire–style chairs, and an English-speaking staff. The comfortably up-to-date rooms have Directoire beds, an "Ile de France" décor upholstered in soft colors, and views over the 18th- and 19th-century buildings in the immediate neighborhood. Each of the 33 rather small rooms has a private bath, minibar, phone, TV, radio, and alarm clock. Doubles range from 410F ($61.90) to 610F ($92.10), depending on the plumbing. Métro: St-Germain-des-Prés.

Saint-Thomas-d'Aquin, 3 rue du Pré-aux-Clercs, 75007 Paris (tel. 42-61-01-22), has been entirely renovated and redecorated. Behind a cream-colored façade with shutters and balconies, the 21-room hotel stands on a relatively traffic-free street between the busy boulevard St-Germain and rue de l'Université. The staff speaks English and gives you a warm welcome. Bedrooms are fresh and modern, with flowery French wallpaper. Amenities include a direct-dial phone and TV as well as private bath or shower, and toilet. Rooms that have insulated windows are serviced by an elevator. Singles are 336F ($50.75), doubles are 436F ($65.85). Continental breakfast is included. Métro: St-Germain-des-Prés or rue du Bac.

Hôtel Agora St-Germain, 42 rue des Bernardins, 75005 Paris (tel. 46-34-13-00), is now one of the best of the moderately priced hotels in this artistic and historical part of Paris. It offers 39 soundproof rooms, each well furnished and equipped with private bath or shower, hair dryer, color TV, minibar, and direct-dial phone. Other amenities include an automatic alarm clock and an individual safety box. Singles range in price from 425F ($64.20) to 500F ($75.50); doubles (either one double bed or twins) rent for 550F ($83.05). Breakfast is the only meal served. Métro: Maubert-Mutualité.

Hôtel du Vieux Paris, 9 rue Git-le-Coeur, 75006 Paris (tel. 43-54-41-66), is one of those hard-to-find little hotels just off the Seine. But this one is worth the search, tucked away in a building dating from 1480, a secret rendezvous for Henri IV and his mistress. Many artists and writers have stayed here, arising the next morning to contemplate the view of Notre-Dame after a short walk along the river. The rooms have been given decorator touches, such as large-patterned wallpaper on the ceilings.

The owner, Madame Odillard, runs a fine operation, renting

21 bedrooms, 14 with private bath or shower. Doubles range from 350F ($52.85) to 400F ($60.40), depending on the plumbing. A simple single costs 180F ($27.20) to 225F ($34). Continental breakfast is included. Métro: St-Michel.

Rooms with Views of Notre-Dame

Hôtel Esmeralda, 4 rue St-Julien-le-Pauvre, 75005 Paris (tel. 43-54-19-20). Esmeralda was the lover of Quasimodo, who used to hunch his way through the towers of Notre-Dame, directly across the river from this hotel. In a small 16th-century storefront, on a quiet square facing a church even older than Notre-Dame, this hotel is one of the most unusual in Paris. It has 19 tastefully wallpapered rooms, many with antiques, as well as views of the cathedral. Exposed timbers still support the narrow walls of this very old house.

You'll reach your room by passing through a small stone-walled lobby and climbing a winding flight of stairs whose massive balustrades are as old as the house itself. This is a popular hotel, and it's usually difficult to get a room in summer. If you do, your favorite chamber might quickly become no. 14. The rooms facing the front are usually bigger. Sixteen of the rooms have a private bath or shower. One or two people in a room with full bath and a view of Notre-Dame pay from 340F ($51.35) to 390F ($58.90). One or two people in a less desirable room with shower are charged only 250F ($37.75), including tax and service. Breakfast is extra. Métro: St-Michel.

Regent's Hôtel, 44 rue Madame, 75006 Paris (tel. 45-48-02-81), is deep in the Left Bank district on a relatively quiet street, one short block from the Luxembourg Gardens. Perhaps its best feature is a little paved patio with beds of flowers, shrubbery, and white wrought-iron furniture. Breakfast is leisurely in this secluded spot. You can meet with friends (or make new ones) in the petit salon.

Thirty-six rooms are offered, with furnishings a mixture of modified modern, antiques, and reproductions. In all cases, they are comfortable, and beds are large and soft. Some doubles and twins with private baths are offered for 425F ($64.20), including continental breakfast and taxes. Métro: St-Sulpice or St-Placide.

Hôtel Lindbergh, 5 rue Chomel, 75007 Paris (tel. 45-48-35-53), honors the late American aviator whose nonstop solo flight across the Atlantic electrified Paris and the world in 1927. Not so long ago, this establishment looked as if nothing had changed since that day, but it now has a modern, elegant exterior and is completely renovated inside. On a somewhat hidden-away Left Bank street two minutes' walk from St-Germain-des-Prés, it's next to a good budget restaurant, off boulevard Raspail. The 26-room hotel offers rooms with private bath or shower along with direct-dial phones. A single with shower rents for 325F ($49.10); a double with shower is 360F ($54.35); a double with complete bath is 440F ($66.45). Breakfast is the only meal served. Métro: Sèvres-Babylone or St-Sulpice.

Hôtel Verneuil St-Germain, 8 rue de Verneuil, 75007 Paris (tel. 42-60-82-14), is a three-star hotel just a few blocks from the Seine on a narrow street lined with antique dealers. Behind its cream-colored façade are 26 cozy rooms that have upholstered walls, exposed beams, marble-tile bathrooms, phones, color TVs, and radios. A bar decorated with French provincial furnishings serves drinks to residents and their guests. If you wish to breakfast here, you can have it in a downstairs room done in stone. Single or double units cost 450F ($67.95) to 580F ($87.60). Métro: rue du Bac or St-Germain-des-Prés.

Hôtel Lenox, 9 rue de l'Université, 75007 Paris (tel. 42-96-10-95), has been a long-standing favorite for those seeking a reasonably priced and desirable nest in St-Germain-des-Prés. Once this was a rather basic little pension. In 1910, in those halcyon years before the "Great War," T. S. Eliot spent a hot summer here on "'the old man's money." Today this much-improved hotel offers 34 comfortably furnished bedrooms, with either a private bath or shower. Rooms are small and snug, some with elaborate ceiling molding. The lobby, with its helpful staff and marble fireplace, sets the tone, and a convivial bar off the main reception area is open daily from 5pm to 2am. Rates, single or double, range from 410F ($61.90) to 550F ($83.05). For 850F, two people can have a double room with a private salon. Many returning guests request the attic duplex with its tiny balcony and skylight. Métro: rue du Bac.

Grand Hôtel Taranne, 153 bd. St-Germain, 75006 Paris (tel. 42-22-21-65). Its enviable location next to the Brasserie Lipp, within the shadow of the tower of St-Germain-des-Prés, makes it a favorite for visitors wanting to be in the heart of a district known for its artistic chic. You'll approach the reception desk via a narrow hallway, at the end of which is a bar and breakfast room.

Upstairs are 35 well-upholstered rooms, each unit slightly different from its neighbor. Some have a scattering of period-style reproductions, a tile- or marble-covered bathroom, a minibar, TV, and phone. The quieter rooms look out over a shadowy courtyard whose walls block out noise from the street. Some of the accommodations have a whirlpool bath and steambath. Both singles and doubles range from 345F ($52.10) to 750F ($113.25). Métro: St-Germain-des-Prés.

Hôtel Louis II, 2 rue St-Sulpice, 75006 Paris (tel. 46-33-13-80). One of the most skillful, and perhaps the most charming, renovations on the Left Bank transformed the interiors of a run-down pair of 18th-century buildings into a chintz-covered rustic fantasy. Its decorators exposed as many of the hand-hewn beams as they could, so that in each of the 20 cozy bedrooms wide expanses of mellowed patina contrast pleasantly with flowered wall coverings and plush carpeting. Many repeat visitors request one of the romantic rooms beneath the slope of the building's eaves for an upgraded version of the kind of attic room where scenes from *La Bohème* might have been staged.

Morning coffee and afternoon drinks are served in an elegant reception salon, where gilt-framed mirrors, bouquets of fresh flowers, and well-oiled antiques add to a refreshingly provincial allure. A visitor's stay is made even more pleasant thanks to the dedicated efforts of the manager, Brigitte Siozade.

Each accommodation contains its own bathroom, phone, minibar, and (if requested) TV. Singles and doubles range from 380F ($57.40) to 550F ($83.05); triples are 680F ($102.70). Métro: Odéon.

Deux-Continents, 25 rue Jacob, 75006 Paris (tel. 43-26-72-46), is the domain of Madame Chresteil, who inherited these two continents—that is, two adjoining buildings. She runs the place with a rare combination of sense and candor, good humor, and kindliness. She's furnished the rooms in modern and not-so-modern, installed telephones, and ensured that there are reading lights over the beds, plus private baths. The prices include taxes, service, and a breakfast tray brought to the room. All rooms have a private bath or shower and a toilet. Rates are 330F ($49.85) to 480F ($72.50) single, 400F ($60.40) to 550F ($83.05) double. A few triples are rented for 600F ($90.60). Métro: St-Germain-des-Prés.

A Bit of Medieval Paris

Hôtel Saint-André-des-Arts, 66 rue St-André-des-Arts, 75006 Paris (tel. 43-26-96-16), is a famous little St-Germain-des-Prés hotel in the midst of several galleries and shops. It housed the Beat Generation of the fifties, the hippies of the sixties, and chances are it'll be around to shelter whatever movement is *au courant* in the year 2000. A half-timbered building, the 34-room hotel (25 with private shower or bath) looks a little bit like medieval Paris. Stone and wood beams help extend the impression inside. Including a continental breakfast, singles with shower and toilet start at 260F ($39.26); doubles with shower and toilet start at 360F ($54.35). Métro: Odéon.

Grand Hôtel des Balcons, 3 rue Casimir-Delavigne, 75006 Paris (tel. 46-34-78-50), is perhaps the best buy on this little street off the Odéon. The lobby is rust-colored and decorated with art nouveau panels. The place is unpretentious. A two-star hotel, it once sheltered Endre Ady (1877–1919), Hungary's greatest lyric poet, who died a victim of alcoholism.

The rooms have been renovated by the owners, Monsieur and Madame Corroyer. They offer 55 compact rooms, each with a private bath, color TV, direct-dial phone, and background music. Depending on the plumbing, singles cost 245F ($37) to 260F ($39.25); doubles, 300F ($45.30) to 330F ($49.85); and triples, 400F ($60.40). Ask for rooms above the street level for greater comfort and security. Métro: Odéon.

Grand Hôtel Moderne, 33 rue des Ecoles, 75005 Paris (tel.

43-54-37-78), near Notre-Dame and the Panthéon, is a successful blend of the Paris of yesterday and that of today. In the heart of the Latin Quarter, this hotel provides a warm welcome by its charming owner, Madame Gibon. She rents 52 comfortably furnished bedrooms with private bath. They are spotlessly maintained and are equipped with minibar, phone, and TV. There are double-glazed aluminum windows in the rooms fronting the rue des Ecoles, which make for a more tranquil atmosphere. Rates are 375F ($56.65) single, 400F ($60.40) double. Métro: Maubert-Mutualité or St-Michel.

---

4. Airport Hotels

AT CHARLES DE GAULLE

Hôtel Sofitel, Aéroport Charles de Gaulle–Zone Centrale, 95713 Roissy-Charles de Gaulle (tel. 48-62-23-23), is just a few minutes from the airport—you can take the free bus service. All 352 of its rooms are air-conditioned and soundproof, and there are enough bars and restaurants to save you from making a difficult trip into Paris. Double-bedded rooms and twins are offered, and all of them contain TVs, phones, private bathrooms, radios, and harmoniously attractive furnishings. A standard single or double costs 670F ($101.15), rising to 750F ($113.25) for the "grand comfort" singles or doubles. For day use only, the single or double rate is 400F ($60.40).

AT ORLY

Hilton International Orly, 267 Orly Sud, 94396 Val-de-Marne (tel. 46-87-33-88), midway between the two terminals at Orly Airport, is one of the most contemporary airport hotels on the continent, with a long "sawtooth" design outside and style and flourish inside. It offers high-level comfort and all the modern conveniences to clients who prefer to spend either their first or last nights near their departure or arrival point. A full range of conference facilities is available, and many of the guests tend to be international businesspeople who prefer the traditional style and efficiency of a Hilton. The hotel has two restaurants, an accommodating bar area, and a wide range of extra service. The hotel is connected by free shuttle bus to the passenger terminals of the nearby airport.

Each of the 380 most comfortable bedrooms has been well insulated against noise, and they contain phone, private bath, air conditioning, multilanguage radio, TV with in-house movies, and access to 24-hour room service. The heart of Paris is about 30 minutes away by taxi anytime except during rush hours. Most clients will find enough to do on the premises, including swimming, ice skating, and tennis courts a few minutes away.

The main restaurant, La Louisiane, features Creole and international specialties in a New Orleans setting. The restaurant is closed on Saturday and in August. Many Parisians come here from the center of Paris just to dine, enjoying such dishes as oysters Rockefeller, seafood or chicken gumbo, and jambalaya.

Singles range from 825F ($124.60) to 970F ($146.45); doubles, 960F ($144.95) to 1,070F ($161.55). Children can stay free in their parents' room.

PARIS DINING

Everything you've ever heard about French cooking is true—it's absolutely superb. And Paris is where you'll find French cuisine at its best. So if fine dining, at any price level, is what you enjoy, then you've come to the right place. All of the world's large cities boast a certain number of fine restaurants, but only in Paris can you turn onto the nearest side street, enter the first ramshackle hostelry you see, sit down at the bare and wobbly table, glance at an illegibly hand-scrawled menu—and get a memorable meal.

But what about the cost? Paris has gained a reputation as being damnably expensive in the food department. True, its star-studded, internationally famous establishments are very expensive indeed. Places like Taillevent, Tour d'Argent, Maxim's, Grand Véfour, Lasserre, and Robuchon are not so much restaurants, but temples of gastronomy, living memorials to the glory of French cuisine. The Grand Véfour, in fact, is officially classed as a local monument and may be altered only under penalty of law. Maxim's was immortalized by Franz Lehar in his *Merry Widow,* and La Tour d'Argent boasts what is widely regarded as the finest wine cellar in the world.

In these culinary cathedrals you pay not only for superb décor and regal service, but also for the art of celebrated chefs on ministerial salaries.

There is also a vast array of expensive restaurants existing almost exclusively on the tourist trade. Their food may be indifferent or downright bad, but they'll have ice water and ketchup to anesthetize your tastebuds, trilingual waiters, and quadrilingual menus. It's these places that are largely responsible for Paris's high-cost reputation, and if you insist on frequenting them you'll find it only too true.

Luckily, there are others. Hundreds of others. For Paris has not only more restaurants than any other city on earth, it also has more good, reasonably priced ones. And they don't take much finding. I counted 18 of them on a single, narrow Left Bank Street.

---

1. Restaurant Notes

Paris restaurants by law add a service charge of around 12% to 15% to your bill (*service compris*), which means you don't have to leave a tip. But it is customary to leave something extra.

Some restaurants include beverage in their menu rates (*boisson compris*). And do try wine with meals. French cooking only achieves palate perfection when lubricated by wine, which is not considered a luxury or even an addition, but an integral part of every meal. Don't—unless you're a real connoisseur—worry about bottle labels and vintages. Some of the most satisfying wines I've had came from unlabeled house bottles. Don't be overly concerned with that red-wine-with-red-meat, white-with-white routine. It's merely a rough guide. When in doubt, order a rosé, which fits almost everything.

French beer, on the other hand, is so anemic that it can't be regarded as an alcoholic beverage. Look on it as a thirst quencher only, like Vichy water.

In many of the less expensive places detailed below, the menu will be printed or handwritten in French only. Don't let that intimidate you. You needn't be timid either about ordering dishes without knowing precisely what they are. You'll get some delightful surprises. I know a woman who wouldn't have dreamed of asking for escargots if she'd realized they were snails cooked in garlic sauce. As it was, she ate this appetizer in a spirit of thrift rather than adventure —and has been addicted to it ever since.

Finally, a word on vegetables. The French regard them as separate courses and eat them apart from the meat dishes. I wouldn't advise you to order them specially, unless you're an exceptionally hearty eater. Most main courses come with a small helping or *garni* of vegetables, anyway.

You'll find a large number of specific dishes explained in the restaurant descriptions. No one, however, can explain the subtle nuances of flavor that distinguish them. Those you have to taste for yourself.

Coffee, in France, is served *after* the meal and carries an extra charge. The French consider it absolutely barbaric to drink coffee along with the courses. Unless you specifically order it with milk (*au lait*), the coffee will be black. In the more conscientious establishments, it is still served as the traditional *filtre,* a rather slow but rewarding filter style that takes a bit of manipulating.

2. The Great Restaurants

ON THE RIGHT BANK

Taillevent, 15 rue Lamennais, 8e (tel. 45-63-39-94), dates from 1946, when the restaurant was founded by the father of present owner Jean-Claude Vrinat. It has climbed steadily in the ranks of excellence since then, and today it is recognized as arguably the most outstanding eating place in Paris in terms of the cuisine, the wines, the service, and the all-around pleasure provided its customers. The setting is a grand 18th-century town house off the Champs-Elysées, once inhabited by the Duke of Morny, with paneled rooms and crystal chandeliers. The name of the restaurant honors a famous chef of the 14th century, who was the author of one of the oldest known books on French cookery. Monsieur Vrinat welcomes guests to his dignified establishment as if they were arriving for a private dinner party. The place is not huge, but that is as the owner wishes, since it permits him to give personal attention to every facet of the operation, seeing to the continuation of the discreet, London-club atmosphere he so carefully maintains. He helps his staff pamper guests while they are eating the fine foods turned out under the direction of Claude Deligne, the chef.

You might begin with aspic de foie gras (dices of liver and veal sweetbreads in aspic jelly with very fine dices of carrots and truffles). Main dish specialties (subject to change, of course) include cassolette de langoustines, agneau aux trois cuissons (three cuts of lamb—feet, breast, and tenderloin—with various sauces). You might follow these with fondant aux deux parfums (an almond toffee Bavarian cream covered with chocolate).

Taillevent's wine list is one of the best in the city. Monsieur and Madame Vrinat make the selections carefully and knowledgeably, providing bottles pleasing to the palate and complementary to the fine cuisine. Count on spending from 850F ($128.35) for a gourmet dinner, plus 15% service. That service, incidentally, is impeccable. Reservations are necessary, and although Monsieur Vrinat likes Americans, it isn't always easy for visitors from the States and other countries to book a table, since the owner prefers to see his clientele comprise about 60% French people. The restaurant is open Monday through Friday from noon to 2:30pm and 7 to 10pm; closed Saturday and Sunday. Métro: George-V.

Lasserre, 17 av. Franklin D. Roosevelt, 8e (tel. 43-59-53-43). What is now this elegant and deluxe restaurant was a simple bistro before the war, a "rendezvous for chauffeurs." Then along came René Lasserre, who bought the dilapidated building and set out to create his dream. His dream turned into a culinary paradise, attracting gourmets from around the world.

Two white-painted front doors lead to the dining rooms on the ground level, including a reception lounge with Louis XVI–style furnishings and brocaded walls . . . most chic. Even the small elevator that takes you to the main dining room upstairs is beautifully lined with brocaded silk. The main salon is two stories high. On each side is a mezzanine. Draped with silk, tall arched windows open onto the street. At a table set with fine porcelain, crystal glasses edged in gold, a silver candelabrum, even a silver bird and a ceramic dove, you sit on a Louis XV–style salon chair and carefully study the menu.

Overhead the ceiling is painted with lamb-white clouds and a cerulean sky. The trick here is that in fair weather the staff slides back the roof to let in the real sky, either moonlight or sunshine. From time to time, Monsieur Lasserre brings in a flock of white doves from his home in the country. Then he releases them in the room. Before that, however, raffle numbers have been attached to their feet.

The food is a combination of French classicism and originality. The presentation of dishes is one of the most winning and imaginative aspects of Lasserre. Always count on high drama. For example, the garni vegetables so often neglected in most restaurants are presented here with flourish. In the hands of some artist back there in the kitchen, vegetables become flowers.

To begin your repast, I'd suggest a specialty, blanc de sandre (zander) à la nage d'etrilles. Among the fish main dishes, try a queues de langoustines (lobster) rôties with an herb-flavored sabayon sauce. Especially recommendable is the steak de Charolais au Bourgueil. For dessert, try a parfait aux noisettes (hazelnuts) grillées, with a honey-flavored sabayon. The cellar of some 180,000 bottles is among the more remarkable in Paris; red wines are decanted into silver pitchers or ornate crystal. It will cost from 800F ($120.80) per person to dine here.

Reservations are a must. Hours Tuesday through Saturday are 12:30 to 2:30pm and 7:30 to 10:30pm; closed Sunday, Monday lunch, and in August. Métro: F. D. Roosevelt.

Robuchon, 32 rue du Longchamp, 16e (tel. 47-27-12-27), is where Joël Robuchon, the chef and proprietor, basks in his reputation as the country's most innovative cook. Some critics say his restaurant is the finest in France. If you're a gourmet, your idea of heaven could well be to hire Monsieur Robuchon to be in charge of your kitchen. He is a master of the cuisine moderne, sometimes called cuisine actuelle, or what is actually being cooked now. Produced here are foods that are light and delicate, with outstanding flavors. In his elegantly understated dining room, where his wife, Janine, presides over the cash register, Robuchon's capable and courteous staff serves dishes that the chef takes pains to make colorful and pleasing to the eye as well as tempting to the palate. He even bakes his own bread fresh every day, and he is known to spend long hours in the kitchen testing out (or inventing) new recipes. He has his own fish and shellfish shipped fresh from Brittany so it doesn't have to "linger" at the Rungis wholesale market.

Among the delectable offerings have been such dishes as kidneys and sweetbreads diced and sautéed with mushrooms, canette rosée (duckling which has been roasted and braised, flavored with such spices as ginger, nutmeg, cinnamon, and other Chinese-influenced touches), shellfish-filled ravioli steamed in cabbage leaves, and chicken for two, poached in a pig's bladder. His mashed potatoes, once labeled "the silliest dish in the world," are hailed here as a masterpiece—and they are. But the chef won't reveal his secret.

A set menu is offered for 790F ($119.30). If you prefer to order à la carte, expect to pay 750F ($113.25) to 1,000F ($151). Hours are 12:30 to 2:30pm and 7:30 to 10:30pm Monday through Friday. Reservations are imperative, and it's wisest to make them six to eight weeks in advance. Some guests make them from the United States before starting their trip to Paris. Monsieur Robuchon likes to have foreign diners, but he prefers to have about half the guest list made up of French customers. The restaurant is closed on Saturday, Sunday, and in July. Métro: Trocadéro.

Le Grand Véfour, 17 rue de Beaujolais, 1er (tel. 42-96-56-27), has been an eating place since the reign of Louis XV, and it has had its ups and downs. Although the exact date of its opening as the Café de Chartres is not definitely known, it is more than 200 years old and is classified as a historical treasure. It got its present name in 1812, when Jean Véfour, former chef to a member of the royal family, owned it. Since that time it has attracted such notables as Napoléon and Danton and a host of writers and artists, such as Victor Hugo, Colette, and Jean Cocteau (who designed the menu cover in 1953).

Amid the arcades of the Palais-Royal, the restaurant had lost its earlier glamour by the coming of the 20th century and was simply a little corner café. It had another "up" period after World War II, under Raymond Oliver, one of the most famous of modern French chefs, but as he aged, it again fell into a decline. Fortunately, Jean Taittinger of the Taittinger Champagne family (they also own the Hôtel de Crillon) purchased the restaurant, and it has now reached —perhaps surpassed—its former glories. The restoration, done under the close eye of the Department of Historical Monuments, involved the cleaning, repairing, and matching of furniture, reweaving of Aubusson carpets, and refurbishing of the painted-silk décor.

Dining here is an experience. From Limoges china, white with a green-leaf border, you can feast at a table bearing a brass plaque with the name of a famous former occupant. The chef, Jean-Claude L'Honneur, produces dishes, some traditional and some new creations, that are limited but choice.

For your appetizer, which the French call *entrées,* select, perhaps, a terrine of chicken liver or cream of lentils with smoked "fruits of the sea." For your main course, you might choose roast monkfish with endive or perhaps a Bresse pigeon flavored with thyme. Desserts are sumptuous, including, for example, a chocolate soufflé Café de Chartres. You'll want to accompany your meal with one or more of the fine wines from the cellar.

Expect to pay 600F ($90.60) to 800F ($120.80) for your à la carte dinner. However, a lunch menu is featured at 305F ($46.05). The restaurant is open Monday through Friday from 12:30 to 2pm and 7:30 to 10pm; closed Saturday and Sunday. Reservations are required. Métro: Louvre.

Alain Senderens' Lucas-Carton, 9 place de la Madeleine, 8e (tel. 42-65-22-90), a Paris landmark from the Belle Epoque era, is today a blend of the old and the new, since it was taken over by one of Paris's top restaurateurs. Senderens has added his own touches to the historic restaurant, which was created during the time of British King Edward VII by an Englishman named Lucas and a talented French chef, Francis Carton. The two dining rooms as well as the private rooms upstairs are decorated with expanses of mirrors, sprays of spring flowers offsetting the carved wooden panels, pristine white ceilings and napery, and art nouveau lighting. If General Pershing, Marshal Foch, General de Gaulle, Winston Churchill, and other leaders in both World Wars were looking around today for a proper site to discuss world affairs over lunch, they would probably opt again for Lucas-Carton, as they once did.

The food they would be served, however, would be different from that of half a century and more ago. Senderens, who bakes his own bread, creates such tasty dishes as fresh cod with eggplant, caviar, and fried zucchini, ravioli filled with scallops and served with thyme-flavored zucchini, and mild smoked salmon with a sprinkling of salmon eggs, plus other delicacies from his own smoker and from the rôtisserie. However, Senderens is constantly searching for new culinary creations so you will have to choose from what he has developed by the time you visit. For dessert, if it is on the menu then, I suggest the hot pineapple fritters, beignets d'ananas Eventhia (named for his wife).

The menu dégustation costs 750F ($113.25). If you order à la carte, expect to pay from 950F ($143.45) for your meal. The restaurant is open Monday through Friday from noon to 2:30pm and 8 to 11:30pm; closed Saturday, Sunday, and holidays. Reservations must be made several days ahead for lunch, several weeks ahead for dinner. Métro: Madeleine.

Maxim's, 3 rue Royale, 8e (tel. 42-65-27-94), is the world's most legendary restaurant. It preserves the era of Belle Epoque. It's not hard to imagine the Gay Nineties when "cocottes," replete with ostrich feathers, perched in their boxes, letting their diamonds sparkle and casting flirtatious glances at handsome, almond-eyed young men. Maxim's was a favorite of Edward VII, then the prince of Wales. He enjoyed the slightly decadent atmosphere, far removed in spirit from the rigid London ruled by his stern mother, Victoria.

The restaurant is known to many North American movie-goers who have never been to Paris. It was the setting for *The Merry Widow,* where John Gilbert "dipped and swayed" with Mae Murray. That memory is kept alive today. You can always be sure the orchestra will play that tune at least once a night. Much later in film history, Louis Jourdan—at that time called "the handsomest man in the world"—took Leslie Caron to the restaurant "the night they invented champagne" in the musical *Gigi.*

Over the years, Maxim's has carried on, only the big names of yesterday—Callas, Onassis, and the like—are long gone. Today, tourists from around the world are likely to occupy once-fabled tables. Clothing-industry giant Pierre Cardin took over the restaurant in 1981. The kitchen has a staff of some of the finest and most talented young cooks in France. Many of them train at Maxim's before going on to open an operation of their own. One of the finest soups I've had anywhere—and it's a great opener to a repast at Maxim's—

is Billi-By soup. It's made with mussels, white wine, cream (of course), chopped onions, celery, and parsley, as well as coarsely ground pepper. Another favorite, the sole Albert, named after the late famous maître d'hôtel, is flavored with chopped herbs and breadcrumbs, plus a large glass of vermouth. Also highly recommended is the Challons duckling in a foie gras sauce. For dessert, try the tarte tatin. As for drinks, everybody at Maxim's orders champagne, or used to in the old days.

After making your reservation, arrive slightly early so you can have a drink in the Imperial Bar upstairs. Formal dress is de rigueur on Friday.

Expect to pay 850F ($128.35) to 1,000F ($151) for an elegant dinner. Maxim's is open seven days a week, except Sunday in July and August. Hours are 12:30 to 2pm and 7:30pm to midnight. It's fashionable to have an after-theater supper here, listening or dancing to the music. The kitchen takes orders until midnight. Métro: Concorde.

Le Vivarois, 192 av. Victor-Hugo, 16e (tel. 45-04-04-31), has been called a revelation by food critics. This restaurant opened in 1966 with a modern décor (including chairs by Knoll), and it was initially popular with the American colony. The American magazine *Gourmet* once hailed it as "a restaurant of our time . . . the most exciting, audacious, and important restaurant in Paris today." It still maintains its standards.

Le Vivarois is the personal statement of its supremely talented owner-chef, Claude Peyrot. His menu is constantly changing. Someone once said, and quite accurately, "the menu changes with the marketing and his genius." He does a most recommendable coquilles St-Jacques (scallops) en crème, and a pourpre de turbot Vivarois. His most winning dish to many is rognons de veau (veal kidneys).

Madame Peyrot is one of the finest maîtres d'hôtel in Paris. She'll guide you beautifully through wine selections so you'll end up with the perfect complement to her husband's superlative cuisine. It is necessary to reserve in advance. Expect to pay from 500F ($75.50) to 600F ($90.60) for a memorable meal. Hours are noon to 2pm and 8 to 10pm; closed Saturday, Sunday, and in August. Métro: Pompe.

ON THE LEFT BANK

La Tour d'Argent, 15-17 quai de la Tournelle, 5e (tel. 43-54-23-31), is a national institution. The view over the Seine and the apse of Notre-Dame is superb. At night, incidentally, Notre-Dame is floodlit, partly at the expense of La Tour d'Argent. Sometimes the lights go off in this penthouse restaurant so that you may enjoy the special illumination of Paris by night.

On the Left Bank, La Tour d'Argent traces its history back a long way. A restaurant of some sort has stood on this ground since 1582. The fame of the establishment was spread during its ownership by Frédéric Delair, who bought the fabled wine cellar of Café

Anglais. He was the one who started the practice of issuing certificates to diners ordering the house specialty, pressed duckling (caneton). The birds, incidentally, are numbered.

Under the sharp eye of its owner, Claude Terrail, the cooking is superb, the service impeccable. Dresden china adorns each table. Although a quarter of the menu is taken up with various ways you can order duck, I assure you that the kitchen *does* know how to prepare other dishes. Especially recommendable are quenelles de brochet homard Lagardère and noisettes de Tournelles. To open your meal, I recommend potage Claudius Burdel, made with egg yolks, fresh cream, chicken broth, sorrel, and butter, whipped together.

Whatever your repast, you'll fare better than those attending the 1870 Christmas dinner during the war with Prussia. Raiding the Paris zoo, the chef offered such delicacies as elephant soup, antelope chops, bear steaks, camel hump, even side dishes of wolves, cats, and rats!

Expect to pay from 750F ($113.25) for a complete meal. The restaurant is open Tuesday to Sunday from 12:30 to 2:30pm and 8 to 11:30pm. You must reserve. Métro: Maubert-Mutualité or Sully-Morland.

---

3. Expensive Restaurants

If you can't afford Maxim's or Tour d'Argent, know that there are many other fine establishments serving remarkable food at prices that are slightly lower than those already previewed.

ON THE RIGHT BANK

Escargot-Montorgueil, 38 rue Montorgueil, 1er (tel. 42-36-83-51). The "golden snail" of Les Halles is as golden as ever, even if the famous market has moved elsewhere. And the Escargot-Montorgueil is firmly entrenched, the building supposedly dating from the days of Catherine de'Medici. The restaurant opened its doors back in the 1830s, and inside it looks it. (The décor has been described as "authentic Louis Philippe.") The greats, such as Sarah Bernhardt, have paraded through here. The food—in the grand bistro tradition—remains consistently good.

Everybody but the regulars appears to order escargots, although this dish doesn't seem to get much attention from the chef. I recommend the pieds de porcs and the feather turbot soufflé. For dessert, the specialty is crêpes flambés. The restaurant is run by Madame Saladin-Terrail, known as Kouikette, sister of Claude Terrail, the guiding hand behind La Tour d'Argent.

Your complete meal is likely to run from 350F ($52.85) per person with wine, not including the 15% service charge. Open from noon to 2pm and 8 to 11pm every day except Monday at lunch, and during part of August. Reservations are imperative. Métro: Les Halles.

Le Sallambier, Hôtel Balzac, 6 rue Balzac, 8e (tel. 45-61-97-22), is the exclusive restaurant of one of the most elegant four-star hotels of Paris, lying just off the Champs-Elysées. From around the world the rich and famous flock to this classically refined restaurant. Here they find service that is impeccably courtly, and a cuisine (thanks to an imaginative chef, Jean-Paul Deyries) that is among the finest in this highly competitive neighborhood of the Eighth Arrondissement. The restaurant is named after Balzac's mother. A quartet of lions peers out from its illuminated ceiling dome whose sides are covered with frescoes that might have been painted by Rousseau or Gauguin.

The well-prepared (and well-received) cuisine features many specialties from southwestern France, as well as an impressive offering of cuisine moderne selections. Specialties are likely to include a papillotte of young rabbit with fennel, a sabayon of langoustines with cauliflower, a cocotte of scallops with cabbage, and grilled filet of beef with a purée of garlic. Try, if it is featured, the veal piccata with spinach. Desserts tend to be elaborate concoctions.

A menu is offered for 195F ($29.45), or you can dine à la carte for 350F ($52.85). The restaurant is open Monday through Friday from 12:30 to 2:30pm and 8 to 11pm; closed in August. Métro: George-V.

Le Céladon, Hôtel Westminster, 13 rue de la Paix, 2e (tel. 42-61-57-46), is one of the finest restaurants in the vicinity of the Opéra and the place Vendôme. At lunch it is busy and bustling, often with outstanding members of the business community of the Second Arrondissement, but in the evening there is rarely any problem in securing a table if you call ahead of time. The restaurant takes its name from the céladon porcelain displayed, an outstanding collection.

You might begin your evening in the bar, Les Chenets, where you are served drinks from 11am until midnight but can also order light but delicious dishes. If you're in the neighborhood, you can also visit in the afternoon for tea or coffee with homemade cakes or pastries. In the evening a barman presents his special cocktail of the day. During apéritif hour, this cozy bar is turned into a piano bar. Its paneling and fireplace are replicas of those in the Gothic Hall at Westminster Abbey.

Le Céladon, of course, is the main attraction. The chef de cuisine, Joël Boilleaut, was previously head chef at the two-star Le Duc d'Enghien in the Paris suburb of Enghien-les-Bains. He offers seasonal specialties, a traditional but light cuisine. The varied and imaginative menu is aided by the professional service. You might begin with an amusing appetizer, then follow with a main course such as a panache of monkfish and salmon flavored with saffron and served with wild rice. After a selection of cheese, you perhaps will be ready for one of the tempting desserts.

Menus begin at 260F ($39.25); à la carte costs around 350F ($52.85). Service is only Monday through Friday from noon to 3pm and 7 to 10pm. Métro: Opéra.

La Grande Cascade, Bois de Boulogne, 16e (tel. 45-06-33-

51), is a garden house—a Belle Epoque shrine for lunch, afternoon tea, or dinner in the heart of Paris's fashionable park. Originally, this indoor-outdoor restaurant was built by Baron Haussmann and was used as a hunting lodge for Napoléon III. At the turn of the century it was converted into a restaurant and drew the chic of its day, including Colette. Picture such a theatrical personality as Mistinguette arriving in a grand carriage, complete with super-wide-brim hat, parasol, and entourage. That was La Grande Cascade that was.

Today's humbler guest can select a table, choosing the more formal interior with its gilt, crystal, and glass roof, or the more popular front terrace. At the latter, under either parasols or portico shelter, you can order a meal, a drink, or an old-fashioned afternoon tea with a generous helping of the chef's favorite cake. Soft lights at night from the tall frosted lamps and the sound of the nearby cascade enhance the romantic feeling of the place.

The restaurant features such à la carte selections as duckling foie gras, fish poached in seaweed and basil, and veal sweetbreads in truffle-flavored butter. A spectacular finish is provided by crêpes soufflées à l'orange.

A complete meal will cost from 500F ($75.50). However, a business lunch costs only 240F ($36.25). Open mid-April through October daily from noon to 3pm and 7:30 to 10:30pm; November to mid-December and mid-January to mid-April, daily noon to 3pm; closed the rest of the year. You must taxi or drive to the restaurant.

ON THE LEFT BANK

Jacques Cagna, 14 rue des Grands-Augustins, 6e (tel. 43-26-49-39). Both the clientele and the food are considered among the most sophisticated and/or grandest in Paris. The establishment is contained in a 17th-century town house whose interior is filled with massive timbers and a delectable color scheme of pinkish beige, plus a series of 17th-century Dutch paintings. The main dining room lies one flight above street level.

A specialty is the Aberdeen Angus beef, aged for a full three weeks, which chef Cagna imbues with a shallot-flavored sauce rich with herbs and seasonings. You might begin with a double-edged salad of Brittany lobster mixed with duck liver and artichoke bottoms, or else a feuilleté of crayfish with mussels in a sherry-flavored morel sauce. Other specialties include tender sweetbreads braised in essence of giant shrimp or a pungent leg of baby lamb with tarragon, perhaps Breton pigeon with honey and sauterne. Desserts are overwhelmingly tempting.

A la carte meals cost 500F ($75.50) to 700F ($105.70). However, an outstanding fixed-price menu is offered at lunch for 235F ($35.50). Meals are served Monday through Saturday from noon to 2pm and 7:30 to 10:30pm; closed in August. Métro: St-Michel.

Le Jules Verne, Tour Eiffel, Champ de Mars, 7e (tel. 45-55-61-44). Today the institution of drinking and dining within the framework of the symbol of Paris is still alive and well. Many visitors view the elevator ride up to the second platform of the Eiffel Tower as one of the highlights of their experience. After the ride, you are ushered into a décor as black as the Parisian night outside, with only strategically placed spotlights set on each of the minimalist tables. The end result seems to bring the twinkling Paris panorama into the restaurant itself.

All of this would be merely a fantasy for ex-aviators and the child in each of us if not for the exquisite food prepared by a culinary team headed by Louis Grondard. The menu changes with the season, but might include a ravioli of sweetbreads with lobster sauce, scallops with sweet-and-sour sauce, duck liver with aged vinegar sauce, filet of turbot with seaweed and a butter flavored with sea urchins, or a cassolette of fresh hot oysters with cucumbers.

Full meals, served only with an advance reservation, start at 550F ($83.05). A fixed-price menu is served only at lunchtime, for 250F ($37.75). The restaurant is open daily from noon to 2:30pm and 7:30 to 10:30pm. Métro: Trocadéro, Ecole-Militaire, or Bir-Hakeim.

Chez les Anges, 54 bd. de Latour-Maubourg, 7e (tel. 47-05-89-86). The encyclopedia *Larousse Gastronomique* reported that "Burgundy is undoubtedly the region of France where the best food and the best wines are to be had." Whether or not that's true, the "House of Angels" does serve some of the finest Burgundian meals in Paris. On the Left Bank, almost opposite the Invalides, Les Anges is worth the trek. It is directed by Jacqueline Delmas and has the ambience of a bistro. Over the years, it has changed very little in cuisine and décor.

Many of the long-time Burgundian dishes are offered, including, as a starter, les oeufs en meurette (eggs in red-wine sauce.) The most classic main dish is sauté de boeuf bourguignon, as well as fricassee of veal kidneys. Other main dishes include suprême de barbue (brill) au beurre de poivrons rouges, a cassolette of scallops with sea urchins, and tranche épaisse de foie de veau (thickly sliced calves' liver). The goat-cheese selection is varied. Desserts are rich, including a sorbet made with fresh strawberries and Cassis.

The average bill is about 300F ($45.30) to 400F ($60.40) per person. Reservations are necessary, especially at lunch when French businesspeople crowd the place. Open daily from noon to 2pm and 7 to 11pm; closed Sunday night. Métro: Latour-Maubourg.

FOR LA CUISINE MODERNE

Many visitors to Paris today are eager to sample La Cuisine Moderne. The aim of the cuisine is to release the natural flavor of food; rich sauces are eliminated and cooking time, which can destroy the best of fresh ingredients, is considerably shortened.

La Cuisine Moderne is an outgrowth of nouvelle cuisine, which flourished in the 1970s and 80s, but is now discredited by some chefs. Indeed, Paul Bocuse, the most famous chef in France, pronounced it "dead." The aim of La Cuisine Moderne is to avoid the excesses of the nouvelle school, yet to stay attuned to light fare with today's weight-conscious and health-conscious diner in mind.

What follows is a random sampling of some of the leading centers where the original, imaginative cuisine moderne is practiced with skill and talent.

Carré des Feuillants, 14 rue de Castiglione, 1er (tel. 42-86-82-82). Alain Dutournier established his reputation as a leading chef de cuisine at Au Trou Gascon, which is now run by his wife, Nicole. He moved his showcase to this restaurant, a beautifully restored 17th-century convent, and immediately became an overnight success. The interior is like a turn-of-the-century bourgeois house, with several small salons. These open onto an inviting skylit interior courtyard, across from which a glass-enclosed kitchen can be viewed (no secrets here). The location near place Vendôme and the Tuileries is platinum.

Monsieur Dutournier likes to call his food a *cuisine du moment.* That suggests a wild, experimental imagination that makes it next to impossible to suggest any specific dishes that might be served on the day of your visit. For example, you might get langoustines with unripened mangoes. He has a whole network of little farms that supply him with the fresh produce from which he weaves his magic spell. He is especially known for his beef butchered from one of the oldest breeds of cattle in France, the *race bazadaise,* and for lamb raised in Pauillac.

The sommelier, Jean-Guy Loustau, has distinguished himself for his exciting *cave* containing several little-known wines along with a fabulous collection of armagnacs. A dozen places in the bar await those who casually walk in without a reservation. There at lunch you can order a special meal for only 230F ($34.75). Otherwise, seating is in a selection of modern dining rooms with a stylish décor, including graphics of vegetables and fruits, the type the Jolly Green Giant might harvest.

A business lunch costs 250F ($37.75), and a six-course seasonal menu goes for 490F ($74). Hours are Monday through Friday from noon to 2pm and 7:30 to 10:30pm, on Saturday from 7:30 to 10:30pm. Métro: Tuileries, Concorde, Opéra, or Madeleine.

Au Trou Gascon, 40 rue Taine, 12e (tel. 43-44-34-26). One of the most acclaimed chefs in Paris today, Alain Dutournier launched his cooking career in the Gascony region of southwest France. His parents mortgaged their own inn so as to allow Dutournier to open a turn-of-the-century bistro in an unchic part of the 12th Arrondissement. At first he got little business, but the word soon spread that this man was a true artisan in the kitchen who practiced the real cuisine moderne and not some of its unfortunate derivatives. Today he has opened another restaurant in Paris, but he left his secret recipes with the kitchen staff. The owner's smiling wife, Nicole, is still there to greet you, and the wine steward has distinguished himself for his exciting *cave* containing several little-known wines along with a fabulous collection of Armagnacs. It is estimated that the cellar has some 350 varieties of wine.

Here you get the true cookery of Gascony, and that means cassoulet, wild salmon with smoked bacon, foie gras (offered from November to June), and Gascon ham cooked farmer's style. Menus cost from 200F ($30.20) to 300F ($45.30), with à la carte meals averaging 400F ($60.40). The restaurant is open Monday through

Friday from noon to 2pm and 7:30 to 10pm; closed around mid-July to mid-August. Métro: Daumesnil.

Restaurant Michel Rostang, 20 rue Rennequin, 17e (tel. 47-63-40-77). Monsieur Rostang is one of the most creative chefs of Paris. He's the fifth generation of one of the most distinguished "cooking families" of France. His family has been connected with the famed Bonne Auberge at Antibes on the French Riviera. From Grenoble, Rostang eventually found himself in Paris in the 17th Arrondissement where the world soon came to the door of what he modestly calls his "boutique restaurant" (nevertheless, it can seat as many as 70 diners).

Small and intimate, the restaurant offers a menu of bourgeois cuisine that changes constantly, depending on Rostang's inspiration. His specialties are likely to include ravioli filled with goat cheese and coated with a sprinkling of chervil bought fresh that morning in the market. If the mood strikes him, he might prepare a young Bresse chicken, considered the finest in France, served with a delicate chervil sauce (as you may have guessed, Rostang is much enamored of fresh chervil). Another specialty worth citing is duckling cooked in its own blood.

From October to March he is likely to offer quail eggs with a coque of sea urchins. He also prepares on occasion a delicate fricassee of sole. Many interesting wines from the Rhône are available, including Châteauneuf du Pape and Hermitage.

Lunch is available for 240F ($36.25). A dégustation menu, at lunch or dinnertime, costs from 460F ($69.45) to 495F ($74.75). Hours are Monday through Friday from noon to 2pm and 7:30 to 10pm, Saturday from 7:30 to 10pm; closed the first two weeks in August. Métro: Ternes.

Guy Savoy, 18 rue Troyon, 17e (tel. 43-80-40-61), serves the kind of food that Monsieur Savoy himself likes to eat, and it does so with consummate skill. When the five or six "hottest" chefs in Europe are named today, he most often is mentioned, and deservedly so. You never know what you are going to be served when you go there, as Monsieur Savoy seems to take his inspiration from the market, and only then when he's right on the spot, selecting his poultry, meat, and fresh vegetables, which he will later blend with his special magic touches.

Don't eat all day; then come here and order his menu dégustation. Although it runs to nine courses, the portions are small; you don't get satiated with food before the meal has run its course.

What will you get? Perhaps red mullet with wild asparagus. Maybe a cassolette of snails flavored with tarragon (no garlic, for a change), or chicken quenelles with chicken livers and cream, the rich-tasting dish sprinkled with strips of delectable black truffles. If you visit in the right season, you may have a chance to order masterfully prepared game such as mallard or venison, even game birds. He is fascinated with the *champignon* in all its many varieties, and has been known to serve as many as a dozen different types of mushrooms, especially in the autumn.

Mr. Savoy is from Grenoble, the son of a French mother and a

Swiss father. Before acquiring his own restaurant, he cooked at some of the great restaurants in France, including Troisgros at Roanne.

To dine at his restaurant will cost from 575F ($86.85) if you order his menu dégustation. On the à la carte, expect to spend from 600F ($90.60) if you sample the specialties. Open Monday through Friday from 12:30 to 2pm and 7:15 to 10:30pm; closed the last three weeks of July. Métro: Charles de Gaulle (Etoile).

La Couronne, Hôtel Warwick, 5 rue de Berry, 8e (tel. 45-63-14-11). Right off the Champs-Elysées, this address was previously recommended as a four-star hotel. However, even if you're not staying there, you may consider patronizing its award-winning restaurant. La Couronne not only offers superb food but an elegant setting amid a scarlet décor with an array of plants, mirrors, and oil murals.

Elegant people from all corners of the earth come here to enjoy the cuisine of Paul Van Gessel. He has a kind of culinary magic, and makes use of only the freshest of ingredients, which he deftly handles with care and finesse. You might begin with his wild rabbit salad with sweet corn and follow with baked salmon in sea salt or else stuffed pork trotters. Served only for two persons, the wild duck in a pepper sauce with turnips is delectable.

A business lunch or dinner is offered for only 210F ($31.70). However, more elaborate menus are also offered, and you can also order à la carte, paying around 350F ($52.85). Service is Monday to Saturday from noon to 2:30pm and 8 to 10:30pm; closed holidays. Métro: George-V.

Chiberta, 3 rue Arsène-Houssaye, 8e (tel. 45-63-77-90), right near place de l'Etoile, has a chef who has stunned some of the gastronomic circles of Paris. He is Jean-Michel Bédier, who once worked with the equally well-known Monsieur Delaveyne at Bougival's Le Camélia. In an elegantly modern setting, Bédier turns out inventive dishes.

The director of this restaurant is Louis-Noël Richard, who has taken this house and turned it into one of the most attractive restaurants in Paris. Each dish is admirably presented and described by the maître d'. The menu changes twice a year, but typical opening courses might include smoked salmon rolled around fresh asparagus and served in a sauce of red pepper and paprika, ravioli with truffles, or salmon tartare. For a main course, you might order a fricassee of scallops with truffles. To finish off, try wild strawberries with honey ice cream covered with raspberry sauce. The wine list is well chosen.

Bédier certainly knows how to turn out a culinary masterpiece, and the service and attention you get here are also winning. However, for all this perfection, you will have to pay a hefty tab, ranging from 400F ($60.40) to 700F ($105.70). The restaurant is open Monday through Friday from noon to 2:30pm and 7:30 to 11pm; closed August. Métro: Charles de Gaulle (Etoile).

L'Ambroisie, 9 place des Vosges, 4e (tel. 42-78-51-45). Bernard Pacaud is one of the most talented chefs in Paris, and his cuisine has drawn world attention. He's come a long way since he was an orphan who, at 14, had to wash dishes. He trained at the prestigious Vivarois before deciding to strike out on his own, first at a Left Bank choice, now at this ideal location in Le Marais on its square evoking memories of Victor Hugo.

His tables are nearly always filled with satisfied diners, who visit to see where his imagination will take him next. His cooking has a certain simplicity yet is at the height of elegance, as it produces subtlety but in natural flavorings that only come about because of the freshness of the products used and his skill in enhancing what nature always offered. His favored dishes include a delectable red-pepper mousse (perhaps the finest you are likely to be served in Paris), braised oxtail, wild salmon breaded and pan-fried (and served with a thin potato pancake), and a salad of mâche with a ballotine of duck. For dessert, the chocolate mousse is velvety smooth, or you might try anything in puff pastry.

Hours are Tuesday through Saturday from noon to 1:45pm and 8 to 10:15pm, Sunday from 8 to 10:15pm. At lunch (the cheapest time to dine here) a set menu is offered for 270F ($40.75); otherwise you are likely to spend from 600F ($90.60) ordering à la carte. Try for a table in the garden. Métro: St-Paul-le-Marais.

Faugeron, 52 rue de Longchamp, 16e (tel. 47-04-24-53), is in the Trocadéro district. Henri Faugeron is an inspired chef. I've followed his career since I first heard of him at Les Belles Gourmandes on the Left Bank and was delighted there with his mastery of French cooking in the classic style. Today the chef and his Austrian wife, Gerlindé, entertain a faithful list of gourmets including artists, diplomats, and business executives.

Faugeron many years ago established this restaurant that is an elegant yet not obtrusive backdrop for his superb cuisine. This creative chef calls his cuisine "revolutionary." He is viewed as a culinary researcher, and his menu always has one or two platters from the classic French table, perhaps a leg of lamb baked seven hours or rack of hare in the traditional French style. Much of his cookery depends on the season and on his shopping for only the freshest ingredients in the market. Game dishes, frogs' legs, oysters, scallops—whatever—Monsieur Faugeron and his chefs prepare food with style. In this he is aided by Jean-Claude Jambon, one of the premier sommeliers of France, indeed of the world.

A business menu, offered at lunchtime only, costs 295F ($44.55), and a dégustation meal goes for 455F ($68.70) to 590F ($89.10), taxes and service included. Hours are Monday through Friday from 12:30 to 2pm and 7:30 to 10pm; closed August. Métro: Iéna or Trocadéro.

FAMOUS BISTROS

Restaurant Pierre, 10 rue de Richelieu, 1er (tel. 42-96-09-17). Its location behind the Comédie-Française is the perfect setting for the kind of richly flavorful bourgeois cuisine for which France is famous. The chef, under the direction of the owners, Nicole and Daniel Dez, prepares updated versions of time-tested recipes that residents of the surrounding neighborhood appreciate highly. A repeat visitor can take a gastronomic tour of France without ever leaving the restaurant, because so many different regions of the country are represented on the menu.

You might begin with a terrine of foie gras, followed by grilled turbot in a Choron sauce or marvelously flavorful preparations of beef. Occasionally, wild duck is featured. The menu changes twice a week. A la carte meals start at 275F ($41.55) and are served daily from noon to 2:15pm and 7 to 10:15pm except on Saturday and Sunday in August. Reservations are necessary. Métro: Louvre.

Emile Zola at the Next Table

Bofinger, 5-7 rue de la Bastille, 4e (tel. 42-72-87-82). A columnist once wrote that whenever she ate her trout with almonds at Bofinger she kept "looking over my shoulder for Emile Zola." Bofinger was founded back in the 1860s, and is thus the oldest Alsatian brasserie in town—and certainly one of the best. It's actually a dining palace, resplendent with shiny brass. Much restored, it looks better than ever. If you prefer, you can dine on an outdoor terrace, weather permitting.

The fashionable make their way at night through the Marais district, right off the place de la Bastille, to this bustling, popular brasserie. In their floor-length white aprons, the waiters bring dish after dish of satisfying fare at reasonable prices.

Choucroûte (sauerkraut) is the preferred dish, accompanied by a vast array of bacon, sausages, and a pork chop. *Tip:* Look for the chef's specials. He features a different one every day, including a superb stew the French call "le cassoulet." Count on spending from 250F ($37.75) per person. It's open daily from noon to 3pm and 7:30pm to 1am. Métro: Bastille.

Le Bistrot de Paris, 33 rue de Lille, 7e (tel. 42-61-16-83). What is that magic element that makes discriminating diners zero in on a little place? Whatever it is, Michel Oliver knows the secret. He is the son of Raymond Oliver, one of the great restaurateurs of France, who ruled supreme for such a long time at the prestigious Grand Véfour at the Palais Royal.

It seems a long-ago summer afternoon when I first strolled into this chic, sophisticated, and elegant bistro, and Monsieur Oliver (the Younger) served me a delicious sweetbreads flavored with orange. He also presented me with his cookbook for children, *La Cuisine est un Jeu d'Enfants,* with an introduction by the late Jean Cocteau.

The various specialties of the Bistrot have changed over the years, but the cookery has consistently remained of high quality, backed up by an impressive wine list. Of course, Monsieur Oliver is no longer in there with those pots and pans, but a trained staff carries on. Count on spending from 330F ($49.85) for a meal. The restaurant is open Monday through Friday from noon to 2:15pm and 7:45 to 11pm, Saturday from 7:45 to 11pm. Métro: Solferino.

A Turn-of-the-Century Brasserie

Brasserie Flo, 7 cour Petites-Ecuries, 10e (tel. 47-70-13-59), is a remembrance of things past. You walk through an area of passageways, stumbling over garbage littering the streets. Then you come upon this sepia world of turn-of-the-century Paris: time-aged mahogany, leather banquettes, brass-studded chairs. Some of the choicest people come here (it's the principal rival of the more celebrated Lipp in St-Germain-des-Prés)—and it isn't even expensive.

The thing to order, of course, is "la formidable choûcroute" (sauerkraut). Don't expect just a heap of sauerkraut; rather, the mound is surrounded by ham, bacon, and sausages. It's bountiful in the best tradition of Alsace. The onion soup is always good, as is guinea hen with lentils. Look for the plats du jour, ranging from roast pigeon to fricassee of veal with sorrel.

An average dinner ranges from 200F ($30.20) to 250F ($37.75). Open daily from noon to 2:45pm and 7pm to 1:30am. Métro: Château-d'Eau or Strasbourg-St-Denis.

---

4. Moderately Priced Restaurants

Deluxe restaurants aside, you'll find any number of less expensive restaurants in Paris whose offerings are among the world's finest. Even so, you should still be prepared to pay a good price for a top-notch meal, providing you stick to an average wine.

I've provided a fairly broad sampling of restaurants in the moderately priced category, but, of course, there are many more. And if you're going to be in Paris for a prolonged stay, one of the joys of such a trip will be to discover others on your own.

ON THE RIGHT BANK

La Fermette Marbeuf 1900, 5 rue Marbeuf, 8e (tel. 47-23-31-31), has a turn-of-the-century décor, reasonable prices, a fine cuisine, and a setting just a short distance from the Champs-Elysées. The hand-painted tiles and stained-glass windows of the twin dining rooms contributed to the establishment's listing as a national historic monument. Guests come here for the fun of it all, as well as for the well-prepared and flavorful cuisine.

Specialties include sweetbreads with a ragoût of wild mushrooms, a basil-flavored filet of sole with fresh noodles, a bavarois of salmon, and several beef dishes. For dessert, try the chocolate cake with a bittersweet icing. A fixed-price menu costs a reasonable 160F

($24.15), while à la carte meals average 280F ($42.30). Reservations are a good idea. Open daily from 12:30 to 3pm and 7:30 to 11:30pm. Métro: F. D. Roosevelt.

Le Petit Bedon, 38 rue Pergolèse, 16e (tel. 45-00-23-66), is traditional but also innovative. The dining room is simply decorated and warm and inviting with only 14 tables. The menu frequently changes. For an appetizer, you might try the salmon, thinly sliced, which has been cured and smoked. A black pepper from South America brings out the right seasoning in the dish. If you visit in early spring, you can order milk-fed lamb from the Dordogne region of France. The lamb is delicate and tender and prepared to perfection. The kitchen is also known to do marvelous twists with Challans duckling. A masterpiece of desserts is a plate of mixed sorbets; not only is its presentation a work of art, but you are allowed to try and guess the flavors.

Expect to spend from 350F ($52.85) for a meal. Le Petit Bedon is open Monday through Friday from 12:15 to 2pm and 7:15 to 10:15pm; closed in August. Reservations are important. Métro: Argentine.

L'Assiette au Boeuf, 123 Champs-Elysées, 8e (tel. 47-20-01-13), offers one of the best food bargains in Paris. You can dine well on an inexpensive cuisine in a glamorous setting. You get simple French food in reproduction Belle Epoque settings. The menus are fixed, and no reservations are accepted. The Champs-Elysées entry has a sidewalk "box," offering dramatic views of the Arc de Triomphe. Much of the food is called cuisine du marché, which means it is based on fresh produce available at the market on any given day. You might be offered a fish casserole or else a tender slice of beef (served rare if you wish), with a sauce on the side, along with a mound of slender pommes frites. There is a wide choice of desserts, including sorbets. Wine can be ordered in four different amounts, including two sizes of carafe.

Menus cost 40F ($6.05) to 98F ($14.80); dessert is extra. In one room, a 160F ($24.15) menu is featured. Hours are from 11am to 1am daily. If you become a L'Assiette au Boeuf aficionado, you'll find other branches of this chain scattered at strategic locations throughout Paris. For the Champs-Elysées version, take the Métro to George-V.

L'Espace, 1 av. Gabriel, 8e (tel. 42-66-11-70). What's probably the most lavish buffet in Paris is served daily in a picnic-style décor of plastic chairs, oilcloth coverings, and decorative parasols, a setting you might find at a California beachside restaurant. In reality, however, nothing could be more French or more central to the hordes of lunchtime diners flocking here from offices in this prestigious neighborhood. It lies midway between the American Embassy and the Champs-Elysées, whose adjacent gardens are exposed to the view of clients who sometimes prefer to dine on an outdoor terrace. The luminary who established this consciously informal place is Pierre Cardin, whose other more formal culinary endeavors have been well documented thanks to his acquisition of Maxim's.

For 167F ($25.20) you'll have access to a buffet of more than 70 hors d'oeuvres, a table rich with salads, vegetables, cold roast meats, and the kind of antipasti you'd expect to find in Italy. The main course is served by a waiter who brings you your choice of a plat du jour. This is followed by a selection from a dessert buffet. Service and drinks are extra (champagne is sold by the glass).

A la carte meals cost from 200F ($30.20). L'Espace is open from noon to 3pm and 8:30pm to 1am serving meals daily, except Saturday at lunch. Métro: Champs-Elysées.

Restaurant Marc-Annibal de Coconnas, 2 bis place des Vosges, 4e (tel. 42-78-58-16). In the Louis XIII style, this restaurant could have been called Bistrot de Henri II (he lost his life on place des Vosges). It could have been called the Victor Hugo restaurant (the novelist lived in an apartment, now a museum, on this square). Instead, it's called Marc-Annibal de Coconnas, honoring some esoteric figure of the 17th century. But what's in a name? Concentrate instead on the superb cuisine, courtesy of Claude Terrail, who also owns that gourmet citadel, La Tour d'Argent. You might begin with Greek-style artichokes with prawns or a cassolette of snails, then follow with sole flavored with ginger or petit salé de canard (duck). In summer, a few guests can enjoy dining outside.

A fixed-price menu goes for 150F ($22.65), with à la carte orders beginning at 260F ($39.25). Open Wednesday through Sunday from noon to 2pm and 7:45 to 10:15pm. Sunday brunch (noon to 3pm) is quite popular. Métro: Bastille or St-Paul.

L'Ambassade d'Auvergne, 22 rue de Grenier-St-Lazare, 3e (tel. 42-72-31-22). The cuisine of the ancient heartland province of Auvergne is set before you in this off-the-beaten-track restaurant near the Pompidou Centre. Although not known for any great number of culinary specialties, the region does provide some rich-tasting cookery.

The chef's wares are best reflected in his typical soupe aux choux (a hearty cabbage-based soup). A personal favorite of mine is the saucisse (sausage) with aligot. Whipped in a copper pot, aligot blends Cantal cheese with cream, garlic, and fresh potatoes, and makes a good side dish. Gastronomes go for the boned breast of veal, which is stuffed and delicately cooked with herbs. It appears on the menu as *la fallette*. The chef has introduced among the more classical dishes some cuisine moderne plates. Specialties include a cassoulet with lentils, a pot-au-feu, confit de canard, and codfish casserole and stuffed cabbage. Some of these specials are featured only on one day of the week.

A complete meal with regional wine will cost from 220F ($33.20). The tavern is open daily from noon to 2pm and 7:30 to 11pm. Métro: Rambuteau.

Julien, 16 rue du Faubourg St-Denis, 10e (tel. 47-70-12-06), offers an opportunity to dine in one of the most sumptuous Belle Epoque interiors in Paris. It stands in an area not too far from Les Halles. It began life at the turn of the century as an elegant place but declined after World War II, becoming a cheap restaurant; however, the décor remained, albeit grimy and unappreciated. From a dingy working-class eating place, it has now been restored to its former elegance, the dirt cleaned off, and the magnificence of the fin-de-siècle dining area brought back to life. Marble and glass gleam in the mirrored, high-ceilinged room, with 15-foot-high murals, peacock-shaped coat hooks, twisted rococo pillars, and paintings of odalisques.

The food served here is traditional bourgeois but without the heavy sauces once used. Excellent prepared dishes include soups such as "Billy-By" (a creamy mussel soup as good as that served at Maxim's), soupe au pistou, and vichyssoise. Among main courses are grilled lobster with whisky, fresh salmon with sorrel, and chateaubriand béarnaise. The wine list contains good and reasonably priced bottles.

Meals start at 250F ($37.75). Julien is open daily from noon to 1:45pm and 7pm to 1:30am. Métro: Strasbourg-St-Denis.

Moulin du Village, 25 rue Royale in the Cité Berryer, 8e (tel. 42-65-08-47), might be an ideal choice if you're strolling along the rue Royale toward the Madeleine district and you can't afford Maxim's (it's just around the corner). This charming little place has a few outside tables, where you can enjoy original, creative, and well-prepared food at reasonable prices. The well-selected wine list is entirely supplied by the renowned Caves de la Madeleine, also in the Cité Berryer.

In an elegant setting with attentive waiters, you can enjoy an à la carte meal for 300F ($45.30) to 400F ($60.40). A fixed-price lunch or dinner costs 180F ($27.20). Dishes likely to be offered are a salad of haddock and smoked eel, duckling with black peppercorns, and chicken with mandarin oranges. You must always reserve a table. Open from 11am to 10:30pm; closed on Saturday night, all day Sunday, and holidays. Moulin du Village adjoins Blue Fox Bar, one of the leading wine bars of Paris (see "Paris Nights"). Métro: Concorde or Madeleine.

Chez Georges, 1 rue du Mail, 2e (tel. 42-60-07-11), is a long and narrow bistro, considered something of a local landmark. At lunch it's heavily patronized by members of the Bourse, the stock exchange that lies only a block away. Georges Constant, the owner, serves what he calls *la cuisine typiquement bourgeoise* or "food from our grandmère in the provinces." If Georges is not there to welcome you, his son, Bernard, and his daughter, Martine, will be. Waiters bring around bowls of appetizers, including celery rémoulade, to get you going. Then you can follow with such time-tested favorites as pot-au-feu (beef simmered with vegetables), a classic cassoulet, or beef braised in red wine. Beaujolais often rounds out the hearty fare.

A meal starts at 175F ($26.45). Open Monday through Saturday from 12:30 to 2pm and 7:30 to 10pm. Métro: Sentier.

Chez André, 12 rue Marbeuf, 8e (tel. 47-20-59-57), on the corner of rue Clement-Marot, is one of the most charming bistros in the neighborhood. A discreet red awning stretches over an array of shellfish on ice; inside, an art nouveau décor includes etched glass and masses of flowers. The interior is a medium-size labyrinth of nooks and cubbyholes. You'll probably be seated elbow to elbow with someone whose picture you've seen in a magazine. The old-fashioned menu is hand-scrawled in purple ink and includes a very French collection of items such as pâté of thrush, roquefort in puff pastry, several kinds of omelets, calves' head vinaigrette, a potage du jour, and an array of fresh shellfish, along with several reasonably priced wines. Desserts might be rum baba, chocolate cake, or a daily pastry.

Full meals begin at 220F ($33.20). Open Wednesday through Monday from noon to 3pm and 7 to 11:30pm; closed August 1 to 25. Métro: F. D. Roosevelt.

Minim's, 76 Faubourg St-Honoré, 8e (tel. 42-66-10-09), is Pierre Cardin's "alimentary boutique" on this fashionable street near the Elysée Palace. It's really an ideal luncheon restaurant for rich suburbanites spending their day shopping, and a good choice for midafternoon tea or a quick, well-prepared snack. The name, of course, is a tongue-in-cheek adaptation of Cardin's acquisition, Maxim's, and like the décor of its counterpart, the tea house is filled with art nouveau lighting fixtures and stained glass.

You dine at small tables near a collection of turn-of-the-century silver maidens that I was told came from the collection of Cardin himself. It's totally appropriate here to order only a plat du jour. These change daily but might include eggplant caviar, carpaccio with salad, and confit de canard (duck). You can also order sandwiches, as well as pastries prepared according to the recipes of Maxim's. Meals cost from 150F ($22.65).

Minim's is open Monday through Saturday from 10am to 6:30pm. A deluxe delicatessen fills an adjoining room, while an arts boutique is upstairs. Métro: Concorde.

Chez Tante Louise, 41 rue Boissy-d'Anglais, 8e (tel. 42-65-06-85), is an intimate little place with a tiny mezzanine, just off the Madeleine and the place de la Concorde. An oil painting on the wall and a bronze plaque on the brown marble façade pay homage to the restaurant's originator, "Aunt Louise," who reigned from the mid-1920s to the mid-1950s.

Today, Elaine and Bernard Lhiabastres carry on in Tante Louise's worthy tradition—they've inherited her secrets. The menu reflects numerous specialties such as foie gras, seafood platter, duck with orange sauce, and game in season. Expect to pay around 280F ($42.30) to 330F ($49.85), including wine. Open Monday through Friday from noon to 3pm and 7 to 10:30pm; closed August. Métro: Madeleine.

Au Pied de Cochon, 6 rue Coquillière, 1er (tel. 42-36-11-75). The onion soup of Les Halles still lures the visitors. Although the great market has moved to Rungis, near Orly Airport, traditions are long in dying. Besides, where in Paris can you be assured of getting a good meal at 3am if not at the famous "Pig's Foot?" The house specialty is the namesake: pig's feet grilled and served with béarnaise sauce, as well as the classic onion soup. Of course, you can sample any of the other tempting fares as well; try the suckling pig St-Eustache. There is another well-known specialty served here too. It is andouillette or chitterling sausage with a béarnaise sauce.

Outside on the street, you can buy some of the freshest-tasting oysters in town. The attendants will even give you slices of lemons to accompany them, and you can down them right on the spot.

You can order à la carte, an average meal costing 300F ($45.30). Au Pied de Cochon is open daily 24 hours. Métro: Les Halles.

ON ILE SAINT-LOUIS

La Taverne du Sergent Recruteur, 41 rue St-Louis-en-l'Ile, 4e (tel. 43-54-75-42), occupies a 17th-century setting on the historic Ile Saint-Louis. But many buildings on this island do that. What makes La Taverne so popular is that it offers an all-you-can-eat meal for 180F ($27.20). You more or less make your own salad with the items placed before you, including black radishes, fennel, celery, cucumbers, green pepper, hard-boiled eggs, and carrots. After that, a huge basket of sausages is brought around, and you can slice as you wish, sampling one or all. The carafe of wine, either red, white, or rosé, is bottomless. Plats du jour, ranging from beef to veal, are changed daily. You usually select from three different items. Next, a large cheese board makes the rounds; and, if you're still upright, you can select chocolate mousse or ice cream for dessert. The narrow dining room is beamed, with leaded-glass windows and ladder-back chairs. Garlic pigtails and oil lamps give it a rustic air.

La Taverne is open daily from 7pm to 2am. Métro: Pont-Marie.

Au Gourmet de l'Isle, 42 rue St-Louis-en-l'Ile, 4e (tel. 43-26-79-27). On the Ile St-Louis is this restaurant, savored by its loyal habitués. The setting is beautiful: a beamed ceiling, candlelit tables. Many Parisian restaurants approach this in décor, but where other establishments on this popular tourist island fall short (in the food department), this little "Gourmet Island" succeeds.

In the window you'll see a sign, "A.A.A.A.A.," which, roughly translated, stands for the Amiable Association of Amateurs of the Authentic Andouillette. These chitterling sausages are soul food to the French. Popular and tasty, too, is la charbonnée de l'Isle, a savory pork with onions. An excellent appetizer is the stuffed mussels in shallot butter.

Your palate will fare as well as your wallet if you order the 100F ($15.10) fixed-price menu. Count on spending from 180F ($27.20) if you order à la carte. Open Friday through Sunday and Tuesday and Wednesday from noon to 2pm and 7 to 10pm. Métro: Pont-Marie.

ON THE LEFT BANK

Le Western, Hilton Hotel, 18 av. de Suffren, 15e (tel. 42-73-92-00). American meat and French wine are what it's all about at Hilton's re-creation of the Old West in Paris. The steaks served at this mixture of cattle ranch and French elegance are imported from Kansas, and are as good as anything you'd find in Abilene. The service, however, is impeccably French and most friendly. Each of the waiters is dressed cowboy-style; the maître d'hôtel is in a sheriff's garb.

Contrary to expectations, this has become one of those chic Parisian places where many of the French go to rubberneck at the unusual (for Europe) costumes and décor. You might begin your meal with a crab cocktail, jumbo shrimp, or a Caesar salad, to be followed by one of the array of grilled steaks, or if not that, a roquefort-stuffed chopped sirloin or a saddle chop of salt-marsh lamb with mint jelly.

The portions are large, but if you are still hungry, there is a selection of French cheese or pastries. At trail's end (according to the menu), you might want a steaming cup of outlaw's coffee (made with Kentucky bourbon instead of Irish whiskey).

A la carte meals average 200F ($30.20). Service is daily from noon to 3pm and 7 to 11pm. Métro: Bir-Hakeim.

Lajarrige, 38 av. de Suffren, 15e (tel. 43-06-49-40), is a bright little restaurant that celebrates the cooking of the southwest of France. Jean-Claude de Lajarrige, longtime restaurateur, presents well-prepared food using the best of ingredients. The menu contains a wealth of good dishes, including a rich foie gras. One of the best specialties is a big cassoulet landais, contrived to let you enjoy the crunchy white beans, the duck confit, and the well-flavored sausages. Another favorite is a duck preparation, magret de canard. This regionally inspired restaurant also has within its premises a food boutique serving conserves, wines, alcohol, and other products. For an apéritif, I'd suggest a fermented brut de pêche (extract of peaches), followed by an appetizer, salade paysanne with chicken livers.

Meals cost from 175F ($26.45). Hours are daily from noon to 2:30pm and 7 to 10pm. Métro: Sèvres-Lecourbe.

La Cagouille, 10-12 place Constantin-Brancusi, 14e (tel. 43-22-09-11), is the domain of the burly Gérard Allemandou, a native of the cognac district. Here you can sample one of the most splendid selections of cognacs from smaller properties ever amassed in Paris. But that's not why everyone comes here. It's because you get some of the freshest and most reasonably priced fish in Paris. Fresh from Rungis, the huge red mullet is grilled to perfection. Salmon steak, however, is usually slightly underdone and served without a sauce (a dieter's dream come true). Ungarnished barnacles, grilled snapper, mussels sautéed in cast-iron pans—you get a Neptunian parade of natural and pure fish here. Peppered butter and sea salt are trademarks of the place; a "teardrop" of butter is the adornment for the accompanying, perfectly steamed vegetables.

Meals cost from 300F ($45.30) to 350F ($52.85), and are served Tuesday through Saturday from 12:30 to 2pm and 7:30 to 10:30pm; closed and from mid-August to mid-September. The décor is ultraclean and minimalist; the "nonwelcome" is bistro-style, but no one seems to mind. Métro: Montparnasse-Bienvenue.

L'Arpège, 84 rue de Varenne, 7e (tel. 45-51-20-02), is currently the rage of Paris because of its young chef, Alain Passard. It sits across from the Rodin Museum, on what was for years the site of the world-famed L'Archestrate, where Passard once worked in the kitchen. He has now gone on to culinary glory on his own. The décor—described by one French food critic as "young, charming, and happy"—is a mere backdrop to what emerges from the kitchen.

The menu is deliberately limited so that chef Passard can give each course his attention. Try, for example, cabbage stuffed with crabmeat or game cock with chicken livers and herb-flavored onions. Sweetbreads are prepared with exotic mushrooms and truffle juice, or you might prefer John Dory with celery juice and asparagus flavored with sage. For dessert, try the chocolate beignets or, strangely, a sugared tomato with a vanilla stuffing. The wine list is something to write home about.

The fixed-price menu at lunch, costing 150F ($22.65), has been called a "steal"—that is, if you can get a table. Of course, beverages, even coffee, are extra, but it's a bargain nevertheless.

A la carte dinners cost from 350F ($52.85) to 450F ($67.95), and service is Monday through Friday from 12:30 to 2pm and 7:30 to 10:30pm, Saturday from 12:30 to 2pm; closed for three weeks in August. Métro: Varenne.

La Gauloise, 59 av. de la Motte-Picquet, 15e (tel. 47-34-11-64), has long been an outstanding favorite in the area. Its fire-engine-red canopy evokes a Parisian bistro of the 1930s. Politicians and athletes in particular love its tobacco-tinged walls—in fact, no one wants anything changed around here. Its owner, Jacques Chalvet, goes to the Rungis market outside Paris every morning to seek only the freshest of ingredients. From his shopping, he composes his *suggestions du marché,* or market selections, to tempt his hungry diners. Fish and shellfish dishes seem to be the favorites. Try, in particular, the bouillabaisse. In summer you can eat outside, beneath parasols, below the rumbling and roar of an elevated subway that the French call "aerien Métro."

A typical meal costs from 280F ($42.30). La Gauloise is open Monday through Friday from 12:30 to 2pm and 7:30 to 11pm. Métro: La Motte-Picquet.

---

5. Budget Restaurants

ON THE RIGHT BANK

L'Etoile Verte, 13 rue Brey, 17e (tel. 43-80-69-34). This "Green Star" is a sign for economy diners. The décor is so simple as to be forgettable, but a large array of well-prepared foods emerges from the kitchen in back, and the staff is helpful. The cookery is that of a typical French bistro menu of long ago: rabbit pâté, veal marengo, fresh oysters, coq au vin in Cahors, sweetbreads with sautéed endive, mussels ravigote, chateaubriand béarnaise, and ris de veau (sweetbreads).

Its least expensive menu, 54F ($8.15), with drink included, is served only from 11am to 8pm. Otherwise, you can order à la carte, with meals costing from 100F ($15.10).

The restaurant is open daily from 11am to 11pm. Métro: Charles de Gaulle (Etoile).

Restaurant Lescure, 7 rue de Mondovi, 1er (tel. 42-60-18-

91), is a small, inexpensive restaurant in the high-priced place de la Concorde district. Right off the rue de Rivoli, the restaurant has been serving good food since 1919. In fair weather, a few sidewalk tables are placed outside; inside, the décor is rustic with an exposed kitchen. Simple, hearty cooking is the rule. For example, you might begin with a pâté en croûte. Main-course house specialties include confit de canard and salmon in a green sauce. My favorite dessert is one of the chef's fruit tarts.

A set menu of four courses costs 90F ($13.60), or else you can count on spending from 175F ($26.45) by ordering à la carte. Open Monday through Friday from noon to 2:15pm and 7 to 10pm; closed two weeks in August. Métro: Concorde.

Le Maquis, 69 rue Caulaincourt, 18e (tel. 42-59-76-07). Montmartre, for all its local color and atmosphere, has never been a great place for dining, with three or four exceptions. However, if you don't mind leaving the place du Tertre and heading on a 12-minute walk down the Butte, you'll be richly rewarded at this attractive restaurant, which has a tiny terrace in the fair-weather months. The menu is limited, but select, and the chef is owner Claude Lesage. Among the tasty courses are sauerkraut of fish, rabbit fricassee, stuffed mussels, coq au vin, a filet of sole served with two butters, and pheasant with cabbage. The desserts are often elaborate concoctions.

I like Le Maquis because it's a bargain. You can dine here for 85F ($12.85) on a set menu served only at lunch, 180F ($27.20) to 210F ($31.70) if you prefer to order à la carte. The restaurant is open Tuesday through Saturday from noon to 2pm and 8 to 10pm. Métro: Lamarck-Caulaincourt.

Le Grand Zinc, 5 Faubourg Montmartre, 9e (tel. 47-70-88-64), may be in an unfashionable quarter, but Paris of the 1880s survives here, as exemplified by the spirit lamps hanging inside. You make your way into the restaurant, passing baskets of seafood. You can inspect the belons or brown-fleshed oysters from Brittany. A traditional favorite and available all year round, these oysters can be purchased inside. The atmosphere is bustling in the tradition of a brasserie.

A full meal goes for only 150F ($22.65). My latest repast began with a selection of crudités (raw vegetables), followed by rognons sautés (fried kidneys), then a coupe de glace, an ice cream dessert. Included also was a quarter of a carafe of vin rouge. Hours are Monday through Saturday from noon to 3pm and 7pm to 1am. Métro: Montmartre.

La Boutique à Sandwichs, 12 rue du Colisée, 8e (tel. 43-59-56-69), is run by two brothers from Alsace, Hubert and Claude Schick. If you're in the Champs-Elysées area, it's a good place to drop in for sandwiches in many types and shapes. You can dine downstairs at the counter, or crowd into the tiny upstairs room, which is extremely active at lunch. Here they offer an unusual specialty, raclette valaisanne à gogo. To make this fondue dish, a wheel of cheese is taken, part of it is melted, then it is scraped right onto your plate. It is served with pickles and boiled potatoes, the latter resting in a pot with a crocheted hat. The other house specialty is pickelfleisch garni (Alsatian corned beef). Naturally, the apple strudel is the dessert everybody orders.

Sandwiches begin at 11F ($1.65). However, if you prefer to order the specialties of the house on the à la carte menu, expect to pay from 100F ($15.10) to 125F ($18.90). There's also a set menu at 65F ($9.80). The restaurant is open Monday through Saturday from 11:45am to 1am; closed August 1 to 20. Métro: F. D. Roosevelt.

La Maison Rose, 2 rue de l'Abreuvoir, 18e (tel. 42-57-66-75). Painted a rosy shade of pink, this building, classified as a historic monument, used to house the atelier of Utrillo. Legend says that Utrillo's friends used to lock him in during his periods of greatest emotional upsets and financial crises so that he could produce something to sell. In time, Aznavour used to sing here. In summer the terrace containing the most desirable tables quickly fills up.

Meals, costing from 175F ($26.45), might include fish soup, confit or magret de canard (duck), foie gras, blanquette de veau a l'ancienne, boeuf bourguignon, and paupiettes of sole à la mousseline. Open in winter daily from 11:30am to 10pm, in summer daily from 11:30am to midnight. Métro: Blanche or Lamarck-Caulaincourt.

ON ILE DE LA CITE

Restaurant Paul, 15 place Dauphine, 1er (tel. 43-54-21-48). This address used to be given out to first-time visitors by in-the-know Parisians who wanted to tell them about that out-of-the-way bistro where no foreigner ever sets foot. Don't you believe it! Chez Paul, on this historic square on the Ile de la Cité, is too good a secret to keep. The food expert, Waverly Root, once wrote of Chez Paul's "resistance to degeneration." And so it remains. The effect inside is much like a cold-water flat. The main-dish specialty is escalope papillotte. Another good order is quenelles de brochet à la Nantua. An old-fashioned dessert is baba à la confiture flambé au rhum.

Your bill will run from 175F ($26.45). Paul is open Wednesday through Sunday from noon to 2:30pm and 7:30 to 9:40pm; closed August. Métro: Pont-Neuf.

ON THE LEFT BANK

La Petite Chaise, 36-38 rue de Grenelle, 7e (tel. 42-22-13-35), is one of the oldest restaurants in Paris, dating from 1680. Very Parisian, it invites you into its ambience of terracotta walls, cramped but attractive tables, wood paneling, and gilt ornate wall sconces. Its special feature is its set meal for 150F ($22.65), which is likely to include such specialties as chicken Pojarski (minced, breaded, and sautéed), noisettes of lamb with green beans, quenelles de brochet (made with pike), trout meunière, escalope de veau normand, and pavé steak with roquefort sauce. The cheese tray, especially the Cantal and Brie, is always respectable, and the desserts are good and rich. Because of the long-enduring fame of this restaurant, it is always necessary to call and reserve a table.

La Petite Chaise is open daily from noon to 2:15pm and 7 to 11pm. Métro: Sèvres-Babylone.

Bourbonnais, 29 rue Delambre, 14e (tel. 43-20-61-73), show-cases the talents of Roger Le Meur in the heart of Montparnasse. Don't come here for the décor, as it is rather unappealing, with consciously heavy and overly rustic furniture. Instead, come for the food: Monsieur Le Meur is a grand chef, some of his culinary inspiration coming from the oldest of his grandmother's recipes. For example, you might enjoy codfish peasant-style or coq au vin with fresh noodles. Perhaps you'll try his foie gras maison or veal kidneys in a mustard sauce. There is also an array of *petits vins* at very reasonable prices.

A set menu at 95F ($14.35) is one of the dining bargains of the street, although you can easily spend 200F ($30.20) or more by ordering à la carte. Open Monday through Saturday from 12:30 to 2pm and 7:30 to 11pm. Métro: Edgar-Quinet or Vavin.

Le Bistro de la Gare, 59 bd. du Montparnasse, 6e (tel. 45-48-38-01). In addition to offering low-cost, well-prepared meals, this unusual establishment, across a busy boulevard from the Montparnasse railway station, has an art nouveau décor that is classified as a national treasure by the government. Its hand-painted tiles were installed in 1903.

Today the crowds who elbow into this place wait for an empty table at the standup bar where an employee offers a free glass of kir to anyone obliged to wait for more than a few minutes. The most popular item is a two-course fixed-price menu, which goes for 70F ($10.55). Menu items are straightforward but flavorful, including several kinds of grilled steak, duck, and terrines. A wide assortment of desserts is offered as well as house wine sold in carafes.

Hours are Monday to Friday from 11:30am to 3pm and 6pm to 1am, Saturday and Sunday from 11:30am to 1pm. Métro: Montparnasse-Bienvenue. Reservations are not accepted. You'll find other members of this popular chain at strategic locations throughout Paris.

Crémerie-Restaurant Polidor, 41 rue Monsieur-le-Prince, 6e (tel. 43-26-95-34), is the most characteristic bistro in the Odéon area, serving the *cuisine familiale.* You might call it a *vieille maison très sympathique.* It still uses the word *crémerie* in its title, an appellation dating back to the early part of this century when it specialized in frosted cream desserts.

In time it became one of the Left Bank's oldest and most established literary bistros. In fact, it was André Gide's favorite and Hemingway, Paul Valéry, Artaud, Charles Boyer, and Jack Kerouac have dined here as well.

The atmosphere is one of lace curtains, polished brass hat racks, and drawers in the back where repeat customers lock up their cloth napkins. Frequented largely by students and artists, who always seem to head for the rear, the present restaurant was founded in 1930 and it's been little changed since then. Overworked but smiling waitresses serve such dishes as pumpkin soup, snails from Burgundy, rib of beef with onions, rabbit with mustard sauce, and veal in white sauce, followed by such desserts as a raspberry or lemon tart.

The menu changes daily, a typical meal costing from 110F

($16.60). Open daily from noon to 2:30pm and 7pm to 1am (until 11pm on Sunday). Métro: Odéon.

Aux Charpentiers, 10 rue Mabillon, 6e (tel. 43-26-30-05), was once the rendezvous of the master carpenters, whose guild was next door. Nowadays it's where the young men of St-Germain-des-Prés take their dates for inexpensive meals in a pleasant atmosphere. Aux Charpentiers keeps alive the fast-disappearing tradition of the neighborhood family dining room—it's like Paris of 30-some years ago.

The restaurant takes up two floors. The street level is more animated, the lower level quieter, better for conversation. Although not especially imaginative, the food is well cooked in the best tradition of cuisine bourgeoise. Appetizers include a rillette of sardines. Especially recommended as a main course is the roast duck with olives. Each day of the week a different plat du jour is offered, with time-tested French home-cooking: petit salé aux lentilles, pot-au-feu, and boeuf à la mode are among the main dishes on the menu. The chef suggests platters of fresh fish daily. There is a large choice of Bordeaux wines direct from the château, including Château Gaussens.

If you order à la carte, count on spending 150F ($22.65) to 200F ($30.20). Open Monday through Saturday from noon to 3pm and 7:30 to 11:30pm. Métro: Mabillon.

Astoin Rive Gauche, 19 rue du Regard, 6e (tel. 45-48-87-67), offers one of the best low-priced meals in the district, according to a coterie of visiting American professors. The establishment's owner developed his high-quality cuisine after traveling to many places, including Vancouver and Texas. Today, Pierre Astoin offers a menu worth a trip. Meals in the mirrored room are served on tables topped with polished slabs of pink granite whose surfaces shimmer from lights clustered along the high ceilings.

The menu changes seasonally, but is likely to offer such dishes as black Angus entrecôte, lamb with cream of fennel, and salmon trout "in the manner of the chef." The dessert specialty is a temptingly caloric marquise of chocolate with a champagne sauce.

A set menu at 145F ($21.90) includes everything but wine and coffee. The customer has a choice from among seven appetizers, nine main courses plus cheese, and six desserts. An à la carte dinner costs from 250F ($37.75). The restaurant is open daily from noon to 2:15pm and 7:30 to 11pm. Métro: St-Placide.

L'Auberge Basque, 51 rue de Verneuil, 7e (tel. 45-48-51-98), is where you'll find excellent food. The owners, Monsieur and Madame Rourre, come from the Basque country near the Spanish border. Their meals reflect the rich cookery of that district and their daily shopping. Among their satisfied diners are some famous sportsmen and French TV stars. You might begin with their Basque pâté, then follow with a pipérade, the famous omelet of the district. They also prepare both magret or confit of canard (duck). Various fresh fish dishes are also served, along with a selection of cheese and fresh fruit tarts. Wines are well chosen.

A set menu of the day is offered for 140F ($21.15). You can also order à la carte, paying from 200F ($30.20). The restaurant is open Monday through Saturday from noon to 2:30pm and 7:30 to 10:30pm. Métro: rue du Bac.

La Cabane d'Auvergne, 44 rue Grégoire-de-Tours, 6e (tel. 43-25-14-75). This self-proclaimed "rabbit hutch" is like a rustic tavern from the Auvergne, an ancient province of France (now divided into départements), which was known as a fertile land of copious and rich cookery. This tiny restaurant on an obscure Left Bank street keeps alive the tradition. Under beamed ceilings, you are served typical regional meals on bare plank tables with provincial stools. The stone and wood-paneled walls are decorated with rustic artifacts. It often gets very popular, so show up early if you want a seat.

The owner, Gilbert Guibert, is the hearty patron of the place, and he keeps the breezy chitchat going. The kitchen specializes in terrines. One is made from marcassin (young boar), another from fricandeau (larded veal loin), yet another from caneton (duckling). Main courses are generous and well cooked. You'll find it an effort to order dessert.

You can enjoy a complete meal for 150F ($22.65) to 200F ($30.20). Hours are Monday from 7:30 to 11:30pm, Tuesday through Saturday from noon to 2:30pm and 7:30 to 11:30pm. Métro: Odéon.

6. Specialty Dining

DINING ODDITIES

La Colombe, 4 rue de la Colombe, 4e (tel. 46-33-37-08), is on one of the smallest streets in old Paris, on the Ile de la Cité, running into the quai aux Fleurs behind Notre-Dame. The house of La Colombe (the dove), dating from 1275, is an idyllic setting for dining. La Colombe has more than a dozen doves providing a unique ambience. It's a favorite with tourists who wish to relax in a peaceful, time-tested atmosphere.

The chef, who has presided over the Colombe kitchen for 20 years, creates such delicacies as duck with pears, tournedos with Périgueux sauce, and veal with mushrooms in a fresh cream sauce. Fresh fish is available every day. The desserts are the chef's specialty: cake Colombe, stuffed crêpes with cream, and profiterole with hot fudge.

A copious gastronomical meal is served for 260F ($39.25), including taxes. Hours are Monday from 7:30pm to midnight, Tuesday through Saturday from noon to 2:30pm and 7:30pm to midnight. Métro: Cité or Hôtel de Ville.

Caviar Kaspia, 17 place de la Madeleine, 8e (tel. 42-65-33-32). How chic can you get, sitting on the second floor of this caviar center, enjoying a view of the columns of the stately Madeleine, while casually tasting Russian caviar and sipping Russian vodka? The English-speaking manager will explain the selections to you and seat you at a tiny table to begin your life of decadence. Should you not want a taste of caviar, you'll also find smoked salmon, foie gras, even a more modest hot borscht and blinis. The more elaborate, such as the smoked salmon and caviar, are priced by the gram, and the tabs on these delicacies fluctuate from week to week—so I won't cite them here, except to say that they are always superexpensive.

Expect to pay from 400F ($60.40) for a taste. A carry-out shop is on the ground floor. Open Monday through Saturday from 9am to 2am, perfect for a late-night snack. Métro: Madeleine.

The Oldest Café in Paris

Le Procope, 13 rue de l'Ancienne Comédie, 6e (tel. 43-28-99-20), was originally opened in 1686 by a Sicilian named Francesco Procopio dei Coltelli. The café today is more of a restaurant than it was originally. It is sumptuously decorated with gilt-framed mirrors, antique portraits of former illustrious clients, crystal chandeliers, banquettes of Bordeaux-colored leather, and marble-topped tables.

Former clients have included La Fontaine, Voltaire, Benjamin Franklin, Rousseau, Anatole France, Robespierre, Danton, Marat, Bonaparte (as a youth), Balzac (who drank endless cups of very strong coffee), and Verlaine (who preferred the now illegal absinthe). There are two levels for dining: the spacious upstairs section or the more intimate street-level room. Fresh oysters and shellfish are served from a refrigerated display. A well-chosen selection of classic French dishes is presented, including baby duckling with spices and "green coffee" or "drunken chicken."

The café is open daily from 8am to 2am, serving a fixed price lunch at noon for 98F ($14.80). An à la carte menu costs from 200F ($30.20). Métro: Odéon.

Androuët, 41 rue d'Amsterdam, 8e (tel. 48-74-26-93). Cheese is king here. Time was when to get invited down to taste the cheese in Monsieur Androuët's cellars was a badge of honor. Now half of Paris and three-quarters of all visiting foreigners who love cheese have probably made their way to this unique restaurant up from the railway station of St-Lazare. *Le fromage* has never been given such attention, or come in such a wide variety, ranging from the mild to what one diner called "a piece laden with enough penicillin to have sufficed for medical supplies for the Allied invasion of Normandy." On the lower level is a luscious shop selling every conceivable variety of cheese from all regions of France.

Reached by elevator, the dining room is on the second landing. It has been redecorated, with wood paneling and pastel colors, and is brightly lit. To reach your table, you pass a vast array of cheeses, the scent of which will activate your taste buds. The atmosphere is a perfect setting for good cooking. As a first course, ravioles de chèvre frais (ravioli stuffed with fresh goat cheese) is highly desirable. A good main dish is filet de boeuf cotentin (beef filet with roquefort sauce flambé with calvados). Cheese fanciers go here to order *la dé-gustation de fromages affinés dans nos caves,* which allows you to sample as many of the 120 varieties of cheese as you wish.

This dégustation costs 200F ($30.20). There is a fixed-price meal costing 200F ($30.20), and you are likely to spend from 275F ($41.55) if you order à la carte.

The restaurant is open Monday through Saturday from noon to 2:30pm and 7 to 10pm. It's best to reserve for both lunch and dinner. Métro: St-Lazare or Liège.

AMERICAN

Joe Allen, 30 rue Pierre-Lescot, 1er (tel. 42-36-70-13). About the last place in the world you'd expect to find Joe Allen is Les Halles, that once-legendary Paris market. But the New York restaurateur long ago invaded Paris with the American hamburger. It easily wins as the finest burger in the city, as Joe originally set out to match those served at P.J. Clarke's in New York.

Joe Allen's "little bit of New York"—complete with imported red-checked tablecloths, a green awning over the entrance, and waiters who speak English—was made possible by "grants" from such fans as Lauren Bacall, whose poster adorns one of the walls. The décor is in the New York saloon style, complete with brick walls, oak floors, movie stills, and a blackboard menu listing such items as black-bean soup, chili, and apple pie. A spinach salad makes a good beginning. The barbecued ribs are succulent as well.

Joe Allen's also makes the claim that it is the only place in Paris where you can have real New York cheesecake or pecan pie. The pecans are imported from the United States. They have a telex linkup with New York, and the two kitchens often swap daily specials and other dishes that have proved successful. Joe claims that (thanks to French chocolate) "we make better brownies than those made in the States." Giving the brownies tough competition is the California chocolate mousse pie, along with the strawberry Romanoff and the coconut cream pie.

Meals cost from 225F ($34) per person. Thanksgiving dinner at Joe Allen's in Paris is becoming a tradition (but you'll need a reservation way in advance). Open daily from noon to 2am. Unless you want to wait 30 minutes at the New York bar, you'd better make a reservation for dinner. Métro: Les Halles.

DANISH

Restaurant Copenhague and Flora Danica, 142 av. des Champs-Elysées, 8e (tel. 43-59-20-41), is the "Maison du Danemark," one of the finest dining establishments along the Champs-Elysées. The good-tasting food of Denmark is served with considerable style and flair. In summer, you can dine outside on the rear terrace, an idyllic spot.

If you want to go Danish all the way, you'll order an apéritif of aquavit and ignore the wine list in favor of Carlsberg or Tuborg, the two best-known beers of Denmark. For an appetizer, you might prefer terrine de canard (duckling) Copenhague. The house specialty is délices Scandinaves, "a platter of joy" of foods the Danes do exceptionally well. The feuilleté Cercle Polaire is a fine finish.

Expect to spend from 350F ($52.85) for a meal, served Monday through Saturday from noon to 2pm and 7:15 to 10pm; closed holidays.

At the Boutique Flora Danica facing the Champs-Elysées you can have a small snack from noon until midnight. Open-faced sandwiches, Danish smørrebrød, with beer go for around 110F ($16.60). Sandwiches, pastries, beer, and aquavit are available in the small delicatessen. Métro: George-V.

RUSSIAN

Dominique, 19 rue Bréa, 6e (tel. 43-27-08-80), is the finest Russian restaurant in Montparnasse, preserving a fin-de-siècle atmosphere, St. Petersburg–style, in its upstairs room. Warning: Don't be tempted to order the Iranian caviar today . . . it's about the same price as sterling silver. The kitchen turns out really superb food. For example, try the familiar borscht and piroshki or the blini with cream. Even the Russian salad makes an interesting beginning. Recommendable main courses include côtelette de volaille (poultry) Dominique. Of course, everything tastes better when washed down with a glass of Zubrovka vodka. It's imported from Poland and is made with a special herb. If you're watching your budget, you can order these specialties downstairs, where there is a counter and bar service, and the prices are not as high.

Meals begin at 300F ($45.30). The restaurant is open daily from 12:15 to 2:15pm and 7:15 to 10:15pm; closed from mid-July to mid-August. Métro: Vavin.

GERMAN

Au Vieux Berlin, 32 av. George-V, 8e (tel. 47-20-88-96), serves the best German food in town. In fine surroundings, at this prestigious address (across the street from the George V hotel), you are served such classic à la carte dishes as Wiener Schnitzel, followed by the typical apfelstrudel. Another interesting specialty the chef does well is filet de porc cooked in beer. Expect to spend from 250F ($37.75) for a meal. The restaurant is open Monday through Saturday from noon to 2:30pm and 7 to 11pm. Métro: George-V.

A JEWISH DELI

Goldenberg's, 69 av. de Wagram, 17e (tel. 42-27-34-79), is a Jewish-delicatessen restaurant in the Champs-Elysées area. Its owner, Albert Goldenberg, is known as "the doyen of Jewish restaurateurs in Paris," and rightly so, since he opened his first delicatessen in Montmartre in 1936. The deli, like many of its New York counterparts, has the front half reserved as the specialty take-out section and the back half for in-house dining. The menu features such specialties as carpe farcie (stuffed carp), blini, cabbage borscht, and pastrami, one of the most popular items. Naturally, everything tastes better if accompanied by Jewish rye bread. For those who want to really get in the spirit, the menu offers Israeli wines as well as French ones.

You'll spend 150F ($22.65) to 200F ($30.20) for a meal. Hours for hot food are daily from noon to 3pm and 7 to 11pm. Métro: Ternes or Charles de Gaulle (Etoile).

VEGETARIAN

Le Jardin, 100 rue du Bac, 7e (tel. 42-22-81-56), offers health-conscious food which is so well prepared that some dedicated meat-eaters sometimes arrive for a taste. You'll dine beneath a greenhouse ceiling in a pleasant room filled with sunlight and plants. An 89F ($13.45) fixed-price meal includes generous portions of salads, grain dishes, vegetables au gratin, and a dessert cheese or pastry. A substantial à la carte meal, with a fish dish, dessert, and wine, costs from 115F ($17.35) per person. Le Jardin is open Monday through Saturday from noon to 3pm and 7 to 10:30pm. Métro: rue du Bac.

Le Grain de Folie, 24 rue de la Vieuville, 18e (tel. 42-58-15-57). Run by a young Frenchwoman, this restaurant has two rooms offering an inviting ambience. They lie one before the other, half-way up the slope of Montmartre's hill. You can take out or eat in amid the relaxed décor. The fixed-price menu goes for 65F ($9.80), including a full array of salads, cereal products, vegetable tarts, and vegetable terrines. Desserts include an old-fashioned apple crumble or a fruit salad. Either the house Beaujolais or a frothy glass of vegetable juice might accompany your meal.

Open daily from 7 to 10pm. It also serves lunch Tuesday to Sunday from 12:30 to 2:30pm. Métro: Abbesses.

La Macrobiothèque, 17 rue de Savoie, 6e (tel. 43-25-04-96). Surrounded by a simple décor appropriately filled with plants, you can enjoy vegetarian specialties in a relaxed and pleasant environment. Set lunches, loaded with rice and vegetables, cost from 41F ($6.20) to 69F ($10.40), with a table d'hôte dinner offered at 69F ($10.40). The restaurant is open Monday through Saturday from noon to 2pm and 7 to 10pm; closed August. Métro: St-Michel or Odéon.

Aquarius, 54 rue Ste-Croix-de-la-Bretonnerie, 4e (tel. 48-87-48-71), is one of the best-known vegetarian restaurants in Le Marais, which has a lot of health-conscious residents who insist on no smoking. Neither wine nor spirits are sold, but you can enjoy a fruit-flavored beverage. Meals, regardless of what you order, seem to overflow with raw or steamed vegetables. A fixed-price menu costs 43F ($6.50), and if you order à la carte you'll pay 75F ($11.35). It is open for lunch, tea, snacks, and dinner Monday through Saturday from noon to 10pm. Métro: Hôtel de Ville.

A GASTRONOMIC STROLL

If the idea of corned beef, pastrami, schmaltz herring, and dill pickles excites you, then strike out for one of the most colorful old neighborhoods in Paris, the **rue des Rosiers** in the Fourth Arrondissement (Métro: St-Paul). There is something of the air of a little village about the place. The blue-and-white Star of David is prominently displayed. Increasingly, North African overtones, reflecting the arrival of Jews from Morocco, Tunisia, and especially Algeria, long ago appeared.

John Russell wrote that the rue des Rosiers is "the last sanctuary of certain ways of life; what you see there, in miniature, is Warsaw before the ghetto was razed . . . Samarkand before the Soviet authorities brought it into line."

The best time to go is Sunday morning when many parts of Paris are sleeping. You can actually wander up and down the street, eating as you go—perhaps selecting an apple strudel, a slice of pastrami on Jewish rye bread, even pickled lemons, smoked salmon, and merguez, the typical smoked sausages of Algeria.

If you want to have a proper sit-down meal, you'll find many spots. The most famous is **Chez Jo Goldenberg,** 4 rue des Rosiers, 4e (tel. 48-87-20-16). Albert Goldenberg long ago moved to fancier quarters off the Champs-Elysées (see above). However, his brother Joseph runs this place. Here you can have stuffed carp or beef goulash. A complete meal begins at 150F ($22.65). Israeli wines are offered. Jewish paintings and strolling musicians add to the ambience of the place. It is open daily from noon to 1am.

This concludes my culinary roundup of Paris, the greatest of all food capitals. If I've omitted your pet hostelry, I offer sincere apologies.

But before departing to other subjects, I'd like to include a line about the humblest of Parisian gastronomic pleasures: the street stalls. You'll see them at most intersections offering such fare as marrons (roasted chestnuts), crêpes (pancakes), and gaufres (waffles). Do yourself a favor and try them.

WHAT TO SEE AND DO IN PARIS

The main attraction of Paris . . . is Paris. You'll make that discovery yourself the moment you start sightseeing. For, unless you're taking an organized tour, you are likely to become so ensnared by the vistas you find en route to a particular sight that you run the risk of never getting there.

No single palace, museum, church, or monument is as captivating as any of the dozen street settings of this city. They work like sirens' songs on a visitor's senses, luring you into hours of aimless rambling when you should be steering resolutely toward some three-star edifice.

I know—it has happened to me more times than I want to remember. And knowing this, I've divided the sightseeing discussion into easy-to-use sections to help you match your interests with all the attractions Paris has to offer.

1. All Around Paris

PLACE DE LA CONCORDE

Regarded by many as the most beautiful urban square in the world, this immense 85,000-square-yard expanse is so vast that your eye can't take it in at one glance. The center of the oval is swarming with cars, a motorist's nightmare, but the hugeness of the place seems to swallow them up.

In the middle, looking pencil-small, rises a 33-century-old obelisk from Egypt, flanked by cascading fountains. Grouped around the outer edges are eight statues representing eight French cities. Near the statue of Brest was the spot where the guillotine stood during the Revolution. On Sunday morning of January 21, 1793, King Louis XVI lost his royal head there, to be followed by 1,343 other victims, including Marie Antoinette and, subsequently, Danton and Robespierre, the very men who had launched the Terror.

The place de la Concorde borders the Tuileries on the east, and on the west the second great showpiece of Paris, the Champs-Elysées.

CHAMPS-ELYSEES

I get a bit tired of repeating "the most in the world," but, of course, this *is* the world's most famous promenade. Pointing from the place de la Concorde like a broad, straight arrow to the Arc de Triomphe at the far end, it presents its grandest spectacle at night.

For the first third, the avenue is hedged by chestnut trees. Then it changes into a double row of hotels and shops, movie houses, office buildings, and block after block of sidewalk cafés. The automobile showrooms, fast-food joints, and gift stores have marred the once-impeccable elegance of this stretch, but this is still the greatest vantage point from which to watch Paris roll and stroll by, preferably while sipping a drink.

TROCADERO

This is actually a series of adjoining sights, which a master touch of city planning has telescoped into one (a characteristic Parisian knack).

From the place du Trocadéro, you can step between the two curved wings of the **Palais de Chaillot** and gaze out on a view that is nothing short of breathtaking. At your feet lie the **Jardins du Trocadéro,** centered by fountains. Directly in front, the Pont d'Iéna spans the Seine. Then, on the opposite bank, rises the iron immensity of the **Tour Eiffel.** And beyond, stretching as far as your eye can see, the **Champ de Mars,** once a military parade ground but now a garden landscape with arches and grottoes, lakes and cascades.

THE SEINE ISLANDS

The "egg from which Paris was hatched," **Ile de la Cité** lies quietly in the shadow of Notre-Dame. The home of French kings until the 14th century, the island still has a curiously medieval air, with massive gray walls rising up all around you, relieved by tiny patches of parkland.

Just behind Notre-Dame, sunken almost to the level of the river, is the **Mémorial de la Déportation,** the monument to the thousands of French men, women, and children who perished in Nazi concentration camps from 1940 to 1945. You step down into a series of granite chambers with narrow, iron-barred windows, horribly reminiscent of the actual killing pens. And just as bare. Hewn into the stone walls are the nightmarish names of the camps, each one like the tolling of a funeral bell: Auschwitz—Bergen-Belsen—Dachau—Buchenwald—Mathausen—Treblinka . . .

Back on ground level, you'll see an iron bridge leading over to **Ile Saint-Louis.** This smaller and quieter of the two river islands has remained somewhat as it was in the 17th century, after it had been divided up into private building lots. Sober patrician houses stand along the four quays, and the fever-beat of the city seems a hundred miles away.

PLACE VENDOME

This is *the* textbook example of classical French architecture, a pure gem set in the fashionable heart of the Right Bank. The pillared palaces encircling the square include the Ritz Hotel as well as the Ministry of Justice. The center is crowned by a 144-foot-high column, erected to commemorate Napoléon's greatest victory—Austerlitz. The actual column is stone, but the enclosing spiral band of bronze was cast from the 1,200 cannon (a fantastic number) captured by the emperor in the battle. The statue on top of the pillar is, of course, Napoléon, restored there after being pulled down twice: once by Royalist reactionaries, the second time by Communard revolutionaries . . . an odd combination.

LE MARAIS

Very few cities on earth boast an entire district that can be labeled a sight. Paris has several. One of them—Le Marais, or the marshland—is the vaguely defined maze of streets north of the **place de la Bastille.**

During the 17th century this was a region of aristocratic mansions, which lost their elegance when the fashionable set moved elsewhere. The houses lost status, but they remained standing. Le Marais is becoming increasingly fashionable by today's standards and many artists and craftspeople are moving in. The government is restoring many of the mansions.

You can take the Métro to the place de la Bastille to begin a stroll around the district. The actual Bastille, of course, is gone now. But as the history books tell us, the mob attacked this fortress on July 14, 1789, sparking the French Revolution. To commemorate the storming, Bastille Day on July 14 is a major French holiday. Once the prison contained eight towers, housing such illustrious tenants as "The Man in the Iron Mask" and the Marquis de Sade.

Be careful of the speeding cars when you cross the square to look at the **Colonne de Juillet.** Surprisingly, it honors the victims of the July Revolution of 1830 that marked the supremacy of Louis Philippe, not the victims of the Bastille.

France honored the bicentennial of the French revolution in 1989 by building the 3,000-seat **Opéra Bastille** on the south side of the square. The Opéra opened in 1990, with five moving stages. The launching of this cultural center, along with major restoration of the area, has turned the formerly dreary Bastille section into a chic neighborhood, rivaling the Marais, which garnered so much publicity in the 1970s and 1980s.

From the place de la Bastille, head up rue St-Antoine, cutting right on rue des Tournelles, with its statue honoring Beaumarchais (*The Barber of Seville*). Take a left again onto the Pas-de-la-Mule, "the footsteps of the mule," which will carry you to the place des Vosges.

Place des Vosges

An enchanted island rather than a city square, this silent, serenely lovely oasis is the oldest square in Paris and—in my opinion—the most entrancing.

Laid out in 1605 by order of King Henry IV, it was once called the "Palais Royale" and was the scene of innumerable cavaliers' duels. The Revolutionary government changed its name but—luckily—left its structure intact. In the middle is a tiny park, and on three sides an encircling arcaded walk, supported by arches and paved with ancient, worn flagstones.

That's all, but the total effect is so harmonious, so delicately balanced between mellow stone and green trees, that it works like a soothing balm on the nerves.

Maison de Victor Hugo

The house at 6 place des Vosges in which Victor Hugo lived and worked from 1832 to 1848 has been turned into a museum devoted to the novelist. You probably know Hugo as a literary giant, but here you'll also see the drawings, carvings, and pieces of furniture he made. The windows of the museum overlook the square. The museum is open Tuesday through Sunday from 10am to 5:40pm (closed legal holidays). Admission is 12F ($1.80), free on Sunday. For information, telephone 42-72-10-16. Métro: St-Paul.

Continuing the Walk

After your visit, you can pick up the trail again by taking rue des Francs-Bourgeois, which will lead you to the **Hôtel Carnavalet,** on the same street. This Renaissance palace—entrance on 23 rue de Sévigné, named after the madame of letter-writing fame—is now owned by the City of Paris, which has turned it into the **Musée Carnavalet.**

Following a stopover here, looking at relics of the French Revolution, you can continue up the same street to the **Palais Soubise,** housing the **National Archives** of France. The palace, at 60 rue des

Francs-Bourgeois, was named for the Princess Soubise, mistress of Louis XIV.

Double back a block to rue Vieille-du-Temple and the **Hôtel de Rohan,** at no. 87. The mansion was once occupied by the fourth Cardinal de Rohan, involved in the diamond-necklace scandal implicating Marie Antoinette. You can see a striking bas-relief depicting a nude Apollo and four horses against a background exploding with sunbursts.

On the same street, at 47 rue Vieille-du-Temple, stands the **Hôtel des Ambassadeurs de Hollande,** where Beaumarchais founded the Rodriguez Hortalez Company financed by the French and Spanish governments to help the American settlers fight the English government, and where he wrote his immortal play, *The Marriage of Figaro.* Again, you have to be content with a look from the outside.

From this street, turn down the **rue des Rosiers** (the street of rose bushes), the main street of the old Jewish quarter of Paris, still filled with kosher delicatessen stores and Hebrew inscriptions.

At the end of this street you'll be on rue Mahler. Take a sharp right onto rue Rivoli, then branch off to the left onto rue St-Antoine.

Hôtel de Bethune-Sully, 62 rue St-Antoine (tel. 42-74-22-22), was begun in 1625. The duc de Sully, Henry IV's minister of finance, acquired it in 1634. He planned to live there with his young bride, who turned out to prefer a more virile lover (Sully was 74 years old). It's very difficult to get inside without special passes unless you're there for the Festival du Marais.

Rue St-Antoine leads into rue François-Miron, where at no. 68 stands the 17th-century **Hôtel de Beauvais,** which was built by Louis XIV as an abode for a lady named Catherine Bellier, allegedly his first-ever mistress. Mozart lived there in 1763, by the way.

Leaving the hotel, continue down the street, turning left onto rue de Jouy, which leads to rue du Figuier and the **Hôtel de Sens** at no. 1. Construction began in 1470 on the mansion for the archbishop of Sens, and it is—other than the Cluny—the only domestic architecture that remains from 15th-century Paris. It was once inhabited by the notorious Queen Margot, wife of Henri IV, who had an interest in young lovers. Today it houses the **Forney Library;** during the day you can walk inside the gate.

QUARTIER LATIN

The Latin Quarter lies on the Left Bank in the Fifth Arrondissement and consists of the streets winding around the University of Paris, of which the **Sorbonne** is only a part.

The logical starting point is the **place St-Michel,** right on the river, decorated by an impressive fountain. This was the scene of some of the most savage fighting during the uprising of the French Resistance in August 1944. Here—as in many, many other spots—you'll see the moving little name tablets, marking the place where a Resistance fighter fell: *"Ici est Tombé . . . le 19 Août 1944. Pour la Libération de Paris."*

Running straight south is the main thoroughfare of the quarter, the wide, pulsating **boulevard St-Michel** (called boul' Mich' by the locals). But we'll turn left and dive into the warren of dogleg alleys adjoining the river—**rue de la Huchette, rue de la Harpe, rue St-Séverin.** Thronged with students, tingling with the spice smells of Arabian, African, and Vietnamese cooking, narrow, twisting, and noisy, the alleys resemble an Asian bazaar more than a European city. This impression is aided by the incredibly garish posters advertising horror movies, belly dancers, and sticky Algerian sweets, the crush of humanity, the honking of cars bullying a path through the swarming crowds.

We emerge at the **Church of St-Séverin** and are back in Paris again. Dating from the 13th century, this flamboyant Gothic edifice acts like a sanctuary of serenity.

Head down **rue St-Jacques** and Paris reasserts itself completely. The next crossing is **boulevard St-Germain,** lined with sophisticated cafés and some of the most avant-garde fashion shops in town.

MONTMARTRE

This name has spread chaos and confusion in many an unwary tourist's agenda. So just to make things clear—there are three of them.

The first is boulevard Montmartre, a busy commercial street nowhere near the mountain. The second is the tawdry, expensive, would-be-naughty, and utterly phony amusement belt along boulevard de Clichy, culminating at place Pigalle (the "Pig Alley" of World War II GIs). The third—the Montmartre I'm talking about—lies on top, and on the slopes, of the actual *mont.*

The best way to get there is to take the Métro to **Anvers,** then walk to the nearby rue de Steinkerque, and ride the curious little funicular to the top. It operates between 6am and 11pm.

Montmartre used to be the artists' village, glorified by masters such as Utrillo, painted, sketched, sculpted, and photographed by ten thousand lesser lights. The tourists, building speculators, and nightclub entrepreneurs came and most of the artists went. But a few still linger. And so does some of the village charm that once drew them. Just enough to give you a few delightful hours, and leave you nostalgic for a past you wish you'd known.

The center point, the **place du Tertre,** looks like an almost-real village square, particularly when the local band is blowing and puffing oompah music. All around the square run terrace restaurants with dance floors and colored lights. Gleaming through the trees is the Basilica of **Sacré-Coeur** (tel. 42-51-17-02). Built in an oddly Asian neo-Byzantine style, the church, which is a center of perpetual prayer, is visited not only by pilgrims from many places but by tourists as well. From the white dome and also from the steps, you get an unsurpassed view of Paris as it lies spread out beneath the "mountain of martyrs" (that is to say, "Montmartre"). The crypt and its dome are open daily from 9am to 6pm. Admission is 20F ($3).

Behind the church and clinging to the hillside below are steep and crooked little streets that seem—almost—to have survived the relentless march of progress. **Rue des Saules** still has Montmartre's last vineyard, plus a cabaret. **Rue Lepic** still looks—almost—the way Renoir and the melancholy van Gogh and the dwarfish genius Toulouse-Lautrec saw it. This—almost—makes up for the blitz of portraitists and souvenir stores and postcard vendors up on top.

The traditional way to explore Montmartre is on foot. However, since it's at the highest elevation in the city, that is too much for many visitors. Those who prefer can take a miniature train along the steep streets on a 45-minute journey. **Le Petit Train de Montmartre** (for information, contact Promotrain, 38 bd. Flandrin, 16e, tel. 45-04-87-47) carries 72 passengers who can listen to an English commentary as they pass the major landmarks. Boarding is at either place du Tertre (the Church of St. Pierre) or place Blanche (near Moulin Rouge). Trains run March to October from 10am to 7pm and cost 25F ($3.80) for adults, half price for children.

PERE-LACHAISE CEMETERY

This graveyard, the largest in Paris, contains more illustrious dead than any other place on earth. Métro: Père-Lachaise.

A map available at the main entrance will help you find the tombs, and they read like a roll call of international renown. There are Napoleon's marshals Ney and Masséna, and the British admiral Sir Sidney Smith who, by holding the fortress of Acre, made the Corsican taste his first defeat.

There are the poets, playwrights, and novelists Beaumarchais, Balzac, Oscar Wilde, Colette, La Fontaine, Molière, Apollinaire, and Daudet, the composers Chopin and Rossini, the painter Corot, the singer Edith Piaf, and a legion more. The tomb of rock star Jim Morrison (1971) has been one of the most-visited graves.

But the most somber note in Père-Lachaise is a piece of wall called **Mur des Fédérés.** It was among the graves of this cemetery that the last-ditch fighters of the Paris Commune—the world's first anarchist republic—made their final desperate stand against the troops of the regular French government in May 1871. They were overwhelmed, stood up against this wall, and shot in batches. All died except a handful who had hidden in vaults and lived for years in the cemetery like wild animals, venturing into Paris at night to forage for food. The cemetery is open from 7:30am to 6pm in summer, 8:30am to 5:30pm the rest of the year. For information, phone 43-70-70-33.

2. Sightseeing Tours

Paris is paradise for free-lance wanderers. But the process takes both time and energy in large quantities, and even if you have both, chances are you'll miss out on some indispensable sights ("What—you *didn't* see the whatyoucallit?").

Therefore, here is a choice selection of conducted tours and trips, designed to combine the maximum of scenery with the minimum of strain. The ideal thing is to use them in combination with your own explorations, but in any case they'll show you the essentials and a few extras.

BY BUS

On a double-decker Cityrama bus, with enough windows for the Palace of Versailles, you're taken on a two-hour introductory ride through the city's streets. You don't actually go inside specific attractions (you can do that on your own later)—rather, you settle for a look at the outside of such places as Notre-Dame and the Eiffel Tower. The language barrier is overcome as individual earphones are distributed, with a canned commentary in ten different languages. In comfortable armchair-like seats, you sit back as Paris unfolds before you.

Coaches depart daily from 9:30am to 2:30pm, leaving every 30 minutes. The day tour cited above costs 110F ($16.60). Another Cityrama tour of the nighttime illuminations leaves at 9pm in winter or 10pm in summer, costing 125F ($18.20) per person.

If you like this form of touring you can inquire at Cityrama about many other tours offered, including one to Versailles and yet another of Paris by night.

These excursions are sold all over Paris, in hotels and at various ticket agencies. Departures are from the bus terminal at 4 place des Pyramides, 1er (tel. 42-60-30-14). Métro: Louvre.

BY BOAT

Bateaux-Mouches (tel. 42-25-96-10) offers luxury cruises on the Seine. The launches vary—some boast a delightful open sundeck; others, well-stocked bars and restaurants. All provide commentaries in five languages, including English.

Departures are from Pont de l'Alma at the place de l'Alma, 8e, on the Right Bank (Métro: Alma-Marceau). Boats leave at least every 30 minutes from 10am to 11:30pm (every 15 minutes in good weather, depending on the demand). Rates are 25F ($3.80) per day all day long for a ride lasting about an hour and 15 minutes. Children pay 15F ($2.25). Luncheon cruises are also popular, costing from 300F ($45.30). There is also a deluxe dinner cruise (formal dress or tie and jacket are compulsory) leaving at 8:30pm at a cost of 500F ($75.50).

3. The Top Attractions

EIFFEL TOWER

Strangely enough, this symbol of Paris wasn't meant to be a permanent structure at all. Erected specifically for the Universal Exhibition of 1889, it was destined to be pulled down a few years later. But by then, wireless telegraphy had appeared on the scene and the 985-foot tower—the tallest on earth—presented a handy signaling station. Radio confirmed its role. During the German advance on Paris in 1914, the powerful beam from the top effectively jammed the enemy's field radios.

You could write a page with nothing but figures about the tower. The plans for it covered 6,000 square yards of paper, it weighs 7,000 tons, contains 2½ million rivets. Its base extends more than . . .

But enough of that. Just stand underneath the tower and look straight up. It's like a rocket of steel lacework shooting into the sky. If nothing else, it is a fantastic engineering achievement.

Gustave Eiffel, "the universal engineer," who had previously constructed hundreds of bridges and even the inner structure of the Statue of Liberty, had the overall responsibility for the project of building the tower. Architects and aesthetes hated it. ("That damned lamppost ruins the skyline.") The Parisians loved it. Almost overnight it became a part of local legendry. A dozen poems were written about it and at least as many ghastly pieces of music, including an "Eiffel Tower Waltz." By 1910 its permanence had been confirmed—the "lamppost" was there to stay.

You can visit the tower in three stages. Taking the elevator to the first landing, at a charge of 14F ($2.10), you'll have a view over the rooftops of Paris. The second landing, costing 30F ($4.55), provides a panoramic view of the city. The third and final stage, 45F ($6.80), gives the most spectacular view, allowing you to identify many monuments and buildings.

The tower is well equipped with restaurants—two dining rooms (one deluxe), a snackbar, and a drinking bar at various levels await your decision. On the ground level, the 1899 lift machinery is open to visitors in the eastern and western pillars. On the first level, a *ciné* museum showing films on the tower is open when the tower is. Eiffel's office has been re-created on the fourth level, with wax figures of the engineer receiving Thomas Edison.

But it's the view that most people desire, and this extends for 42 miles, theoretically. In practice, weather conditions tend to limit it. Nevertheless, it's fabulous, and the best time for visibility is about an hour before sunset. For information, telephone 45-50-34-56. Métro: Trocadéro, Ecole-Militaire, or Bir-Hakeim.

NOTRE-DAME

The Cathedral of Paris and one of civilization's greatest edifices, this is more than a building—it's like a book written in stone and wood and glass. It can be read line by line, the Virgin's Portal alone telling four different picture stories. The doors of Notre-Dame did, in fact, take the place of religious texts during the ages when few of the faithful were literate.

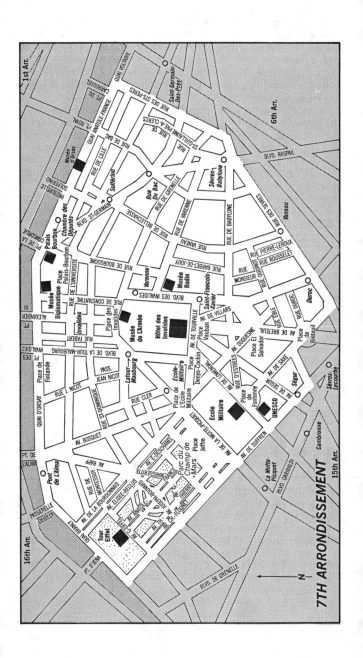

The cathedral replaced two Romanesque churches (Ste. Mary and St. Stephen), which stood on the spot until 1160. Then Bishop Maurice de Sully, following the example of Suger, the abbot of St. Denis, undertook the new structure, and building continued for more than 150 years. The final result was a piece of Gothic perfection, not merely in overall design but in every detail. The rose window above the main portal, for instance, forms a halo 31 feet in diameter around the head of the statue of the Virgin.

More than any other building, Notre-Dame is the history of a nation. Here, the boy-monarch Henry VI of England was crowned king of France in 1422, during the Hundred Years War when—but for Joan of Arc—France would have become an English dominion. Of course, that is how history is viewed in the English world. A French historian, on the other hand, might point out that the Plantagenets were French, not English, and that England would have become a French/Anjou dominion.

Here, Napoléon took the crown out of the hands of Pope Pius VII, and crowned himself and Josephine emperor and empress.

Here, General de Gaulle knelt before the altar on August 26, 1944, to give thanks for the liberation of Paris—imperturbably praying while sniper bullets screeched around the choir galleries.

Because of the beauty of its ornaments and of its symbolic meaning of redemption of all evil, Notre-Dame is a joyous church. However, those devils and gargoyles grinning from its ledges add a genuinely macabre touch. You can almost see Victor Hugo's hunchback peering from behind them.

There are many cathedrals larger than Notre-Dame, but the interior has a transcending loftiness that makes it seem immense. The flat-topped twin towers flanking the entrance rise to 225 feet. You can climb the 387 steps, leading to a magnificent view, Wednesday through Monday from 10am to 4:30pm. You can visit the tower for 22F ($3.30) or 9F ($1.35) in winter. Incidentally, on national holidays and feast days, you can hear the brass thunder of the "Bourdon," the 16-ton bell that hangs in the South Tower. Requiring an entrance fee of 15F ($2.25) for adults and 3F (45¢) for children, the **Treasury (Trésor)** is open Monday to Saturday from 10am to 6pm and Sunday from 2 to 6pm.

The cathedral is generally open from 8am to 7pm. However, it is advised to refrain from visiting during Sunday mass from 10am to 1pm. Free organ concerts are given each Sunday at 5:45pm. For information, telephone 43-26-07-39. The complete address is 6 place du Parvis Notre-Dame, 4e, but it's such a landmark, no one needs a street number to find it. Métro: Cité, Hôtel-de-Ville, or Maubert.

Approached through a garden behind Notre-Dame is the **Memorial to the Deportation,** jutting out on the very tip of the Ile de la Cité. Birds chirp nowadays, the Seine flows gently by—but the memories are far from pleasant. It is a memorial to French martyrs of World War II, who were deported to camps like Auschwitz and Buchenwald. In blood-red are the words: "Forgive, but don't forget." The memorial can be visited daily from 10am to noon and 2 to 7pm. Admission is free.

ARC DE TRIOMPHE

This is the third of the trio of great Paris symbols, the largest triumphal arch in the world and the centerpiece of the entire Right Bank. It stands as the focus of 12 radiating avenues on the place Charles de Gaulle (formerly the place de l'Etoile), giving it an unequaled position and making it pretty difficult to reach for the uninitiated. The best—in fact, the only—way to get there through the traffic is to use the underground passage leading from the Champs-Elysées.

The arch was begun on Napoléon's orders in 1806 to commemorate the victories of his Grande Armée. But it was not completed for another ten years, when the Grande Armée had long been shattered. Ever since then, the arch has born witness to France's defeats as well as its triumphs.

Twice—in 1871 and 1940—German troops tramped through it in their moments of victory. And twice—in 1919 and 1945—Allied armies staged victory parades through those buttresses.

The arch is 162 feet high and 147 feet wide—a stone fanfare of military glory . . . and its price. It's ornamented with martial scenes and engraved with the names of the 128 victories of Napoléon and the 600 generals who participated in them.

But underneath burns the Flame of Remembrance that marks the tomb of France's Unknown Soldier. The effect at night is magical—if only that light weren't burning for millions of young men who lost their lives in war.

Open April to September, daily from 10am to 5:30pm; October through March, daily from 10am to 4:15pm. Admission is 25F ($3.80). For information, phone 43-80-31-31. Métro: Charles-de-Gaulle (Etoile).

HOTEL DES INVALIDES

This is not a "hotel," rather a palace and a church combined, which today houses a great museum, dozens of military administration offices, and the **tomb of Napoléon.**

The monumental ensemble was originally built by Louis XIV as a stately home for invalid soldiers (hence the name). There are still a few living there, but most of the enormous space is taken up by the **Musée de l'Armée** (see "Museums and Exhibitions"), various army bureaus, and the crypt beneath the dome in the rear that makes it one of Paris's greatest showpieces.

It's a shrine, and, like most shrines, impersonal. Napoléon rests in a sarcophagus of red granite on a pedestal of green granite. Surrounding the tomb are 12 figures of victories. The pavement of the crypt consists of a mosaic of laurel leaves.

It took 19 years for the British to release the body of their most illustrious prisoner, who had originally been buried near his house of banishment. Finally, on December 15, 1840, Napoléon's second funeral took place in Paris. The golden hearse was taken through crowds of mourners who had braved a snowstorm to pay their last respects to the nation's hero.

The same golden dome also covers the tombs of Napoléon's brothers, Joseph and Jerome, his son (who was never crowned), and Marshal Foch, who led the Allied armies to victory in 1918. Métro: Latour-Maubourg, Varenne, or St-François-Xavier.

THE CONCIERGERIE

The most sinister building in France squats on the north bank of the Ile de la Cité (near the Pont au Change) and forms part of the huge Palais de Justice, 1 quai de l'Horloge, 1er (tel. 43-54-30-06). Its name is derived from the title *concierge* (constable), once borne by a high official of the Royal Court. But its reputation stems from the Revolution.

Even on warm days, a chill wind seems to blow around its two bleak towers, and the gray, massive walls feel eternally dank. Here, as nowhere else in Paris, you can see the tall, square shadow of the guillotine.

The Conciergerie was the country's chief prison after the fall of the Bastille. When the Reign of Terror got under way, the Conciergerie turned into a kind of stopover depot en route to the "National Razor."

You forget everything else as you enter those courtyards and passages. There are the splendid remnants of a medieval royal palace in there, complete with refectory and giant kitchen. But the only features that imprint themselves on the mind are the rows of cells and the doghouse hovel in which prisoners—shorn and bound— sat waiting for the dung cart that was to carry them to the blade.

First came the "aristos"—led by Marie Antoinette, the duc d'Orléans, brother of the king, and the notorious Madame du Barry. Then came the moderate liberals known as "Girondins." Then followed the radicals with their leader Danton. At their heels were the ultra-radicals along with their chief, the frozen-faced Robespierre. Finally, as the wheel turned full circle, it was the turn of the relentless public prosecutor Fouquier-Tinville, together with the judges and jury of the Revolutionary Court.

They all had their brief stay in those cells, followed by the even briefer ride to the guillotine. Among the few who stayed there but lived to write about it was America's Thomas Paine, who remembered chatting in English with Danton.

The Conciergerie is open April to September, daily from 9:30am to 6:30pm; October to March, daily from 10am to 5pm. Admission is 24F ($3.60) in summer, 12F ($1.80) in winter. Métro: Cité, Châtelet, or St-Michel; RER: St-Michel.

La Sainte-Chapelle

Within the same building complex, but spiritually a thousand miles away, is La Sainte-Chapelle. One of the oldest, most beautiful, and most unusual churches in the world, it was built in 1246 for the express purpose of housing the relics of the Crucifixion, which had been sent from Constantinople at tremendous expense. But the rel-

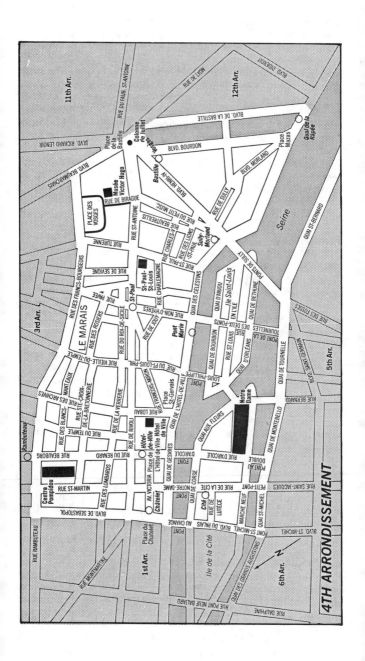

ics were later transferred to Notre-Dame, leaving La Saint-Chapelle as an empty showcase, albeit a magnificent one.

Actually, it consists of two separate churches, one humble, the other superb. The lower chapel was for the servants, the upper for the gentry—and one glance will tell you the difference. The gentry, in fact, were the royal household, and you can still see the small grated window from which Louis XI could participate in the service without being noticed.

The outstanding feature of the chapel, though, is the stained glass. Fifteen windows flood the interior with colored light—deep blue, ruby red, and dark green—and depict more than a thousand scenes from the Bible.

Sainte-Chapelle, Palais de Justice, 4 bd. du Palais, 4e (tel. 43-54-30-09), is open April to September, daily from 9:30am to 6:30pm; October to March, daily from 10am to 5pm. Admission is 25F ($3.80). Métro: Cité or St-Michel.

PANTHEON

At the place du Panthéon, this strangely splendid cross between a Roman temple and a Gothic church has at some time been both and is now neither. But it towers impressively on the Left Bank as one of the city's most illustrious landmarks.

Originally the site of a Roman temple, which grew into a medieval abbey, it was constructed as the Church of Ste-Geneviève in the 18th century, finishing up with the capitol-like dome, as well as noble Roman pillars.

Then the Revolutionary government decided to convert it into a purely patriotic shrine for the nation's greats. Under Napoléon it again became a church. Since 1885, however, it has reverted to being a nonreligious temple—a worthy receptacle for those the nation wished to honor.

The interior is stark and bare, with an austere grandeur all its own. It houses the tombs of Rousseau and Voltaire, of Victor Hugo and Emile Zola, of Louis Braille, and of the African Felix Eboué, who rallied his Equatorial colony to the colors of de Gaulle at a time when no other French administrator dared to do so.

The Panthéon is open June through September, daily from 10am to noon and 2 to 6pm; to 4:30 pm the rest of the year. Admission is 22F ($3.30). For more information, telephone 43-54-34-51. Métro: St-Michel or Monge.

LA MADELEINE

Much more than somber Notre-Dame, this is the patron church of Paris, reflecting the mood, character, and charm of the city. Standing at the most fashionable focal point, between the Opéra and place de la Concorde, it could pass as a handsome palace just as well.

Begun as an 18th-century church, the Madeleine was—at some stage or other—earmarked as a Napoleonic "Temple of Glory," a library, stock exchange, theater, municipal building, court-house, and the Bank of France. Only in 1842 was it finally completed as a house of worship.

Yet despite these dubious beginnings, it became an outstand-ingly beautiful edifice—superlative when the west doors are open and the light is streaming in. The interior is roofed by three domes, lined with 52 Corinthian pillars, and decorated with rich, lively reli-gious scenes.

Once a month there is a concert here, sometimes an exception-al one. Métro: Madeleine.

CITE UNIVERSITAIRE

This is the only one of the sights listed in this section that is still in the building stage. But then it has been since 1925, and will prob-ably continue so for another half century. For the city's great international students' campus isn't really meant ever to be com-pleted. Its purpose is to keep on growing and expanding as long as the space lasts and the students keep coming.

Sprawling just south of Montsouris Park on the Left Bank, this city of colleges, pavilions, and hostels resembles a nonbickering United Nations or a scholastic World's Fair. Only two-thirds of the students living here are French; the rest come from 83 different countries and are housed in buildings suggesting their national ori-gins.

The community center—something like a city hall—is the huge Maison Internationale, built from the funds contributed by John D. Rockefeller, Jr. It has a theater, swimming pool, meeting hall, and club rooms.

All around this center lie the students' buildings, some of them architectural gems. Both the Swiss and the Brazilian pavilions were designed by Le Corbusier. There is also a British college, a Japanese hostel, a Moroccan college, a Norwegian house, and the elegantly French Institut Agronomique. Take a look—perhaps you'd like to enroll! Métro: Cité Universitaire.

THE SEWERS OF PARIS (LES EGOUTS)

Some say Baron Haussmann will be remembered mainly for the vast, complicated network of sewers he erected. The *égouts* of the city, as well as telephone and telegraph pneumatic tubes, are con-structed around a quartet of principal tunnels, one of them 18 feet wide and 15 feet high. It's like an underground city, with the street names clearly labeled. Further, each branch pipe bears the number of the building to which it is connected (guides are fond of pointing out Maxim's). These underground passages are truly mammoth, containing pipes bringing in drinking water and compressed air as well as telephone and telegraph lines.

That these sewers have remained such a popular attraction is something of a curiosity in itself. They were made famous by Victor Hugo's *Les Misérables*. "All dripping with slime, his soul filled with a strange light," Jean Valjean in his desperate flight through the sewers of Paris is considered one of the heroes of narrative drama.

Tours begin on the Left Bank at Pont de l'Alma (Métro: Alma-Marceau; RER: Pont de l'Alma). A stairway leads into the bowels of the city. Often, you have to wait in line for about a half hour. Tours are possible on Saturday and Wednesday from 11am to 5pm; times may change when the weather is bad (storms can make the sewers dangerous). Admission is 20F ($3). A documentary movie on the sewer system is offered, as well as a museum. For information, phone 47-05-10-29.

---

4. Museums and Exhibitions

There are people—and you might agree with them—who find visiting museums in Paris redundant. Why sacrifice the sunshine to pursue art and culture through dim museum corridors when every Seine-side stroll brings you vistas the masters have painted and every city square is a model of architectural excellence?

If that's your view, stick with it. Of the almost 100 highly worthy Paris museums, only one is a requirement for the world traveler: the **Louvre.** Some say that the **Musée d'Orsay** should also be singled out for that honor. But all the rest can be guiltlessly left to people with serious and specific interests, or saved up for that proverbial (and inevitable) rainy day or for your next trip here.

Paris museums fit into three categories: city museums, national museums, and those run by private organizations. The municipal and national museums have fairly standard hours. They are often closed on Tuesday and national holidays. Fees vary, but half-price tickets are usually provided to students, children ages 3 to 7, and extra-large families or groups. If you want to museum-hop in earnest, pick a Sunday, when the majority of the museums let you in for half price.

Whatever time of the year you come, Paris seems to be deeply involved with one or another outstanding exhibition—touted madly from the lampposts by huge and colorful posters. The largest and most comprehensive are showcased at the **Grand Palais,** between the Seine and the Champs-Elysées on avenue Winston Churchill, built for this purpose for the 1900 Exposition. More modest collections are set out across the street in the **Petit Palais.** In the halls and museum rooms across the city, there are at least 15 special shows on any given week—a Chagall retrospective, Giacometti sculptures, Art of the Workers' Movement, the public life of Napoléon. Fees charged depend on the exhibit.

INFORMATION

To find out what's showing while you're in town, stop into the **Welcome Office,** 127 av. des Champs-Elysées, 8e (tel. 47-23-61-72). Métro: Charles de Gaulle (Etoile). Here, you can pick up a free copy of the English-language booklet "Paris Weekly Information," published by the National Tourist Office. Hours are daily from 9am to 8pm in summer, daily from 9am to 6pm in winter.

SPECIAL PASSES

Marketing Challenges International, 10 East 21st St., New York, NY 10010 (tel. 212/529-8484), offers a money-saving museum pass called **La Carte.** With La Carte you can visit 60 museums in Paris, including the Louvre and the Musée d'Orsay, at one low price—and with no waiting in line for tickets. A one-day pass is $10; a three-day pass, $20; and a five-day pass, $30. (Prices for La Carte are subject to change, of course, but probably not by much.)

ART MUSEUMS

The Louvre

The largest palace in the world, housing a collection of up to 300,000 works of art, the Musée du Louvre, rue de Rivoli, 1er (tel. 42-60-39-26), is both impressive and exhausting.

There's so much to see, so many endless hallways to get lost in, that—regardless of how much you may enjoy exploring a museum on your own—here I suggest you start with the guided tour. At least do so until you get the lay of the land. You can always go back and see what you missed. Or sit down in one favorite room and spend the day. Tours in English are given Wednesday through Saturday and Monday at 11:30am and 3:30pm; the 90-minute tour is 25F ($3.80).

Entrance to the museum is through I. M. Pei's 71-foot-high glass pyramid in the Louvre's courtyard. First announced in 1983 by French president Mitterrand, the modern structure opened in 1990 to acclaim by some, denunciation by others. The pyramid shelters an underground complex of shops and restaurants and, most importantly, increases the gallery space of the Louvre by an astonishing 80%. It also provides garages for all those tour buses that previously created havoc on rue de Rivoli. In addition, automatic ticket machines here help relieve those long, long lines of former days.

The museum buildings are immensely interesting in themselves. French kings have lived on this site by the Seine since the 13th century, but much of the present grand residence was built by Napoléon I and his nephew, Napoléon III. The palace was converted to a museum after the Revolution; the royal arts collections provided the first exhibits. The palace rooms don't function perfectly as skillfully lit museum rooms (for which the Louvre apologizes), but they provide sumptuous settings, which at times even compete with the displays.

Be sure to see at least the highlights of the collection. To the left of the main entrance, at the crest of a graceful flight of stairs, stands the *Winged Victory*, cloak rippling in a wind that blew two centuries before the birth of Christ. In the Department of Greek Antiquities, on the ground floor, stands the supple statue of *Venus de Milo*, the warm marble subtly tinted by sunlight. Upstairs, in the Salle des Etats, covered with bulletproof glass and surrounded by art students, photographers, and awe-struck tourists, hangs the gently chiding portrait *Mona Lisa*.

Altogether, there are six museum departments: Egyptian Antiquities, Oriental Antiquities (the world's most complete collection), Greek and Roman Antiquities, Objets d'Art and Furniture, Paintings, and Sculpture.

There are so many other things to see as well: six more da Vincis (near the *Mona Lisa*), voluptuous Titians, Franz Hals's *The Gypsy*, the enormously lifelike Egyptian *Seated Scribe*. But one can't even start to list the items in this museum. Nor could you see them all if you took three days and brought your lunch. The only blessing is that there is a cut-off point—the collection doesn't go beyond the 19th century.

The Louvre is open Wednesday through Monday from 9:45am to 5pm; the Greek section, containing the *Venus de Milo* and the *Winged Victory*, is open until 6:30pm; some rooms are closed between 12:30 and 2:30pm. Métro: Louvre.

Musée de l'Orangerie des Tuileries

After the Louvre, walk to the river edge, to the place de la Concorde, 1er (tel. 42-97-48-16). Often set aside for special exhibits, this museum, a gem among art galleries, has an outstanding collection of art and one celebrated display: Claude Monet's exquisite *Nymphéas* (executed between 1890 and 1921), a light-filtered tangle of lily pads and water, paneling the two oval, ground-floor rooms whose construction was supervised by the artist himself.

The renovated building also shelters the Walter-Guillaume collection, which includes more than 24 Renoirs, including *Young Girl at a Piano*. Cézanne is represented by 14 works, notably *The Red Rock*, and Matisse by 11 paintings. Rousseau's nine works are highlighted by *The Wedding*, and the dozen paintings by Picasso reach their brilliance in *The Female Bathers*. Other outstanding paintings are by Utrillo (10 works in all), Soutine (22), and Derain (28).

The collection can be viewed Wednesday through Monday from 9:45am to 5:15pm. Admission is 15F ($2.25); half price on Sunday. Métro: Concorde.

Musée d'Orsay

Standing across the Seine from the Louvre, the defunct but handsome neoclassical rail station, the Gare d'Orsay, 1 rue de Bellechasse, 7e (tel. 40-49-48-14), has been transformed into one of the greatest art museums in the world.

The museum houses thousands of pieces of sculpture and

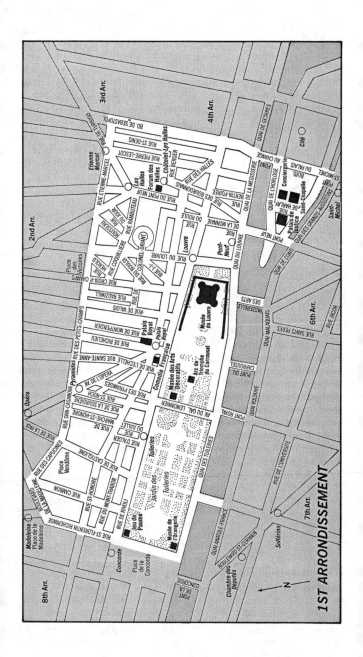

1ST ARRONDISSEMENT

painting in 80 different galleries. It also displays Belle Epoque furniture, photographs, objets d'art, architectural models, even a cinema. A detailed and wide-ranging panorama of international art is presented from the period between 1848 and 1914, from the birth of the Second French Republic to the dawn of World War I. It is a repository of art and civilization of the century just past.

A monument to the Industrial Revolution, the Orsay station, once called "the elephant," is covered by an arching glass roof, flooding the museum with light. The museum displays works ranging from the creations of academic and historic painters such as Ingres to romanticists such as Delacroix, to neorealists such as Courbet and Daumier. In a setting once used by Orson Welles to film a nightmarish scene in *The Trial,* based on a Kafka work, are displayed the impressionists and post-impressionists, including Cézanne, Van Gogh, and the Fauves, along with Matisse, the cubists, expressionists, and the abstract painters. You get the sunny wheatfields by Millet, works from the Barbizon School, the misty landscapes of Corot, and brilliant-hued Gauguins.

But it is mainly the impressionists that keep the crowds lining up. The impressionists, unified in opposition to the dictatorial Académie des Beaux-Arts, chose for their subject matter the world about them, ignoring ecclesiastical or mythological scenes, and insisted on bathing their canvases in light. They painted the Seine, Parisians strolling in the Tuileries, even railway stations such as the Gare St-Lazare (some critics considered Monet's choice of the latter unforgivable vulgarity). The impressionists were the first to paint the most characteristic feature of Parisian life: the sidewalk café, especially in what was then the artists' quarter of Montmartre.

Perhaps the most famous painting displayed from this era is Manet's *The Picnic on the Grass,* which, when it was first exhibited, was decried as *au grande scandale des gens de bien.* Painted in 1863, it depicts a forest setting with a nude woman and two fully clothed men. Two years later, his *Olympia* created another scandal, showing a woman lounging on her bed and wearing nothing but a flower in her hair and high-heeled shoes. Attending her is a black maid. Zola called Manet "a man among eunuchs."

One of Renoir's brightest, most joyous paintings is here—the *Moulin de la Galette,* painted in 1876. Degas is represented by paintings of racehorses and dancer; his 1876 café scene *Absinthe* remains one of his most reproduced works. Paris-born Claude Monet was fascinated by the changing light effects on Rouen Cathedral, and in a series of five paintings he makes the old landmark live as never before.

One of the most celebrated works is by an American, James McNeill Whistler, represented by *Arrangement in Gray and Black: Portrait of the Painter's Mother.* It is said that this painting heralded the advent of modern art, although many critics denounced it at the time as "Whistler's Dead Mother" because of its funereal overtones. Today the painting has been hailed as a "veritable icon of our consciousness." As far as Whistler was concerned, he claimed he made "Mummy just as nice as possible."

Open Tuesday, Wednesday, Friday, and Saturday from 10am to 6pm; Sunday from 9am to 6pm; Thursday from 10:30am to 9:45pm. From June 20 to September 20, the museum opens at 9am. Admission is 23F ($3.45) for adults, 12F ($1.80) ages 18 to 24 and over 60 (under 18 admitted free). Métro: Solferino; RER: Musée d'Orsay.

Centre Georges Pompidou

It was Georges Pompidou's dream to create a large cultural center in Paris that would include every form of 20th-century art. As president of France (in 1969), he launched the project for a "temple devoted to art" on the Plateau Beaubourg, east of boulevard de Sébastopol, 4e (tel. 42-77-12-33). That center was finally inaugurated in 1977 by yet another French president, Valéry Giscard d'Estaing.

The building housing the center has been called "the most avant-garde building in the world" because of its radical exoskeletal design, but Parisians are more likely to refer to it as "the refinery." The colorfully painted pipes and ducts that crisscross the transparent façade are actually the practical housings for the intricate electrical, heating, and telephone systems that service the center. Even the escalators are housed in wormlike tubes on the outside of the building. Thus the vast interior has no need for walls, and a grand feeling of open space is created. When walls are needed for exhibits, moving partitions are rolled into place.

All this uniqueness has made the Pompidou Center Paris's favorite sightseeing attraction, surpassing even the Eiffel Tower in the number of tourists who visit.

The **Musée National d'Art Moderne (National Museum of Modern Art)**, can be entered on the fourth floor. It offers a large collection of 20th-century art, including French and American masterpieces from the Fauves up to abstract and expressionist works. All the trends of modern art are displayed on two floors in well-lit rooms of varying sizes.

Featured are works by such artists as Max Ernst (a sculpture, *The Imbecile*), Kandinsky, Vuillard, Bonnard, Utrillo, Chagall, Dufy, Juan Gris, Léger, and Pollock, as well as sketches by Le Corbusier and stained glass by Rouault. Modern sculpture includes works by Alexander Calder, Henry Moore, and Jacob Epstein. Galeries Contemporaines, on the ground floor, demonstrates the trends in artistic activity today. Special exhibitions and demonstrations are constantly being staged in the Grande Galerie. Guided tours are available.

In addition to the modern art museum, the center contains the largest consulting library in Paris, with more than a million volumes and documents. Its Center of Industrial Design contains exhibits and research facilities in the field of architecture, space planning, publishing, and visual communications. A cinémathèque offers visitors a historical tour of filmmaking. The top-floor restaurant and cafeteria offer a panoramic view of Paris.

The Centre Georges Pompidou is open Monday and Wednesday through Friday from noon to 10pm, Saturday and Sunday from 10am to 10pm. Admission is 50F ($7.55) for an all-day pass, which permits you access to any part of the center; admission to the museum of modern art only is 24F ($3.60); free admission Sunday morning. Métro: Rambuteau.

Musée Picasso

When it opened at the beautifully restored Hôtel Salé (salt mansion), 5 rue de Thorigny, 3e (tel. 42-71-25-21), the press hailed it as a "museum for Picasso's Picassos." And that's what it is. Almost overnight it became one of the most popular attractions in Paris. The greatest Picasso collection in the world, acquired by the state in payment of inheritance taxes totaling around $50 million, consists of 203 paintings, 158 sculptures, 16 collages, 19 bas-reliefs, 88 ceramics, and more than 1,500 sketches and 1,600 engravings, along with 30 notebooks.

The paintings include a remarkable 1901 self-portrait and such masterpieces as *Le Baiser* (the kiss), painted at Mougins on the Riviera in 1969, and the 1970 *Reclining Nude and the Man with a Guitar*. It's easy to stroll through the handsome museum seeking your own favorite work (mine is a delightfully wicked one, *Jeune Garçon à la Langouste,* or young man with a lobster, painted in Paris in 1941). The museum owns several intriguing studies for *Les Demoiselles d'Avignon,* the painting that initiated cubism.

Many of the major masterpieces such as *The Crucifixion* and *Nude in a Red Armchair* should remain on permanent view. However, because the collection is so vast, temporary exhibitions, such as one featuring the studies of the Minotaur, are opened to the public at the rate of two a year. In addition to Picasso's own art, works by other masters from his private collection are displayed, including the contributions of such world-class artists as Cézanne, Rousseau, Braque, Matisse, André Derain, and Joan Miró. Picasso was fascinated with African masks, and many of these are on view as well.

The mansion was constructed in 1656 by Aubert de Fontenay, who collected the dreaded salt tax in Paris. The museum is open Wednesday from 9:15am to 10pm, Thursday through Monday from 9:15am to 5:15pm. Admission is 21F ($3.20). Métro: St-Paul, Filles-du-Calvaire, or Chemin-Vert.

Musée d'Art Moderne de la Ville de Paris

At 11 av. du Président Wilson, 16e (tel. 47-23-61-27), this museum houses the City of Paris collections of 20th-century art and also organizes temporary exhibitions. Other sections of the museum are: **ARC**, which shows work of young artists and new trends in contemporary art, and the **Musée des Enfants,** with exhibitions and animations for children. The museum is open Tuesday through Sunday from 10am to 5:30pm, until 8:30pm on Wednesday. Admission is 25F ($3.80), 15F ($2.25) for students and children. Métro: Iéna or Alma-Marceau.

Musée de Cluny

An enchanting museum, with some of the most beautiful medieval art extant, the Musée de Cluny, 6 place Paul-Painlevé, 5e (tel. 43-25-62-00), stands back from the intersection of boulevards St-Michel and St-Germain in a walled courtyard—one of the two Gothic private residences of the 15th century left in Paris.

Dark, rough-walled, and evocative, the Cluny is devoted to the church art and castle crafts of the Middle Ages, jewelry (votive crowns of the Visigothic kings and a golden altar from Basel), sculpture, stained glass, and tapestries—among them the world-famed series of *The Lady and the Unicorn* gracefully displayed in a circular room on the second floor. The painstakingly depicted *Life of St. Stephen* hangs in the shadowy chapel, while a third series is concerned with the colorful life at court. The building also includes the remains of an A.D. 200 Roman bathhouse with a well-preserved *frigidarium.*

The Cluny is open Wednesday through Monday from 9:45am to 12:30pm and 2 to 5:15pm. Admission is 15F ($2.25), 8F ($1.20) on Sunday. Métro: Cluny-Sorbonne.

Musée National Auguste Rodin

Auguste Rodin, the man credited with freeing French sculpture of classicism, once lived and had his studio in the charming 18th-century mansion Hôtel Biron, 77 rue de Varenne, 7e (tel. 47-05-01-34), across the boulevard from Napoléon's Tomb in the Hôtel des Invalides. Today the house and garden are filled with his works, a soul-satisfying feast for the Rodin enthusiast.

In the cobbled Court of Honor, within the walls as you enter, you'll see *The Thinker* crouched on his pedestal to the right of you; *The Burghers of Calais* grouped off to the left of you; and to the far left, the writhing *Gates of Hell*, atop which *The Thinker* once more meditates. There's a third *Thinker* inside the museum before a second-floor window. In the almost too-packed rooms, men and angels emerge from blocks of marble, hands twisted in supplication, and the nude torso of Balzac rises up from a tree. Wander back from the house through the long wooded garden where more sculptures await you under the trees.

The Musée Rodin is open Tuesday through Sunday from 10am to 6pm (until 5:15pm October through March). Admission is 18F ($2.70), half price on Sunday. Métro: Varenne.

Musée des Arts Decoratifs

In the northwest wing of the Pavillon de Marsan of the Louvre, at 107 rue de Rivoli, 1er (tel. 42-60-32-14), the museum offers a treasury of furnishings, fabrics, wallpaper, objets d'art, and other items that add up to displays of styles of living from the Middle Ages to the present day. Notable are the art deco boudoir, bath, and bedroom done in the 1920s for couturier Jeanne Lanvin by designer Rateau. This and other displays from 1900 to 1925 are on the first floor, together with collections of contemporary art and a 1900 room.

For many people the first floor holds the most interest, as it contains the prestigious collection of the works of Jean Dubuffet that the artist donated to the museum. Decorative art from the Middle Ages to the Renaissance are on the second floor, while rich collections from the 17th, 18th, and 19th centuries occupy the third and fourth floors. The fifth floor contains specialized centers of the museum, such as wallpaper and drawings, and documentary centers detailing fashion, textiles, toys, crafts, and glass trends.

The museum is open Wednesday through Saturday from 12:30 to 6pm, Sunday from 11am to 6pm. The admission price depends on the temporary exhibitions. Métro: Louvre.

Musée Guimet

A splendid collection of artworks from India, Indochina, Afghanistan, Tibet, China, and Japan is featured at Musée Guimet, 6 place d'Iéna, 16e (tel. 47-23-61-65), and its annex at 19 av. d'Iéna. Included are the entire Far East collection of the Louvre, bronzes dating back to 1300 B.C., plump and placid Buddhas, and ancient Indian figurines of religious import. Many of the monuments are displayed with maps of the area where they were unearthed, plus photographs of the excavation. The jewels of the collection are on the first floor in the Rousset collection, and in the Michel Calmann room on the top floor (take the elevator), which contains some lovely porcelain pieces, pottery statues, plates, and vases, dating from the earliest Chinese dynasties, including many from the Tang Dynasty.

The museum is open Wednesday through Monday from 9:45am to 5:15pm. Admission, to both the museum and its annex, is 15F ($2.25), half price on Sunday. Métro: Iéna.

Musée Eugène Delacroix

From 1857 through 1863 the great Romantic painter Delacroix had his final studio at 6 place de Fürstenberg, one of the most bewitching small squares in all Paris. The artist's apartment and rear-garden "atelier" have been transformed into a museum of his work (tel. 43-54-04-87). This is no poor artist's shabby studio, but the very tasteful creation of a solidly established man. Sketches, lithographs, watercolors, and oils are hung throughout, and a few personal mementos remain, including a lovely mahogany paint box.

The museum is open Wednesday through Monday from 9:45am to 5:15pm; closed holidays. Admission is 10F ($1.50). Métro: St-Germain-des-Prés.

To see the work that earned Delacroix his sure niche in art history, go to the Louvre for such passionate paintings as his *Liberty Leading the People on the Barricades,* or to the Church of St. Sulpice (Métro: Mabillon) for the famed fresco, *Jacob Wrestling with the Angel,* among others.

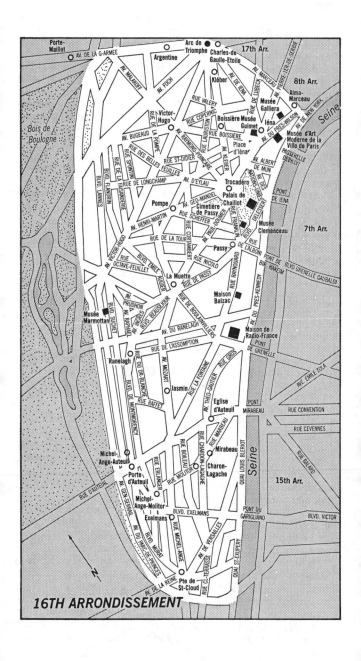

16TH ARRONDISSEMENT

Musée Marmottan

Time was when nobody but a stray art scholar ever visited the museum at 2 rue Louis-Boilly, 16e (tel. 42-24-07-02), on the edge of the Bois de Boulogne. Nowadays it is quite popular. The rescue from obscurity actually occurred on February 5, 1966, when the museum fell heir to more than 130 paintings, watercolors, pastels, and drawings of Claude Monet, the painter considered the father of impressionism. A gift of Monet's son, Michel, an octogenarian safari-lover who died in a car crash, the bequest was valued at the time at $10 million. Of the surprise acquisition, one critic wrote, "Had an old widow in Brooklyn suddenly inherited the fortune of J. P. Morgan, the event would not have been more startling."

The owner of the museum, the Académie des Beaux-Arts, was immediately embarrassed with a lack of space. The Marmottan was just a small town house, adorned with First Empire furniture and objets d'art (although it did own Monet's *Impression: Sunrise,* which named the movement). The house had once been owned by a dilettante, Paul Marmottan, who had donated it, along with his treasures, to the academy. The solution was to go underground.

Now you can trace the evolution of Monet's art, especially his eternal obsession with water lilies. Presented are about 30-odd pictures of his house at Giverny that inspired him so much. Exceptional paintings include his celebrated 1918 *The Willow,* his 1905 *Houses of Parliament,* his undated *African Lilies,* as well as paintings by Monet's masters, Boudin and Delacroix, and by his fellow impressionists (see especially a portrait of the 32-year-old Monet by Renoir). You can also see the extensive collection of miniatures donated by Daniel Waldenstein.

The museum is open Tuesday through Sunday from 10am to 5:30pm. Admission is 25F ($3.80). Métro: La Muette.

Musée Jacquemart-André

This 19th-century town house at 158 bd. Haussmann, 8e (tel. 45-62-39-94), with its gilt salons and elegant winding staircase, contains one of the best small collections of 18th-century decorative art in Paris. The building and its contents were a bequest to the Institut de France by the late Madame Nélie Jacquemart-André, herself an artist of some note. She and her husband, Edouard André, formed a fine collection of rare French decorative art, adding to it a rich collection of painting and sculpture from the Dutch and Flemish Schools, as well as paintings and objets d'art from the Italian Renaissance and the 18th-century French School.

Enter through an arcade, which opens onto an inner courtyard. Through the main entrance, flanked by two stone lions, is a world of paintings, antiques, Gobelin tapestries, Savonnerie carpets, Slodtz busts, Della Robbia terra-cottas, and Donatello torchères. Many of the greatest painters of the Northern Schools and the Italian Renaissance are represented: Rembrandt *(The Pilgrim of Emmaüs),* Van Dyck, Rubens, Tiepolo, and Carpaccio. The art of 18th-century France is well represented by the works of Watteau, Fragonard, and Boucher.

Open Wednesday through Sunday from 1:30 to 5:30pm; closed August. Admission is 35F ($5.30). Métro: St-Philippe-du-Roule.

By Invitation Only

The presidential palace, the **Palais de l'Elysée,** occupies an entire block along the chic Faubourg St-Honoré. But you have to have a personal invitation from the president to visit inside.

The palace was built in 1718 for the comte d'Evreux and knew many owners before becoming the residence for the presidents of the Republic in 1873. Madame Pompadour purchased it and in time bequeathed it to the king when she had "the supreme delicacy to die discreetly at the age of 43." Voltaire presented the world premiere of his play, *The Chinese Orphan,* here. After her divorce, Josephine spent a brief time here. Napoléon III lived here as president from 1848 until he went to the Tuileries as emperor in 1852. Distinguished English visitors have also been lodged here, everybody from Wellington to Queen Victoria to Queen Elizabeth II.

The palace contains many works of art, including 18th-century Beauvais tapestries, paintings by Leonardo da Vinci and Raphael, Louis XVI furnishings, plus a grand dining hall built for Napoléon III, a lavish ballroom, a portrait gallery, and the former Orangerie of duchesse du Berry, which has been converted into a winter garden.

Musée Cernuschi

Bordering on the Parc Monceau, this small museum at 7 av. Vélasquez, 8e (tel. 45-63-50-75), is devoted to the arts of China. It's another one of those mansions whose owners stuffed them with an art collection, then bequeathed them to the City of Paris. The address was quite an exclusive one when the town house was built in 1885.

Inside there is of course a bust of Cernuschi, a man whose generosity and interest in the Far East was legend in his day. The collections include a fine assortment of neolithic pottery, as well as bronzes from the 14th century B.C., the most famous perhaps the tiger-shape vase. Jades, ceramics, and funereal figures are exceptional, as are pieces of Buddhist sculpture. Most admirable is a Bodhisattva originating from Yun-kang (6th century). Rounding out the exhibits are some ancient paintings, the best known being *Horses with Grooms,* attributed to Han Kan (8th century, Tang Dynasty). The museum also houses a good collection of contemporary Chinese painting.

The museum can be visited Tuesday through Sunday from 10am to 5:40pm. Admission is 12F ($1.80), free on Sunday except for exhibitions. Métro: Monceau or Villiers. Bus: 30 or 94.

Musée Nissim-de-Camondo

At 63 rue de Monceau, 8e (tel. 45-63-26-32), near the Musée Cernuschi, this museum is a jewel box of elegance and refinement, evoking the days of Louis XVI and Marie Antoinette. The pre–World War I town house was donated to the Museum of Decorative Arts by Comte Moïse de Camondo (1860–1935) in memory of his son, Nissim, a French aviator killed in combat in World War I.

Entered through a courtyard, the museum is like the private home of an aristocrat two centuries ago—richly furnished with needlepoint chairs, tapestries (many from Beauvais or Aubusson), antiques, paintings (the inevitable Guardi scenes of Venice), bas-reliefs, silver, Chinese vases, crystal chandeliers, Sèvres porcelain, Savonnerie carpets, and several busts by Houdon (in an upstairs bedroom). The Blue Salon, overlooking Parc Monceau, is impressive. You wander without a guide through the gilt and oyster-gray salons.

The museum can be visited Wednesday through Sunday from 10am to noon and 2 to 5pm; closed May 1, Christmas, and New Year's Day. Admission is 15F ($2.25) Métro: Villiers.

Musée Zadkine

This museum, at 100 bis rue d'Assas, 6e (tel. 43-26-91-90), near the Luxembourg Gardens and boulevard St-Michel, was once the private residence of Ossip Zadkine, the sculptor. Now the collection of this famous artist has been turned over to the City of Paris for public viewing. Included are some 300 pieces of sculpture, displayed both in the museum and in the garden, which gives a rural charm to the heart of the city. In addition, some drawings and tapestries are also exhibited.

Open Tuesday through Sunday from 10am to 5:30pm. Admission is 12F ($1.80). Métro: Luxembourg or Vavin.

HISTORICAL MUSEUMS

Musée Carnavalet

In the Marais district at 23 rue de Sévigné, 3e (tel. 42-27-21-13), the museum covers the history of the city to the present time. There are rooms filled with models of the old quarters of Paris—detailed down to the lace on the cap of the baker's girl. You can see the Bastille, of which there is now not a trace. One room is crammed with signposts of the 17th and 18th centuries, designed to let the unlettered know that here at the sign of the tree worked a carpenter, and here where a pig was portrayed you could buy your cold cuts. The striking collection of memorabilia from the French Revolution includes the chessmen with which Louis XVI passed time while imprisoned in the Temple, as well as the boyish diary of the dauphin and some effects of Marie Antoinette.

There is more, such as antique furniture of various periods.

The mansion that houses the exhibits, built in 1545, is considered a prime example of Renaissance architecture. The tour continues across the courtyard at the Hôtel le Peletière de Saint-Fargeau. There, exhibits cover the time of the Revolution up to the present.

The museum is open Tuesday through Sunday from 10am to 5:40pm. Admission is 15F ($2.25). Métro: St-Paul or Chemin-Vert.

When you leave the museum, take a few moments to walk up rue des Francs-Bourgeois two blocks to the aged arcades of the **place des Vosges,** where you may sit and rest a while within the fenced park or visit the home of Victor Hugo. Alternatively, turn right down rue des Francs-Bourgeois and walk three long blocks to the majestic Palais Soubise (Archives Nationales, 60 rue des Francs-Bourgeois, 3e), where an elegant 18th-century apartment contains the **Musée de l'Histoire de France** (tel. 40-27-61-78), created in 1867. What you see are mainly documents—some so gloriously inscribed they become works of art—chronicling the history of France from its origins. The building vies in interest with the displays within. It is open Wednesday through Monday from 1:30 to 5:45pm. Admission is 12F ($1.80), 8F ($1.20) on Sunday.

Musée de l'Armée

In the Hôtel National des Invalides, 7e (tel. 45-55-30-11, ext. 3769), is the finest military museum in the world—outdistancing even Britain's Imperial War Museum in amassed martial relics. Its collection of arms dates back so far it seems to include the first rock thrown by Neolithic man. The museum sets out the war paraphernalia of every age—bronze spearheads and medieval crossbows, intricately engraved armor and doughboy drabs—leading up with a flourish and the recorded strains of "Tipperary" to the bugle that sounded the cease-fire on November 7, 1918, before the general cease-fire on November 11, 1918. The shrinelike aura is distressing. The detail is fascinating.

The west wing, on your right as you enter the courtyard, houses suits of armor, especially in the new so-called Arsenal—arms belonging to the kings and dignitaries of France. The Salle Orientale in the west wing shows arms from the Far East and from Muslim countries of the Mideast, from the 16th to the 19th centuries. Turkish armor (see Bajazet's helmet) and weapons, as well as Chinese and Japanese armor and swords, are on exhibit. Moreover, the west wing houses exhibits from World Wars I and II.

You can gain access to the Musée des Plans-Reliefs through the west wing. It is a unique collection in scale model of French towns and monuments.

The east wing, on your left, shows objects dating back to the 17th century and predating 1914. Off the entrance hall in the hushed Salle Turenne (a plaque at the door cues you to proper respect) fly the battleflags of France, including those of Bonaparte's regiments and some shredded remnants of standards from 1940. Opposite, in the Salle Vauban, 18 mounted figures illustrate the showy uniforms of the French Cavalry. Go upstairs to view souvenirs of the French Revolution campaigns, next to the bed in which Napoléon died, as well as the personal effects from his island exile.

The gloss of the show tends to veil the truth that war is a matter of death and heartbreak. But occasionally it comes through, simply and effectively, as in the display of a silvery cuirass, pierced by a jagged wound the size and shape of a softball—the breastplate of a Carabinier downed by a cannon at Waterloo.

The Army Museum is open October through March, daily from 10am to 5pm; April through September, daily from 10am to 6pm. Napoléon's Tomb stays open until 7pm in the summer. Admission is 23F ($3.45) for adults, half price for students and those under 18. The ticket, valid for two consecutive days, covers admission to the Musée de l'Armée, Napoléon's Tomb, and the Musée des Plans-Reliefs.

Musée National des Monuments Français

Up the hill from the modern art museum, in the complex of the Palais de Chaillot on the Trocadéro, is this unusual and strangely atmospheric museum, place du Trocadéro (tel. 47-27-35-74). There are no original works of art in this museum. Instead, the sculptures are full-scale plaster casts, which enable you to study at eye level such exalted creatures as the sword-brandishing angel on the Arc de Triomphe. But most fascinating are the meticulously reproduced (even the colors are aged) murals from the most ancient abbeys and churches in France—all in reconstructed settings. Within the awesome museum with its echoing crypts, you can view the great works now in the cathedrals of Chartres, Reims, and Amiens, without even losing sight of the Eiffel Tower outside the museum-room windows.

The National Museum of French Monuments is open Wednesday through Monday from 9am to 6pm. Admission is 15F ($2.25), 8F ($1.20) for children. Métro: Trocadéro.

A LITERARY MUSEUM

Maison de Balzac

This unpretentious house on the slope of a hill in Passy, a residential district of Paris, was the home—or more accurately, the hideaway—of the great French novelist Honoré de Balzac from 1840 to 1847. At 47 rue Raynouard, 16e (tel. 42-24-56-38), the Balzac museum is almost completely unfurnished, but it does contain mementos, documents, manuscripts, and other items associated with the writer. Throughout the house are scattered caricature drawings of Balzac, whose amusing appearance and eccentric dress lent itself to ridicule. Among the better-known mementos is the famed Limoges coffeepot that Balzac's "screeching owl" kept hot during the long nights while he wrote *La Comédie Humaine*. Also enshrined here are Balzac's writing desk and chair.

The house contains a library of special interest to scholars, as well as a small courtyard and garden. While the main entrance is on rue Raynouard, the back door leads to rue Berton—a fortunate situation for Balzac who often had to make hasty retreats from his many creditors.

The museum is open Tuesday through Sunday from 10am to 5:40pm. Admission is 12F ($1.80). Métro: Passy or La Muette.

A SCIENCE MUSEUM

Cité des Sciences et de l'Industrie

A center of science and industry has risen at La Villette, 30 av. Corentin-Cariou, 19e (tel. 46-42-13-13). When its core was originally built in the 1960s, it was touted as the most modern slaughterhouse in the world, but when the site was abandoned as a failure in 1974, its echoing vastness and unlikely location on the northern edge of the city presented the French government with a problem. In 1986 the converted premises opened as the world's most expensive ($642-million) science complex, designed "to modernize mentalities" as a first step in the process of modernizing society.

The Cité des Sciences et de l'Industrie is both an educational institution and a true "city," with activities, facilities, and services. Visitors can take an active role in learning about science, technology, and industry—and have fun as well.

The museum is set in the largest city park of Paris, with 136 acres of green expanses, twice the size of the Tuileries. A flatland has been turned into futuristic forms, with many walkways, and red steel pavilions scattered throughout. Here you'll find a belvedere, a video workshop for children, and information about exhibitions and events, along with a café and a restaurant.

The Cité itself consists of a permanent exhibition, "Explora," several temporary exhibitions, an "Inventorium" for children (ages 3 to 12), a multimedia library, as well as a planetarium. Explora, spread over three upper levels of the building, covers 322,800 square feet. The 31 display areas revolve around four themes: the universe, life, matter, and communication.

The Inventorium could be nicknamed "the children's kingdom," as it offers children an approach to science and technology through games and discovery exhibitions. Temporary exhibitions range from the invention of time to scientists of the enlightment. In the planetarium, the astronomic simulator in the 280-seat amphitheater is capable of reproducing a sky studded with 10,000 stars.

Opposite the Cité is the Géode, a geodesic dome that's the closest thing to 3-D cinema in Europe.

Visiting hours are Saturday, Sunday, and holidays from noon to 8pm; Tuesday, Thursday, and Friday from 10am to 6pm; and Wednesday from noon to 9pm. Admission is 30F ($4.55); children must pay an additional 15F ($2.25) for the Inventorium; everyone is charged a supplement of 15F ($2.25) to visit the planetarium. Showtimes at the Géode are Tuesday and Thursday at 10am and

6pm, Wednesday and Friday through Sunday at 10am and 9pm; admission is 40F ($6.05). Métro: Porte de la Villette.

A TAPESTRY MUSEUM

Manufacture des Gobelins

If you enjoyed seeing the tapestries at the Musée de Cluny, you might also enjoy watching how they are made. Tapestry work is still being done at Les Gobelins, 42 av. des Gobelins, 13e, in the same way and on looms like those used at the founding of the factory in 1662. You can tour the workshops where weavers sit behind huge screens of thread, patiently thrusting stitch after stitch into work that may take up to three years to complete.

The tours are given in French only on Tuesday, Wednesday, and Thursday between 2 and 2:45pm. Admission is 16F ($2.40). Métro: Gobelins. For information, get in touch with Caisse Nationale des Monuments Historiques, 62 rue Saint-Antoine, 4e (tel. 48-87-24-14).

5. A Garland of Gardens

You'll be astonished to hear that Paris boasts far less parkland than, for instance, New York or London. You don't notice it because the rows of trees along every boulevard create the illusion of vast green spaces. The impression is conscientiously fostered by the municipality, which replaces each tree the moment it dies (unlike certain other city governments, whose main ambition seems to be to hack down and pour concrete over as many trees as possible).

JARDIN DES TUILERIES

Stretching along the right bank of the Seine, from the place de la Concorde to the court of the Louvre, this exquisitely formal garden was laid out as a royal pleasure park in 1564, but thrown open to the public by the French Revolution. Filled with statues and fountains and precisely trimmed hedges, it's just a bit too artificial for comfort. The nicest features are the round ponds on which pleasantly disorderly kids sail armadas of model boats. Métro: Tuileries.

JARDIN DU LUXEMBOURG

This is the Left Bank equivalent of the Tuileries, bordering the boulevard St-Michel. A masterpiece of Renaissance landscaping with a jewel of a central pond, it faces the Palais de Luxembourg, the senate building of the French Republic. More intriguing than the senators, however, are the throngs of university students who come here to do their outdoor cramming and, incidentally, to enlarge their acquaintance with the opposite sex. Métro: Odéon.

PARC MONCEAU

The most fashionable park in Paris lies in the plush district northeast of the Arc de Triomphe. It has a colonnade of artificial Roman ruins, a Chinese bridge, a tiny river, and a great many upper-class toddlers guarded by nurses and amiable dogs. Métro: Monceau or Villiers.

BUTTES-CHAUMONT

Napoléon III transformed an abandoned quarry into an artificial lake with an island in the middle, raised a mountain, and erected a suspension bridge. The park is rather like a stage setting, but a delightful one, and more of a fun place than the formalized Tuileries. Métro: Buttes-Chaumont.

BOIS DE VINCENNES

Stuck on the southeastern fringe of the city, this is a big, popular patch of woodland with fine trees, two boating lakes, and a racecourse. Its zoo you'll find described in "Kids' Paris." A favorite spot for family outings, it adjoins the 14th-century Castle of Vincennes, which is open to visitors. Métro: Picpus.

JARDIN DES PLANTES

The botanical garden of Paris is set in a rather drab area near the Gare d'Austerlitz on the Left Bank. It contains a not-too-difficult maze and more than 11,000 different plants. Also, it offers the Museum of Natural History and a little zoo.

BOIS DE BOULOGNE

Covering 2,500 acres, this area of woods, lakes, playgrounds, and sportsfields is Paris's favorite outdoor amusement zone. Bordering on the northwestern edge of the city, the Bois is no longer quite the promenade of top-class elegance it was in the "Gay Nineties." But on race days at Longchamp, you can still admire the best-dressed women of the capital displaying their finest dresses. Otherwise it's relaxed and bourgeois, with family groups and lovers enjoying the lakes and waterfalls and discreetly hidden glens. To read about the compact Jardin d'Acclimation, see "Kids' Paris." Métro: Les Sablons.

6. Cool for Kids

Paris is a grown-up town, dedicated to adult pleasures, and I don't know an adult who won't say *"Vive!"* to that. French children are expected to earn their future privileges by studying Latin quietly for long hours and being unfailingly polite to their superiors in age and wisdom. Family outings almost invariably include a four-course dinner at some special restaurant, relished as thoroughly by *la petite fille* of seven as by her mama and papa.

So there are fewer special spots for children in Paris than there are, say, in Amsterdam or Copenhagen. But there are *some,* plus others that will charm both sides of the generation gap equally. When you're weary of dragging the kids on your rounds, forcibly inculcating culture, try refreshing the family spirit with a few of these.

MUSEUMS

The only problem for parents in Paris museums is that all the exhibits are identified in French and unless you managed to struggle past that silly aunt's plume in high school or are an expert on the subject under study, you aren't going to distinguish yourself with explanations.

Perhaps no museum in Paris is more geared to receive and delight children than that of **Cité des Sciences et de l'Industrie,** 30 av. Corentin-Cariou, 19e (tel. 46-42-13-13). It has entire areas set aside just for them. Of course, many of its exhibits will enthrall both adult and child equally. For a full description, see "Museums and Exhibitions," above.

If your kids have seawater in their veins, take them to the **Musée de la Marine** in the Palais de Chaillot, 16e (tel. 45-55-31-70), which features a kaleidoscopic collection of models, maps, figureheads, and whole craft, tracing the development of shipping from Columbus's *Santa Maria* to the present. The most magnificent item on show is the actual "Boat of the Emperor," a gilt-crowned, oar-driven longboat built in 1811 for Napoléon's trip to Anvers. The museum is open Wednesday through Monday from 10am to 6pm; admission is 20F ($3). Métro: Trocadéro.

The Palais de Chaillot also contains the **Musée de l'Homme** (tel. 45-53-70-60), a large and important collection of artifacts illustrating the way different peoples live the world around. There is plenty of scope here for a little instructive lecturing. In the rooms dealing with anthropology and paleontology, you can point out characteristics all human races share and view such fascinating fossils as the skeleton of the Cro-Magnon Menton man. Other displays deal with prehistoric Africa. Less needful of elucidation is the rich collection of costumes, weapons, tools, jewelry, and household goods from every corner of civilization—Eskimo sleds, African totems, a sinuous gold-spangled matador's suit contrasting with the heavy garb of the Slovak peasant.

Open daily from 9:45am to 5:15pm. Admission is 16F ($2.40). Métro: Trocadéro.

The desire to compare the **Musée Grévin,** 10 bd. Montmartre, 9e (tel. 47-70-85-05), to Madame Tussauds of London is almost irresistible. Grévin is the number-one waxworks of Paris, having opened in 1882. From Charlemagne to the mistress-collecting

Napoléon III, it shows memorable moments from French history in a series of tableaux.

Depicted are the consecration of Charles VII in 1429 in the Cathedral of Reims (Joan of Arc, dressed in armor and carrying her standard, stands behind the king); Marguerite de Valois, first wife of Henri IV, meeting on a secret stairway with La Molle, who was soon to be decapitated; Catherine de' Medici with the Florentine alchemist Ruggieri; Louis XV and Mozart at the home of the Marquise de Pompadour; and Napoleon on a rock at St. Helena, reviewing his victories and defeats.

Two shows are staged frequently throughout the day. The first, called the "Palais des Mirages," starts off as a sort of Temple of Brahma, and through magically distorting mirrors, changes into an enchanted forest, then a fête at the Alhambra at Granada. A magician is the star of the second show, "Le Cabinet Fantastique"; he entertains children of all ages.

The museum also presents contemporary personalities in the sports world as well as the leaders of many countries. One display presents 50 of the world's greatest film actors.

The museum is open daily from 1 to 7pm (the ticket office closes at 6pm); during French school holidays, from 10am to 7pm. Admission is 42F ($6.35), 28F ($4.25) for children under 14. Métro: Montmartre or Richelieu-Drouot.

Among the other museums frequented by the children of Paris is the **Musée National d'Histoire Naturelle,** 57 rue Cuvier, 5e (tel. 40-79-30-00), in the Jardin des Plantes. Its history dates back to 1635, when it was founded as a scientific research center by Guy de la Brosse, physician to Louis XIII, but that period is a fleeting moment compared to the eons of history covered inside the huge museum complex. In the Galleries of Paleontology, Anatomy, Mineralogy, and Botany, your little genius can trace the history and evolution of life on earth, wondering at the massive skeletons of dinosaurs and mastodons, and staring fascinated at the two-headed animal embryos floating forlornly in their pickling jars. Within the museum grounds are tropical hothouses containing thousands of species of unusual plant life along with small animal life in simulated natural habitats.

These galleries are open Wednesday through Monday from 10am to 5pm. Admission is 25F ($3.80), 6F (95¢) for children. Métro: Jussieu or Austerlitz.

Budding scientists will delight in the **Palais de la Découverte** in the Grand Palais on avenue Franklin D. Roosevelt, 8e (tel. 43-59-16-65)—if they know French, that is. This is a full funhouse of things to do: displays to light up, machines to test your muscular reactions, live experiments to watch. White-coated technicians give more than 50 lectures a day using a large number of experiments in physics, chemistry, and biology. You can also visit and listen in on astronomy, space, geology, genetics, medicine, and other lectures. You can find special temporary exhibitions, and there is a planetarium. But, as I've said, all is in French. If your little science nut is fanatical enough, take him or her anyway. He or she can explain the exhibits to *you.* Scientific films are shown daily.

The museum is open Tuesday through Sunday from 10am to 6pm. Planetarium shows are held at 11:30am and 2, 3:15, and 4:30pm on weekdays, with an additional one at 5:45pm on Saturday and Sunday. Admission is 20F ($3); admission to the planetarium show is an additional 13F ($1.95). Métro: F. D. Roosevelt or Champs-Elysées-Clemenceau.

PARKS AND ZOOS

The definitive children's park in Paris is the **Jardin d'Acclimation,** a 25-acre zoo-cum-amusement park on the northern edge of the Bois de Boulogne, 16e (tel. 40-67-90-82). This is the kind of place that satisfies tykes and adults alike—but would be regarded in horror by anyone in his or her teens. The visit starts with a ride from Porte Maillot to the Jardin entrance, through a stretch of wooded park, on a jaunty, green-and-yellow narrow-gauge train. Inside the gate is an easy-to-follow layout map. The park is circular, and if you follow the road in either direction it will take you all the way around and bring you back to the train at the end.

En route you will discover a house of funny mirrors, an archery range, miniature golf, zoo animals, an American-style bowling alley, a puppet theater (only on Thursday, Saturday, Sunday, and holidays), playground, hurdle-racing course, and a whole conglomerate of junior-scale rides, shooting galleries, and waffle stalls. You can trot the kids off on a pony or join them in a boat on a mill-stirred lagoon. Let Asterix and Obelix be your hosts in a real Gallic village, just like the ones that covered France at the time of the Romans. Fun to watch (and a superb idea for American cities to copy) is "La Prévention Routière," a miniature roadway operated by the Paris police. The youngsters drive through it in small cars equipped to start and stop and are required by two genuine Parisian gendarmes to obey all street sign and light changes.

The Jardin d'Acclimation is open Monday through Saturday from 10am to 6:30pm, on Sunday until 7:30pm. Entrance to the park is 7F ($1.05). Métro: Sablons.

There is a modest zoo in the Jardin des Plantes, near the natural history museum. But without a doubt, the best zoo this city has to offer is in the **Bois de Vincennes**—on the outskirts, but quickly reached by Métro. This modern zoo displays its animals in settings as close as possible to their natural habitats. Here you never get that hunched-up feeling about the shoulders from empathizing with a leopard in a cage too small for stalking. The lion has an entire veldt to himself, and you can view each other comfortably across a deep protective moat. On a cement mountain reminiscent of Disneyland's Matterhorn, lovely Barbary sheep leap from ledge to ledge or pose gracefully for hours watching the penguins in their pools at the mountain's foot. The animals seem happy here and are consequently playful. Keep well back from the bear pools or your drip-dries may be dripping wet. Open Monday through Saturday from 9am to 5:30pm, until 6pm on Sunday. Admission is 30F ($4.55), 15F ($2.25) for ages 4 to 10. Métro: Porte Dorée.

The large inner-city parks all have playgrounds with tiny merry-go-rounds and gondola-style swings. If you're staying on the Right Bank, take the children for a stroll through the **Tuileries,** where there are donkey rides, ice-cream stands, and a marionette show. At the circular pond, you can rent a toy sailboat. On the Left Bank, equivalent delights exist in the **Luxembourg Gardens.** If you take in the gardens of the **Champ de Mars,** you can combine a donkey ride for the children with a visit to the nearby Eiffel Tower for the entire family.

PUPPET SHOWS

You can take in a puppet show while visiting the above-mentioned parks—but, once again, all the words are French. Still, they're a great Paris tradition and worth seeing, if only for the joy of sharing a French child's typical experience. The shows are given in the Tuileries at 3:15pm on Wednesday, Saturday, and Sunday, all summer long. At the Luxembourg Gardens, you'll see puppet productions of sinister plots set in Gothic castles and Asian palaces. Prices vary depending on the extravagance of the production. Some young critics think the best puppet shows are held in the Champ de Mars. Performance times in both the Luxembourg Gardens and the Champ de Mars vary with the day of the week and the production being staged. But all are colorfully and enthusiastically produced—and received. You may have to whisper the story line to your monolingual offspring as you go along, but when Red Riding Hood pummels the Wolf over the head with an umbrella, they'll be contorted in glee like the rest of the half-pint audience. That's international kid-talk.

In the tradition of the famous French guignols, puppet shows are staged at **Guignol du Parc de Choisy,** 149 av. de Choisy, 13e (tel. 43-66-72-39), on Wednesday as well as Saturday and Sunday at 3:30pm. Admission is 8F ($1.20). Métro: Tolbiac.

MONTMARTRE

On Sunday afternoon whole French families crowd up to the top of the Butte Montmartre to join in the fiesta atmosphere. Start by taking the Métro to Anvers and walking to the **Funiculaire de Montmartre.** You'll run the gamut of several balloon-sellers before you get there. The funiculaire is a small, silvery cable car that slides you gently up the steep, grassy hillside to the Sacré-Coeur on the hillcrest. Once up top, follow the crowds to the **place du Tertre,** where a Sergeant Pepper–style band will usually be blasting off-key and where you can have the kids' pictures sketched by local artists. Funny how even the shyest child will preen when a crowd is watching.

Signs lead from the place du Tertre to the **Musée de Cire de la Butte Montmartre,** 11 rue Poulbot, 18e (tel. 46-06-78-92), a wax museum illustrating the history of Montmartre. All the neighborhood characters—Toulouse-Lautrec, Renoir, Liszt, Chopin—make their somewhat stiff appearances in settings of their time. One of the tableaux represents *Le Bateau Lavoir,* the Montmartre meeting place of painters since 1830.

Admission is 25F ($3.80) for adults, 15F ($2.25) for children. There are guided tours in English if the demand is large enough. It is open daily from 10:30am to noon and 2:30 to 5:15pm in summer; on Wednesday, Saturday, and Sunday from 2:30 to 5pm November 11 to Easter. Before returning to the cable car, take in the views of Paris from the various vantage points and have an ice cream in an outdoor café on the square. Métro: Abbesses.

PARIS SHOPPING

Should you buy anything in Paris? Are there any good buys? Is there any item purchased here that you can't duplicate better back home?

Shopping abroad can be fraught with pitfalls. It's conceivable that you might buy something here, then find a comparable item for less in your own home city. But not everyone has access to the wide and multifarious offerings found in Paris. There are items unique to France that are not easily found in America.

There is also the joy of bringing "something back from Paris," a reminder of your stay. A purchase made at home will be no substitute for memories of strolling along one of the chic boulevards of Paris, browsing in the smart boutiques, and finally, purchasing a scarf or handbag.

Naturally, as everywhere, you'll have to be careful, even shrewd, in your shopping. It's easy to buy something shoddy anywhere in the world. On the other hand, if you're careful and adventurous, you'll find many quality items.

1. Shopping Tips

BEST BUYS

Perfumes in Paris are almost always cheaper than in the States. That means all the famed brands—Guerlain, Chanel, Schiaparelli, Jean Patou. Cosmetics bearing French names, such as Dior and Lancôme, also cost less. Gloves, too, are a fine value.

Paris, with the possible exception of London, is stocked with more antiques and "curios" than any city of Europe—the world, for that matter. Whether you dream of art or art deco or furniture familiar to Napoléon III, you'll find it in Paris. Big names in crystal such as Lalique and Baccarat don't exactly sell cheaply, but are usually under the world market averages.

Of course, many visitors come to Paris just to shop for fashion. From Chanel to Yves St. Laurent, from Nina Ricci to Sonia Rykiel, the city literally overflows with fashion boutiques ranging from haute couture to daringly modern dress. Likewise, going hand in glove, fashion accessories in Paris are among the finest and best designed in the world. If you don't believe me, then ask Louis Vuitton or perhaps Céline.

French lingerie may be every woman's dream. The top lingerie designers sell in Paris. Galeries Lafayette and Printemps have large sections.

TAX REFUND

If you've been here less than six months, you are entitled to a refund on the value-added tax (VAT) on purchases made in France to take home—under certain conditions. These export discounts range from 20% to 30%, but it depends on the item purchased, of course. The *détaxe,* or refund, is allowed on purchases of goods costing more than 1,200F ($181.20) in a single store, but it's not automatic. For United Kingdom residents and Common Market citizens, the figure is almost 2,400F ($362.40). Food, wine, and tobacco don't count, and the refund is only granted on purchases you carry with you out of the country, *not* on merchandise you have shipped back home.

Here's what you must do:

Show the clerk your passport to prove you're eligible for the refund. You will then be given an export sales document in triplicate (two pink sheets and a green one), which you must sign. You'll also be given an envelope addressed to the store. Go early to your departure point, as there are sometimes queues waiting at the booth marked "détaxe" at French Customs. If you're traveling by train, go to the détaxe area in the station before boarding. You can't get your refund documents processed on the train. The refund booths are outside the passport checkpoints, so you must take care of that business before you proceed with the passport check.

Only the person who signed the documents at the store can present them for the refund. Give the three sheets to the Customs official, who will countersign and hand you back the green copy. Save this in case problems arise about the refund. Give the official the envelope addressed to the store (be sure to put a stamp on the envelope). One of the processed pink copies will be mailed to the store for you. Usually you will be reimbursed by check in convertible French francs sent by mail to your home; sometimes the payment is made to a credit-card account. In some cases, you may get your refund immediately, paid at an airport bank window. If you don't receive your tax refund in four months, write to the store, giving the date of purchase and the location where the sheets were given to

Customs officials. Include a photocopy of your (green) refund sheet.

AIRPORT TAX-FREE BOUTIQUES

Another decision: Should you do your shopping within the city proper or wait until you fly out to make some of your purchases? In the tax-free shops at Orly and Charles de Gaulle airports, you will get a minimum discount of 20% on *all* items and up to 50% off on such items as liquors, cigarettes, and watches. Among the stock on sale: crystal and cutlery, French bonbons, luggage, wines and whiskies, pipes and lighters, filmy lingerie, silk scarves, all the name perfumes, knitwear, jewelry, cameras and equipment, French cheeses, and antiques. Remember that what you buy must travel with you.

U.S. CUSTOMS

You're allowed to bring back into the United States overseas purchases with a retail value of $400, providing you have been out of the country at least 48 hours. However, you must have claimed no similar exemptions within 30 days. After your duty-free $400 is exceeded, a tax of 10% is levied on the next $1,000 worth of items purchased abroad. Amounts of more than $1,400 are subject to duty at various rates according to U.S. Customs regulations. If you're 21 or older, you can bring back 200 cigarettes, 100 cigars (providing they're not from Cuba), and one liter of alcohol.

You pay no duty on antiques or art, if such items are 100 years old or more, even if they cost $4 million or more. In addition, you're allowed to send one gift a day to family or friends back home, providing its value does not exceed $50. Perfumes costing more than $5, liquor, cigarettes, and cigars can't be sent duty-free.

BUSINESS HOURS

Shops are *usually* open Tuesday through Saturday from 9am to 7pm, but the hours can vary greatly. Small shops sometimes take a two-hour lunch break. The flea market and some other street markets are open on Saturday, Sunday, and Monday. That intriguing sign on shop doors reading *Entrée Libre* means you may browse at will. *Soldes* means "sale." *Soldes Exceptionelles* means they're pushing it a bit.

2. Right Bank Shopping

THE DEPARTMENT STORES

Printemps, 64 bd. Haussmann, 9e (tel. 42-82-50-00), is the city's largest department store. Actually, it consists of three stores connected by bridges on the second and third floors. Go to Brummell for clothing for men, both sports and dress. Printemps de la Maison is mainly for records and books, furniture, and housewares, while Printemps de la Mode sells clothes for women, young people, and children. The ground floor is mainly for perfume, cosmetics, gifts, and Paris handcrafts. The perfumery at Printemps is one of the largest in Paris, maybe *the* largest. Interpreters stationed at the Welcome Service in the basement will help you claim your discounts, find departments, and make purchases. International customers are also invited to one of the store's fashion shows held under the historic 1923 glass dome every Tuesday at 10:15am throughout the year, every Tuesday and Friday at 10:15am from March through October. The store is open Monday to Saturday from 9:30am to 6:30pm. Métro: Havre-Caumartin.

A landmark in the Parisian fashion world and a beautiful example of the city's Belle Epoque architecture, **Galeries Lafayette,** 40 bd. Haussmann, 9e (tel. 42-82-34-56), is one of the leading department stores of the world. A special entrance marked "Welcome" brings you to English-speaking hosts available to assist you with your shopping needs. The department store includes the Galfa Club men's store, Lafayette Sports, and the main store, featuring the latest in international fashion designs, unusual gifts, perfumes, and quality housewares. Finish your shopping day with an exceptional view of Paris on the Galeries Lafayette rooftop terrace. The store is open Monday to Saturday from 9:30am to 6:30pm. Métro: Chausée d'Antin or Opéra.

A much more economical and family-oriented department store is **La Samaritaine,** 19 rue de la Monnaie, 1er (tel. 40-41-20-20). It has a little bit of everything—and some good clothing buys. A restaurant on the premises serves meals Monday through Saturday from 11:30am to 3pm. The store itself is open Monday, Wednesday, Friday, and Saturday from 9:30am to 7pm; and Tuesday and Thursday from 9:30am to 8:30pm. Métro: Pont-Neuf.

LES HALLES

Now that Les Halles is going through a rebirth, the produce market having long moved elsewhere, a growing number of fashionable boutiques have taken over, opening on the side streets. These avant-garde boutiques include the following:

Sara Shelburne, 10 rue du Cygne, 1er (tel. 42-33-74-40), is what happens when a law graduate switches to couture. This is a luxurious ready-made boutique for women, with colorful dresses, separates, hostess gowns, coats, knits, and sexy evening wear. An interesting detail: Sara designs and makes most of her fabrics: machine-washable combed-wool knits and Egyptian cottons for daytime; dyed-to-match silks, velvets, and lace for evening. She will make garments to your measurements for the same price as ready-to-wear within two days. In addition to her one-of-a-kind wedding-dress department that attracts people from all over the world, Sara Shelburne has added a collection of handmade shoes coordinated with the colors of her clothes, in suede, leather, or covered in the

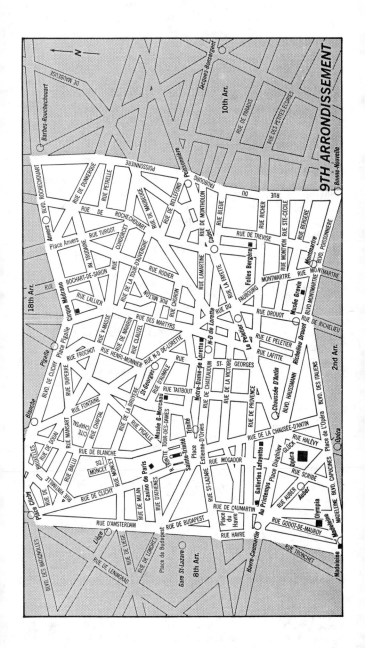

9TH ARRONDISSEMENT

same silk as a dress. Hours are 10am to 7pm Monday to Saturday. Métro: Les Halles or Etienne Marcel.

SPECIALTY SHOPS

Trousselier, 73 bd. Haussmann, 8e (tel. 42-66-97-95), is a century old. At first you'll think it's simply a florist shop, with some artfully displayed sprays. But look again or touch—and you'll see that every flower is artificial, shaped in silk and hand-painted by people who pursue this famous French craft in the workshops in the rear. And what exquisite work! Everything is lifelike in the extreme. One cluster will bear a bud, a full-blown flower, and then one just past its prime and fading at the edges. The prices reflect the high quality. Hours are 2 to 6pm Monday and 10am to 6pm Tuesday to Saturday. Métro: Havre-Caumartin.

At the place de la Madeleine stands one of the most popular sights in the city—not the church, but **Fauchon,** 8e (tel. 47-42-60-11), a vast shop crammed with gastronomical goodies. Never have I seen faces so rapt—not even before the *Mona Lisa*—as those of Parisians gazing at the Fauchon window display. Plump chickens coated in a glazing of sliced almonds, a thigh of lamb opening out like a cornucopia, filled with bright, fresh vegetables made to look like fruits. It's the French version of the Garden of Eden.

English-speaking hosts will assist you, if needed. In the fruit-and-vegetable department you'll find such items as rare mushrooms and fraises des bois (wild strawberries). The pastry and confectionary store features different types of pastry, candies, and a self-service stand-up bar. The candies, incidentally, are divine, including glazed tropical fruits, whisky truffles, stuffed dates, and chocolate-dipped ginger. After seeing the self-service bar, you'll probably decide to stay for lunch. Go first to the display case, make your decision, then tell the cashier what you want. She'll give you a check for each item which you in turn surrender to the serving woman. You may order an omelet, a shrimp salad, or even a club sandwich. A *coupe* of ice cream makes a soothing dessert. A simple meal can be composed for 230F ($34.75) to 280F ($42.30). Also on the premises is a cocktail department, a gifts department, a selection of porcelain and table settings, and an impressive collection of very drinkable wines.

Fauchon is open Monday through Saturday from 9:40am to 7pm. A "Mini-Fauchon," selling mainly food products, is open Monday to Saturday from 7 to 10pm. Métro: Madeleine.

Across the square is **rue Royale,** the street of the legendary Maxim's. Along rue Royale you can turn right onto the **Faubourg St-Honoré,** that platinum strip of the city where the presidential palace shares space with the haute couture houses of Lanvin and Courrèges.

Lanvin, 22 rue du Faubourg St-Honoré, 8e (tel. 47-63-80-21), specializes in women's fashions and accessories. On the second floor, Lanvin's marvelous haute couture dresses are presented in the house's salon. On the first floor, chic and contemporary *prêt-à-porter* (ready-to-wear) day and evening dresses and ensembles are to be found together with beautiful Lanvin shawls. Hours are Tuesday to Friday from 9:30am to 6:30pm. Métro: Concorde.

Hermès, 24 rue du Faubourg St-Honoré, 8e (tel. 42-65-21-60), is a legend, of course. The shop is especially noted for its scarves, made of silk squares that are printed with antique motifs. Three well-known Hermès fragrances, two for women and one for men, make excellent gift choices. The gloves sold here are without peer, especially those for men in reindeer hide, doeskin, or supple kid. The leather-goods store at Hermès is the best known in Europe. The craftspeople working on the premises turn out the Hermès handbag, an institution that needs no sales pitch on these pages. Hermès is open Monday through Saturday from 10am to 6:30pm. Métro: Concorde.

Céline, 24 rue François 1er, 8e (tel. 47-20-22-83), is one of the best choices for ultraconservative, well-made clothes that Parisian women say almost never wear out. There's also a selection of elegant shoes and handbags. The store is open Monday to Friday from 9:30am to 6:30pm. Métro: F. D. Roosevelt.

Of course, there are others—so many others! You can visit **Christian Dior,** world-famous for its custom-made haute couture, at 26-32 av. Montaigne, 8e (tel. 40-73-54-44), with a wide selection of both women's and men's ready-to-wear, sportswear, and accessories, including separate salons for shoes and leather goods, furs, children's clothing, and a variety of gift items, genuine and costume jewelry, lights, and pens, among other offerings. Hours are Monday to Saturday from 10am to 6pm. Métro: F. D. Roosevelt.

The spirit of **Chanel** lives on, and her shop at 31 rue Cambon, 1er (tel. 42-61-54-55), across from the Ritz, is more than ever in business with haute couture, a landmark design showcase of classical French fashion. Prices, of course, are celestial. The shop also sells accessories, perfumes, cosmetic lines, and watches. Hours are Monday to Saturday 10am to 7pm. Métro: Concorde or Tuileries.

For Chanel's ready-to-wear, which is more reasonably priced but still very expensive, try the shop at 42 av. Montaigne, 8e (tel. 47-23-74-12). It is said that every woman—at least those who can afford it—should own a "basic Chanel," and that it will never go out of style. Accessories are also sold here. Hours are Monday to Saturday from 9:30am to 6:30pm. Métro: F. D. Roosevelt.

Pierre Cardin boutiques seem to pop up on every corner. You can't help notice at least one. Two major ones are **Pierre Cardin Couture,** 27 av. Marigny, 8e (tel. 42-66-92-25; Métro: Champs-Elysees-Clemenceau), and **Pierre Cardin Prestige,** 29 rue du Faubourg St-Honoré, 8e (tel. 42-65-36-91; Métro: Concorde). The range of styles is vast, from ultraconservative to what used to be called "way out." Both stores are open Monday to Saturday from 10am to 1pm and 2 to 7pm.

Pierre Cardin, 59 rue du Faubourg St-Honoré, 8e (tel. 42-66-92-25), carries a large assortment of ready-to-wear clothing for the well-dressed man, backed up with some of the finest accessories in Paris. There's also an excellent and often unusual selection of men's shoes. Of course, everything is expensive. Hours are Monday to Saturday from 10am to 1pm and 2 to 7pm. Métro: Concorde.

Van Cleef & Arpels, 22 place Vendôme, 1er (tel. 42-61-58-58), is the headquarters of a store that was established around the turn of the century. A premier jewelry store of world renown (and numerous branches), its motto is: "There is nothing a man in love can refuse to the woman who makes him happy." This exclusive shop is known for its special settings and also carries a range of deluxe watches. Open Monday to Friday from 9:30am to 1pm and 2:30 to 6pm. Métro: Opéra or Tuileries.

Gucci, 2 and 27 rue du Faubourg St-Honoré, 8e (tel. 42-96-83-27), is one of the world's largest showcases for this fabled Italian designer, with his trademark red-and-green trim in leather goods. Gucci makes fine shoes and handbags, as well as other items, including wallets, gloves, and clothing. This outlet has an excellent selection of scarves and two-piece ensembles. Its sweaters are especially outstanding. Hours are Monday to Saturday from 9:30am to 6:30pm. Métro: Concorde.

Louvre Reproductions

A boutique at 107 rue de Rivoli, 1er (tel. 42-61-01-88), is connected with the **Musée des Arts Décoratifs,** and offers a variety of handsome household goods, some of them exact copies of items displayed in the museum. Craftspeople have copied faïence, molded crystal, art nouveau jewelry, porcelain boxes, scarves, and other items of fine workmanship and great beauty. The shop is open Monday through Saturday from 12:30 to 6pm, Sunday from noon to 6pm. There is no charge for admission, and you can find interesting items in low to expensive price ranges. Métro: Louvre.

Hats

One of the most distinguished outlets for classic handmade hats for both men and women is the chapeliers of **E. Motsch,** 42 av. George-V, 8e (tel. 47-23-79-22), right off the Champs-Elysées. This sedate corner store, in business since 1887, offers almost every type of headgear, ranging from berets to Scottish tam-o'-shanters. The section for women contains some of the most stylish, if conservative, hats in Paris. Hours are Monday through Saturday from 9:30am to 1pm and 2 to 6:30pm. Métro: George-V.

Books

W. H. Smith & Son, 248 rue de Rivoli, 1er (tel. 42-60-37-97), is the English bookshop in Paris. Books, magazines, and newspapers published in the English-speaking world are widely available. You can get *The Times* of London, of course, and the *New York Times* is available every Monday. You'll find many American magazines, too. There's a fine selection of maps if you plan to do much touring. Across from the Tuileries, W. H. Smith also has excellent reference books, language books, and a special children's section. Open Monday to Saturday from 9:30am to 7:30pm. Métro: Concorde.

Engravings

Carnavalette, 2 rue des Francs-Bourgeois, 4e (tel. 42-72-91-92), off the place des Vosges in the Marais, sells unusual one-of-a-kind engravings, plus a large collection of satirical 19th-century magazines and newspapers whose illustrations people buy for framing. Hours are Wednesday through Monday from 10:30am to 7pm. Métro: St-Paul.

Perfume

Freddy of Paris, 10 rue Auber, 9e (tel. 47-42-63-41), near the American Express office and the Opéra, offers discounts of up to 40% on all name-brand perfume, cream, novelties, gifts, handbags, scarves, ties, and costume jewelry. Open Monday to Friday from 9am to 6:30pm. Métro: Auber or Opéra.

The outside of **Michel Swiss,** 16 rue de la Paix, 2e (tel. 42-61-61-11), looks like many of the ultra-chic façades near the place Vendôme. But once you get inside (there's no storefront window), you'll see the major brands of luxury perfume, makeup, leather bags, pens, neckties, fashion accessories, and giftware. All items are discounted by 25%, plus an additional tax discount for non-EC residents amounting to 18.6% to 28% depending on the product. The store is two flights above ground level, and is reached by a small elevator. It might be a good idea to avoid the crowds who pile in here at lunchtime. It is open Monday through Saturday from 9am to 6:30pm. Métro: Opéra.

Antiques

Le Louvre des Antiquaires, 2 place du Palais-Royal, 1er (tel. 42-97-27-00), is the largest antique center in Europe, attracting collectors, browsers, and those interested in everything from Russian icons to 19th-century furniture to art deco. The center stands across from a giant parking lot at the side of the Louvre. Housing some 240 dealers, the showrooms are spread across 2½ acres of well-lit modern salons. The building, a former department store, was erected in 1852, according to Napoléon's plans for the rue de Rivoli. Down an enormous flight of skylit stairs, past a café and reception area, you enter the inner sanctum where you find the dealers operating Tuesday through Sunday from 11am to 7pm. Métro: Louvre.

China, Porcelain, and Crystal

Au Grand Siècle, 31 rue La Boétie, 8e (tel. 45-63-25-96), is a small, elegant shop filled to the brim with antique and reproduction furniture, silver, and crystal, especially Daum, Baccarat, and Swarovski. There is a splendid collection of lamps and small gifts. Lladró porcelain is also sold here. No low-price merchandise is offered, but it is a memorable shopping experience. Open in summer, Monday to Friday from 9:30am to 6:30pm; off season, open Monday from noon to 6:30pm, Tuesday to Saturday from 9:30am to 6:30pm. Métro: Miromesnil.

Lalique, 11 rue Royale, 8e (tel. 42-65-33-70), is directed today by the granddaughter of the original founder, René Lalique, a silver-smith who launched the shop during the Belle Epoque era. Known around the world for its glass sculpture and decorative lead crystal, the shop sells a wide range of merchandise at prices slightly lower than the celestial prices charged abroad. Open Monday and Saturday from 9:30am to noon and 2 to 6:30pm, Tuesday to Friday from 9:30am to 6:30pm. Métro: Concorde.

Baccarat, 30 bis rue de Paradis, 10e (tel. 47-70-64-30), purveyor to kings and presidents of France since 1764, produces world-renowned full-lead crystal requested by and created for perfectionists. A visit here is worth the time, even for visitors not intending to purchase, as there is a museum of the company's most historic models on premises. Open Monday through Friday from 9am to 6pm, Saturday from 10am to noon and 2 to 5pm. Métro: Château d'Eau, Poissonière, or Gare de l'Est.

Limoges-Unic, 12 and 58 rue de Paradis, 10e (tel. 47-70-54-49), sells a wide stock of Limoges china such as Ceralane, Haviland, and Bernardaud, as well as Villeroy & Boch, Hermès, Dior, Lanvin, Lalique, Daum, St. Louis, and Sèvres crystal, Christofle & Ercuis silverware, and many other items for table decoration. It's open Monday through Saturday from 10am to 6:30pm. Métro: Gare de l'Est or Poissonnière.

Bath Fixtures

Raymond, 100 rue du Faubourg St-Honoré, 8e (tel. 42-66-69-49), is one of the principal outlets for Porcelaine de Paris in the city. And if you're shopping for what might be the most elegant bathroom fixtures in the world, including basins and faucets fashioned from hand-painted porcelain, they have it here. They'll mail your purchases anywhere in the world. Near the Elysée Palace, the store is open Tuesday through Friday, from 9:30am to 6:30pm, Saturday from 9:30am to 12:30pm and 2 to 6:30pm; closed during August. Métro: Concorde or Champs-Elysées-Clemenceau.

Stationery

Cassegrain, 422 rue St-Honoré, 8e (tel. 42-60-20-08), opened right after World War I, and it's been attracting letter writers ever since. It is considered by many the premier stationery shop in the city. Beautifully engraved stationery, most often in traditional patterns, is offered, although businesspeople can also get their business cards engraved to order. Lots of other items for the desk—many suitable for gifts—are for sale as well. Métro: Concorde. Cassegrain also has a shop at 81 rue des Saints-Pères, 6e (tel. 42-22-04-76; Métro: Sèvres). Both stores are open Monday to Friday from 9:30am to 6:30pm, Saturday from 9:30am to 1pm.

Toys and Kids' Stuff

Au Nain Bleu, 406 rue St-Honoré, 8e (tel. 42-60-39-01). Any child you love is expecting a present from Paris, and at the "Blue

Dwarf" you'll be bedazzled by the choice. Browse through this paradise of playthings that has been in business for a century and a half. It's a world of toy soldiers, stuffed animals, games, model airplanes, technical toys, model cars, even a "Flower Drum Kit." Puppets come in all shapes, sizes, and costumes. Hours are Monday to Saturday from 9am to 6:15pm. Métro: Concorde.

Tableware and Bed Linen

Au Bain Marie, 10 rue Boissy d'Anglas, 8e (tel. 42-66-59-74), between Hermès at Faubourg St-Honoré and the Hôtel Crillon, is one of Paris's best choices for all kinds of new and antique table and bedroom linen, some of it painstakingly embroidered. The two floors of merchandise include virtually everything that might touch a dining table, including tableware of many different styles, inspired by many different eras. There's also a collection of books relating to food and wine, and a good selection of bathroom towels. It's open Monday through Saturday from 10am to 7pm. Métro: Concorde.

Champagne

Maison du Champagne, 48 rue des Belles Feuilles, 16e (tel. 47-27-58-23), is where all Paris lines up outside to buy its holiday bubbly. In addition to more than 90 labels of champagne, the shop has rare and fine burgundies and Bordeaux dating back to the turn of the century, as well as cognacs and armagnacs from the 19th century, plus Eau de Vie. Owner-connoisseur Charles Delmare will guide you in your selection. This delightful boutique opens Tuesday through Saturday at 10am, closes its doors for lunch at 1pm, and reopens from 3 to 8pm. Métro: Victor-Hugo or Dauphine.

Chocolate

La Maison du Chocolat, 225 rue du Faubourg St-Honoré, 8e (tel. 42-27-39-44), is filled with racks and racks of chocolates, priced individually or by the kilo. Each is made from a blend of as many as six different kinds of South American and African chocolate, and flavorings include just about everything imaginable. Chocolate pastries are also sold. Everything here is made in the super-modern facilities in the establishment's cellars before being sent up on an old-fashioned dumbwaiter. Robert Linxe, the owner, maintains hours Monday through Saturday between 9:30am and 7pm; closed August. Métro: Ternes.

Dalloyau, 99-101 rue du Faubourg St-Honoré, 8e (tel. 43-59-18-10). When it was established in 1802, the newly rich bourgeoisie of Paris rushed to its doorstep to enjoy the luscious chocolate suddenly flooding the market from France's colonial plantations. Today, still very much in business, the shop can ship its chocolates, elegantly packaged, anywhere you specify. In addition to a variety of chocolates in a bewildering array of sweetnesses, it sells pastries, petits-fours, and cakes. The shop is located near some of the most fashionable clothing stores in Europe, provoking endless calorie-induced guilt from the appearance-conscious women browsing through the shops nearby. Métro: Champs-Elysées-Clemenceau.

Boutiques

Josephine Fisse, 5 rue Clément-Marot, 8e (tel. 47-23-45-27), close to the corner of the avenue Montaigne, is a super-chic, super-expensive boutique that carries the latest fashions of six of the most fashionable designers in France and Italy, including Sonia Rykiel. It is designed in a high-tech format. The store is open Monday through Saturday from 10am to 7pm. Métro: F. D. Roosevelt.

Cadolle, 14 rue Cambon, 1er (tel. 42-60-94-94). All of Paris nostalgically remembers the founding mother of this store, Hermine Cadolle, as the person who in 1889 invented the brassiere. Today the store is managed by Hermine's great-great- and great-great-great-granddaughters, Alice and Poupie Cadolle. This is the place to go for a made-to-order or a ready-to-wear fit. For custom-made fit, it is best to make an appointment long in advance, preferably before leaving for France or at least as soon as you arrive. Custom-made whalebone corsets are still available, and the night-gowns range from the demure to the scandalous. There is also a fashionable collection of bathing suits. This is the home of Cadolle's fine perfume, Le No. 9. It is open Monday through Saturday from 9:30am to 1pm and 2 to 6:30pm. Métro: Concorde or Madeleine.

CUT-RATE SHOPPING

Paris no longer caters to just the well-heeled in its boutiques. Many formerly high-priced items are often on sale at tabs cut from 20% to 40% of their original price when displayed in a store along the Champs-Elysées. Several shops have opened that offer leftover merchandise from some of the better-known fashion houses. Of course, the famous labels have been cut out, but it's still the same clothing.

Discount houses tend to be crowded, often bustling, and a bit rushed. At each of the following stores, however, at least one of the employees speaks English.

Anna Lowe, 35 av. Matignon, 8e (tel. 43-59-96-61), is considered the premier boutique in Paris for the discriminating woman who wishes to purchase high-quality clothing—but at discount prices. The boutique lies only half a block from rue du Faubourg St-Honoré, where haute couture is much more expensively priced. All items sold by Anna Lowe (a former model herself) have the designer's label still attached, including Chanel, Valentino, Givenchy, and Guy Laroche. Prices are often one-half the normal selling price of a garment. The merchandise does not contain factory rejects or seconds. Some of the clothing is models' samples. Alterations are done for a nominal price, often within two or three days. The shop is open Tuesday through Saturday from 9:30am to 6pm. Métro: Concorde.

Mendès (Saint-Laurent), 65 rue Montmartre, 2e (tel. 42-36-83-32). Many of the fashion-conscious, but also budget-conscious, women of Paris come here to buy ready-to-wear lines of Saint-Laurent called "sportswear." Sometimes discounts on "last season's" clothing average as much as 50%. There are no dressing rooms, no alterations, and no exchanges or refunds, but that doesn't prevent a battalion of determined women from buying clothes from the winter collection at reduced prices after the middle of January. Clothes from the summer collection become available after mid-July. All of the activity takes place on two floors of a building at the edge of the garment district. The store is open Monday through Thursday from 9:30am to 5:30pm, Friday and Saturday to 4:30pm. Métro: Les Halles.

---

3. Left Bank Shopping

Eiffel Shopping, 9 av. de Suffren, 7e (tel. 45-66-55-30), offers you a free glass of cognac while you browse through the designer collection (Dior, Saint-Laurent, Lanvin, Cartier, Chanel, to name just a few) of handbags, ties, scarves, watches, sunglasses, jewelry, perfumes, Lalique crystal, and much more. This tax-free shopping center, only one block from the Eiffel Tower, offers top-quality merchandise at discount prices, and all the salespeople are bilingual. It's open Monday through Saturday from 9:15am to 8pm, and on Sunday from 11am to 8pm. Métro: Bir-Hakeim.

Rigodon, 13 rue Racine (a street branching off from place de l'Odéon), 6e (tel. 43-29-98-66), is a puppet-and-doll world for every child, even for those who are children only at heart; but they're dolls to look at, not to play with. Hanging from the ceiling is one of the most varied collections of puppets in Paris. They come in all characters, sizes, and prices, and include everything from angels to witches on broomsticks to bat women with feather wings. Rigodon also makes porcelain dolls. The painting on the faces and the costumes are unique for each model, be it a queen with all her power or the amazon of the hunt. There are marionettes (with strings) from French artisans. Hours are Tuesday to Saturday from 9:30am to 6:30pm. Métro: Odéon.

Schmock Broc, 15 rue Racine, 6e (tel. 46-33-79-98), is a specialty shop run by Mlle Clement Nadine, who is one of the city's leading collectors of the increasingly fashionable art nouveau and art deco accessories. Her boutique is on the Left Bank near the Odéon Théâtre. The glorious, more flamboyant world of yesterday comes alive here, as you explore the collection of jewelry, lighting fixtures, whatever the owner herself has discovered on her frequent shopping expeditions. The shop is open Tuesday through Saturday from 9:30am to 6pm. Métro: Odéon.

The **Amon Gallery** (Galerie d'Amon), 28 rue St-Sulpice, 6e (tel. 43-26-96-60), just off the Luxembourg Gardens and the Church of St-Sulpice, has a permanent exhibition of glasswork, with a wide range of items from France and abroad. Madeleine and Jean-Pierre Maffre display items in blown glass, blown engraved glass, molded glass, and paperweights by top artisans. Open Tuesday through Saturday from 11am to 7pm. Métro: Odéon.

At the place de l'Odéon, you strike out again—this time down **rue de l'Odéon,** which contains the kind of items you might pick up at the Flea Market. You can also walk to **rue de Tournon,** 6e, one of the most interesting streets for shopping on the Left Bank.

After walking back along rue de Tournon for a while, you can cut onto rue de Seine, 6e, where art nouveau posters are sold cheek-by-jowl with genuine old masters. You pass along the **Buci street market,** where you can gather the makings of an unforgettable picnic under the shrill guidance of vendors.

The **Galerie Documents,** 53 rue de Seine, 6e (tel. 43-54-50-68), contains one of the most original collections of old posters (1870 to 1930) in Paris. Many of them are inexpensive, although you could easily pay 1,200F ($181.20) for an original. Your selection will be mailed back home in a tube. Hours are Monday from 2:30 to 7pm and Tuesday to Saturday 10am to 12:30pm and 2:30 to 7pm. Métro: Odéon.

Shakespeare and Company, 37 rue de la Bûcherie, 5e (no phone), is the offshoot of the famous bookstore founded by the legendary Sylvia Beach, who was called a "mother confessor to the Lost Generation." Her shop was on rue de l'Odéon. Hanging out in the shop in days of yore, you were likely to encounter everybody from Gertrude Stein to Ernest Hemingway to F. Scott Fitzgerald. In more recent decades you might have attended an autograph party for the late diarist, Anaïs Nin. Henry Miller called the store "a wonderland of books." It is not slick like any modern chain, and the history associated with it, the rich traditions, are still maintained by the gruffly warm-hearted owner, George Whitman, who is originally from Boston. Open daily from 11am to midnight. Métro: St-Michel or Maubert-Mutualité.

Aux Muses d'Europe, 64 rue de Seine, 6e (tel. 43-26-89-63), sells a collection of antique lace dresses of rare beauty, as well as contemporary clothing (1900 to 1950) and accessories. With items collected from all over France by the mother-daughter team of Marguerite and Katia Belleville, the shop has appeared in nationwide television broadcasts in Japan and frequently welcomes actresses who need to dress in period costume. The shop is not large, but the clothing racks stretch up to the ceiling. They also sell linens, accessories, costume jewelry, bags, and gloves (1940 to 1950). Ask to see the lace-trimmed baby dresses as well. It is open Monday from 2:30 to 7pm, Tuesday to Saturday from 11am to 7pm. Métro: Odéon or St-Germain-des-Prés. At the end of rue de Seine, you can walk along the quays for galleries filled with graphics. On the river side of the street, open stalls dispense tourist prints, postcards, second-hand books, and funky antique postcards—but few real bargains or finds.

Le Monde en Marche, 34 rue Dauphine, 6e (tel. 43-26-66-53), has a large assortment of creative playthings for children at reasonable prices, including music boxes and little tin animals. Hours

are Tuesday through Sunday from 10:30am to 7:30pm. Métro:
Odéon.

CUT-RATE SHOPPING

Mouton à Cinq Pattes, 8 rue St-Placide, 6e (tel. 45-48-86-26),
in the Montparnasse area, with another outlet in the St-Germain
neighborhood at 19 rue Grégoire-de-Tours, 6e (tel. 43-29-73-56),
offers heavily discounted creations of several well-known women's
designers, usually with their labels removed. A few storefronts away
from the first of these, you'll find a similar system for men's clothing, with discounts matching those of its sister store. It's called
Annexe, 48 rue St-Placide, 6e (tel. 45-48-86-26). The management
also maintains two branches for children, both named **Nuage-
Rouge,** at 10 rue St-Placide (tel. 45-48-86-26) and at 26 rue des
Canettes, 6e (tel. 43-26-52-32). Here, designer garments, *sans
etiquettes,* for toddlers and pre-teenagers are sold in imaginative
combinations at discounted prices. Métro for the above outlets:
Mabillon or Odéon.

The rock-bottom cheapest of the stores in this mini-chain is the
Mouton à Cinque Pattes, 18 rue St-Placide, 6e (no phone; Métro:
St-Placide), where even the goods on sale are on sale. These garments might have been somewhat "picked over," but you'll find
clothes priced for as low as 30F ($4.55), a price almost certain to
whisk them off the racks within the week. Open Monday from 2 to
7pm, Tuesday through Saturday 10am to 7pm.

Au Fil de Laure, 7 rue Sédillot, 7e (tel. 47-05-46-31), near Les
Invalides, is a reduced-price outlet for late-model and used clothing
from some of the biggest designers in Paris. The staff speaks English
and is happy to answer your questions. It is open daily except Sunday from 10:30am to 7pm. Métro: Ecole-Militaire.

---

4. Markets

A landmark, the **Marché aux Puces** (Flea Market) is both
adored and abused. Even if you don't purchase one item (an unlikely possibility), it's an experience to be savored. This is a complex of 2,500 to 3,000 open stalls and shops on the fringe of Paris,
selling everything from antiques to junk, from new to second-
hand clothing. Occupying a vast triangular area, it is spread over
half a mile and is almost impossible to cover entirely in just one
visit.

The market is open only on Saturday, Sunday, and Monday. To
reach it by Métro, take the train to Porte de Clignancourt. Bus 56
also goes to this point. When you emerge, turn left and cross boulevard Ney, then walk north on avenue de la Porte de Clignancourt.
The first clues showing you're there will be the stalls of cheap cloth-

ing along that street. As you proceed, various streets will tempt you to walk down them. Some of these streets are narrow, lined with little shops that start pulling out their offerings around 9am and start bringing them in around 6pm. Monday is the traditional day for bargain seekers, as there is smaller attendance at the market and a greater desire on the part of the merchants to sell.

Naturally, you are supposed to bargain. Nobody pays the first price quoted. Many don't even pay the second or third price. Of course, a little basic French helps too. The sound of an English-speaking voice is known to drive the price up right away. In addition to the permanent stalls, there are "dropcloth" peddlers as well. They spread out their wares on canvas or sheets (and are predictably viewed with scorn by the permanently installed vendors).

The big question everybody asks is, "Do you get any real bargains at the Flea Market?" Or, conversely, "Will you get fleeced?" Actually, it's all comparative. Obviously, the best buys have been skimmed by dealers (who often have a prearrangement to have items held for them). It's true, the same merchandise in the provinces of France will sell for less. But from the point of view of the visitor who has only a few days to spend in Paris—and only half a day for shopping—the Flea Market is worth the experience.

Many of the items are a tremendous social comment on the discards of society. For example, "junk" discarded in garbage cans in the 1920s often commands high prices today. Incidentally, if goods are stolen in Paris or elsewhere, they often turn up at the Flea Market.

The **Marché aux Timbres** draws the avid stamp collectors. Nearly two dozen stalls are set up on a permanent basis under shady trees on the eastern edge of Rond Point, off the Champs-Elysées. The variety of stamps is almost unlimited—some common, some quite rare. The market is generally held on Thursday, Saturday, and Sunday from 10am to 7pm. Take the Métro to Champs-Elysées-Clemenceau.

The **Marché aux Fleurs** (Flower Market), is the bouquet treat of Paris. Artists love to paint it; photographers love to click away. But for the most part, travelers go there to refresh their souls, enjoying a feast of fragrance. The stalls are ablaze with color, each a showcase of flowers, usually from the French Riviera (those that escaped a fate of being hauled to the perfume factories of Grasse). The Flower Market is on the Ile de la Cité in the Fourth Arrondissement, at the place Louis-Lépine, along the Seine, in back of the Tribunal de Commerce. The market is open daily from 8am to 4pm. Métro: Cité.

The **Marché aux Oiseaux (Bird Market),** also at place Louis-Lépine on Ile de la Cité, comes alive with feathered creatures every Sunday from 9am to 7pm. Even if you don't plan to buy a rare parrot, you'll want to go for a look. From the Louvre to the Hôtel de Ville, you can visit the small stalls with vendors along the Seine. Métro: Cité.

La Cour aux Antiquaires, 54 rue du Faubourg St-Honoré, 8e (tel. 47-42-43-99), near the Elysée Palace, is an elegant Right Bank arcade frequented by the most discerning Parisians and international designers. At some 18 shops you can peruse the offerings, including antiques, paintings, and objects of art (usually from the 16th to the 20th century). Each store operates independently Monday from 2 to 7pm and Tuesday to Saturday from 10:30am to 7pm. The complex also prints a catalogue. Métro: place de la Concorde.

PARIS NIGHTS

1. THE PERFORMING ARTS
2. THE CLUB AND MUSIC SCENE
3. CAFES AND BARS
4. MOVIES

With five national theaters, including a new opera house and 55 theaters of lesser renown, Paris is both the hub of French culture and host to all the best on the international circuit. Whatever the season, the choice is fantastic: top pop stars, French classics, chamber concerts, lavish music-hall spectaculars. In one cavernous hall, an American singer might be belting out a standard to a packed crowd of Parisians, while in a shabby Left Bank lane, a young playwright anxiously watches his first work performed on the same small stage that launched Ionesco or Beckett.

Contemporary Paris has less nudity than London, less vice than Hamburg, and less drunkenness than San Francisco. Nevertheless, the quantity and the variety of Paris's nocturnal pleasures still beat those of any metropolis on earth. Nowhere else will you find such a huge and mixed array of clubs, bars, discos, cabarets, jazz dives, music halls, and honky-tonks, ranging—in the subtlest of gradations—from the corniest tourist traps to the most sophisticated connoisseurs' fare.

And to leave out cafés from any description of Paris would be like writing about London without mentioning a pub.

1. The Performing Arts

The only limitation to your enjoyment of French theater is language. Those of you with modest French can still delight in a lively, sparkling Molière at the Comédie-Française. But those with no French at all might prefer an evening that is longer on melody and shorter on speech.

Announcements of shows, concerts, even the opera programs are plastered all around town on kiosks. A better way to find out what's playing is to consult *Pariscope, Une Semaine de Paris,* a weekly entertainment guide that includes a section of arts, with full listings of theaters, concerts, and more.

Ticket agents are dotted all over Paris but clustered thickest near the Right Bank hotels. Avoid them if possible, because you'll get the least expensive tickets at the theater box offices. Remember to tip the usher who shows you to your seat. This holds true in movie houses as well as theaters. Performances start later in Paris than in London or New York—anywhere from 8 to 9:30pm—and Parisians tend to dine after the theater. You don't have to follow suit, since many of the modest, less expensive restaurants close as early as 9pm.

OPERA AND BALLET

All of Paris is buzzing with news of the opening of **Opéra de Paris Bastille,** place de la Bastille, 120 rue de Lyon, 4e (tel. 43-43-96-96), which was inaugurated in July 1989 with the presentation of a few concerts. After several initial conflicts, which were widely publicized around the musical world, the curtains rose on March 17, 1990, with the presentation of a Hector Berlioz's *Les Troyens.*

The building was designed by Canadian architect Carlos Ott, with curtains created by Issey Miyake, the Japanese fashion designer. The opera's full facilities are not scheduled for completion until sometime in 1992, although small-scale performances will be presented in the interim period. The main hall, when completed, will be the largest of any opera house in France, with 2,700 seats. The building also contains three additional concert halls, the smallest of which is an intimate room containing only 250 seats. Both traditional opera performances and symphony concerts will be presented here.

In honor of certain French holidays, several concerts are presented free of charge, but prices for musical events usually range from 85F ($12.85) to 450F ($67.95). For reservations, call 40-11-16-16. To reserve by mail, write to Opéra de Paris Bastille, 120 rue de Lyon, 75012 Paris.

The most glorious thing about **Opéra de Paris Garnier,** place de l'Opéra, 9e (tel. 47-42-53-71), is the building itself. It was designed by a young architect who entered a contest in the heyday of Napoléon III's Second Empire; he adorned the façade with marble and sculptures, including *The Dance* by Carpeaux. The greats of the world, including Sarah Bernhardt, came and went here. But l'Opéra has given way in its stellar operatic performances to the new l'Opéra Bastille. Closed for renovations in 1990, l'Opéra should emerge in its new reincarnation as a premier stage for ballet and musical concerts. Prices range from 40F ($6.05) to 300F ($45.30). Métro: Opéra.

For light opera productions, go to **Opéra-Comique,** place Favart, 2e (tel. 42-96-12-20). The opera is closed in summer; the rest of the year the box office is open daily from 11am to 6:30pm two weeks before a performance is scheduled. Métro: Richelieu-Drouot.

The **Théâtre Musical de Paris,** place du Châtelet, 1er (tel. 42-21-00-86), stages more reasonably priced opera and ballet performances than either l'Opéra or l'Opéra Bastille. Known for its good acoustics, it offers tickets beginning at 65F ($9.80). Métro: Châtelet.

CONCERTS

The concertgoing public is kept busy year-round in Paris, with daily offerings taking up full newspaper columns. Organ recitals are featured in the churches (the largest organ is in Saint-Sulpice); jazz shatters the peace of the city's modern art museum.

The best orchestra in France belongs to Radio France, and top-flight concerts with guest conductors are presented in the **Radio France Auditorium,** 116 av. Président Kennedy, 16e (tel. 42-30-15-16). Tickets for performances of the Orchestre National are 110F ($16.60), 70F ($10.55) for the Orchestre Philharmonique. Métro: Passy.

Salle Pleyel, 252 rue du Faubourg St-Honoré, 8e (tel. 45-63-88-73), is host to the Orchestre de Paris. The season runs from September to Easter. The location is a few blocks northeast of the Arc de Triomphe. Prices range from 50F ($7.55) to 200F ($30.20). Métro: Ternes.

Opera, ballet, and concerts are performed at the **Théâtre des Champs-Elysées,** 15 av. Montaigne, 8e (tel. 47-23-47-77). Both national and international orchestras appear here. The box office is open Monday through Saturday from 11am to 7pm. Prices vary, but seats begin at 50F ($7.55). Métro: Alma-Marceau.

One of the largest concert halls is the **Théâtre National de Chaillot,** place du Trocadéro, 16e (tel. 47-27-81-15), with programs announced on big showboards out front. (Prices range from 70F ($10.55) to 130F ($19.65). Métro: Trocadéro.

MUSIC HALLS

That old music-hall format of sing a little, dance a little, juggle a few balls, and sprinkle generously with jokes, is very much alive and doing well in Paris today. The combination, slickly carried off, adds up to a top value in entertainment for the visitor.

The first-rank city music hall offering packed programs of professional talent and international stars is the **Olympia,** 28 bd. des Capucines, 9e (tel. 47-42-82-45). The Olympia is the cavernous hall where the likes of Charles Aznavour make frequent appearances. On one occasion Yves Montand appeared, but you had to reserve a seat four months in advance. A typical lineup would include an English rock duo singing its latest record hit, a showy group of Italian acrobats, a well-known French crooner, a talented dance troupe, a triple-jointed American juggler/comedy team (doing much of their work in English), plus the featured Big Name, all laced together neatly by a witty emcee and backed by an onstage band. Tickets dip as low as

120F ($18.10) and climb up to about 180F ($27.20). Shows are presented Tuesday through Sunday at 8:30pm. Métro: Opéra.

THEATER

If you've a taste for fine theater, don't let the language barrier scare you off—spend at least one night of your Paris stay at the **Comédie-Française,** place du Théâtre-Français, 1er (tel. 40-15-00-15). Nowhere else will you see the French classics—Molière, Racine—so beautifully staged in their own language. As a national theater established for the purpose of keeping the classics in the cultural mainstream and promoting the most important among contemporary authors, the Comédie-Française usually prices its tickets from a low of 19F ($2.85) up to 186F ($28.10). Métro: Louvre.

English Theatre of Paris, 55 rue de Seine, 6e (tel. 43-26-63-51), a small theater, presents a changing schedule of English-language plays. In a storefront on a well-known street in the Latin Quarter, it can make for an exciting, offbeat evening. Call the theater for a schedule of what it is presenting and when. Admission is 100F ($15.10) for a regular seat, 70F ($10.55) for a stool. Métro: Odéon.

2. The Club and Music Scene

The most remarkable thing about the famed nightlife of Paris is its unremarkable normalcy. It's simply part of the city routine continued after dark. There's none of the vacuum period you find in American towns between the time offices close and the theaters start. Paris keeps humming on much the same beat until around one or two in the morning, when it finally curls up for a brief slumber. The main boulevards remain thronged, noisy, and traffic-clogged at all hours without a noticeable break.

The chief cause of this cycle is the younger set's habit of not going home after work, meeting in cafés instead. But quite apart from this, Parisians tend to work later, date later, eat later, and get to bed later than Anglo-Americans. One reason for this is undoubtedly their long midday break.

Paris today is still a nirvana for night owls, even though some of its once-unique attractions have become common. The fame of Parisian nights was established in those distant days of innocence when Anglo-Americans still gasped at the sight of a bare bosom in a chorus line, and free love was something you only whispered about in polite transatlantic circles.

Some of the best and most genuinely Parisian attractions are, unfortunately, outside the scope of this book. They are the so-called *boîtes* in which chansonniers sing ballads and ditties intended only for local consumption. A few performers, like Edith Piaf and Juliette Greco, graduated to international fame from these places.

But the lyrics that delight the patrons there are so slangy, so topical-ly witty, so heavily laced with verbal innuendoes and double-entendres that they're incomprehensible to foreigners. Your French wouldn't just have to be good, but Pigalle-perfect. In which case you aren't likely to be reading this guidebook.

Luckily, there are hundreds of other establishments where lin-gual ignorance is of no consequence. Sometimes it can even be an advantage, because the verses perpetrated by, say, a French rock group are every ounce as inane as their Stateside brethren's.

Many of the Right Bank—but few of the Left Bank—hostelries are lavishly sprinkled with mademoiselles whose job it is to push a man's tab up to astronomical heights. They're incompara-bly more skillful at it than American hookers; you could be in for a staggering bill including champagne, cigarettes, candy, teddy bear, and what-have-you. Under their gentle touch, an evening that might have cost you the equivalent of $5 can rapidly mount up to $200 and more—much more. Don't be afraid to respond with a firmly polite no to an unsolicited approach. The reaction is usually a regret-ful Gallic shrug, and she'll rarely try again. That way you'll retain control of your night's expenditure.

The other general rule to remember is that the Right Bank, by and large, is plusher, slicker, and more expensive than the Left, which contains more of the avant-garde entertainment, the younger clientele, and a minimum of professional "companions."

THE DISTRICTS

L'Etoile

The region around the Arc de Triomphe and along the Champs-Elysées is the most glamorous—and expensive—of the city's night haunts, home of the Lido and the world's greatest strip spot, the Crazy Horse Saloon.

Most of the action is found in the side streets off the Elysées, such as avenue George-V, rue de Marignan, and rue du Colisée, plus half a dozen others. Clubs here are as svelte as mink coats and almost as expensive . . . Paris at its most seductive.

L'Opéra

The heart of the tourist center is almost as sparkling as the above. It extends from the boulevard des Italiens in the northeast to the posh part of the rue de Rivoli in the southwest. It contains Harry's Bar (with shades of Hemingway) as well as Le Slow Club in rue de Rivoli, an authentic haven for jazz aficionados.

Around here, the entertainment spots are rather more widely spaced than elsewhere, not cheek-by-jowl as in Montmartre. Neon signs are discreet instead of blazing, and you get fewer of the moto-rized prostitutes smiling from their car windows.

Adjoining this region to the east is a huge and intriguing sec-tion catering almost entirely to the locals. Starting at boulevard Montmartre and stretching to the place de la République, the spots become solidly French, lower-middle-class, and parochial—a crowded, cluttered, slightly sleazy, and lively playland for under-paid Parisians.

You'll need more than a smattering of French to follow proceedings in the music halls and variety shows here, so I haven't included any of them in my listing. But if you have a spare evening, it might be fun to amble around there and see for yourself how little the French person's idea of "popular entertainment" differs from ours.

Montmartre

Snaking along the foot of the actual mountain, the garish, rainbow-hued, raucous, and jostling ribbon of bright lights provided by boulevard de Clichy, place Pigalle, and the surrounding alleys is probably the best-known and most frequently cursed of the tourist regions. It is also the most dangerous. A great many places here are simply sucker traps, lavish in promise, lilliputian in delivery, using the stalest of conmanship to milk you of more than you intended to spend.

Take the trick habitually sprung by some of the wayside strip cabarets. The notice outside quotes low admission fees. But once inside, you discover that there's also a stiff one-drink minimum. This surprise sting is also displayed (the law is pretty strict hereabouts), but in such a darkened corner that only a bat could read it.

The sloping side streets boast bars strung together like fake pearls on a necklace. Most of them carry English or German labels, and all of them are equipped with an ample quota of sociable lasses ready to quadruple a man's bill.

However, there are a few raisins in the Montmartre pie. I'll help you pick them out when we get down to particulars later.

St-Germain-des-Prés

Centering around the church of that name, this is undoubtedly the most stimulating entertainment district in Paris. Although touristy and chichi in patches, it has somehow managed to retain enough genuine local color to avoid becoming a cardboard backdrop. Some of the bars and cafés are at least as amusing as the actual nightclubs—thanks to the cosmopolitan population of students, artists, writers, sculptors, and professional expatriates.

The best spots are mostly away from the main boulevards St-Germain and St-Michel, and crowd the ramshackle back streets like rue de l'Abbaye, rue de Seine, and rue Monsieur-le-Prince. The weekend crush is murder, particularly in the discos, but on Wednesday and Thursday nights you have room to breathe as well as look around.

Quartier Latin

This is the eastern neighbor of the above, the dividing line running—very roughly—along boulevard St-Michel. The Latin Quarter, revolving around the Sorbonne, is similar to St-Germain, but more so—the streets older and grayer, the crowds more academic, the atmosphere less smartly sophisticated. Prices—perhaps —are a fraction lower.

The Quarter houses a pseudomedieval cabaret installed in a medieval dungeon. It also boasts a couple of the best jazz dives in town, for contrast. And more bars, bistros, and boîtes than you can count are found here.

Montparnasse

Southwest of the above sections, this curiously contradictory area has as its centerpiece the futuristic Gare Montparnasse, France's most modern railroad terminal. The district looks drab and ordinary, lacking both the elegance of the Right Bank and the charm of the Left. Yet for a quarter century it was *the* literary and artistic portion of Paris, stamping ground for a fabulous constellation of celebrities that included Picasso, James Joyce, Augustus John, Chagall, Ernest Hemingway, Mary McCarthy, and F. Scott Fitzgerald.

Currently Montparnasse has regained some of its old magnetism, which may account for its checkered complexion.

The **Maine-Montparnasse Tower,** 33 av. du Maine, 15e (tel. 45-38-52-56), overshadows the Left Bank quarter of Montparnasse where Gertrude Stein once reigned at her Saturday-evening gatherings. The tower, completed in 1973, covers an entire block and houses some 80 shops, including Galeries Lafayette, and more than 200 offices. Its floors are serviced by rapid elevators, which speed visitors from the lobby to the top floor in less than 40 seconds. Sightseers go to Montparnasse 56, the covered, glassed-in observation deck on the 56th floor, where a panoramic view of Paris opens from every side. A ticket includes an audio-visual presentation of the girls and glamour of Paris, expositions of how the tower was built, and highlights of the Paris skyline far below. The Belvedere bar-café, good for lunch, a quick snack, or a drink, is also in the Montparnasse 56 complex. The charge for the elevator to the 56th floor is 33.50F ($5.10) for adults and 20F ($3) for children under 15. These prices include access to the open-air roof terrace on the 59th floor, almost 700 feet above the streets of Paris. Montparnasse Tower 56 is open in summer, daily from 9:30am to 11pm; in winter, daily from 10am to 10pm.

Also on the 56th floor is **Le Ciel de Paris,** Tour Montparnasse, 33 av. de Maine, 15e (tel. 45-38-52-35), the highest restaurant in the city, where for 220F ($33.20), you can enjoy an array of French and Continental dishes. When you have finished your meal, if you wish, the waiter will give you a ticket for entrance into Montparnasse 56. Le Ciel de Paris is open daily from noon to 3pm and 7pm to midnight. Reservations are suggested but not essential ordinarily. There is no charge to take the elevator going directly to the restaurant from the lobby. The Métro stop for the tower is Montparnasse-Bienvenue.

Before starting the round of establishments, let me repeat that this is a town for genuine night owls. Few spots get swinging before 11pm and most acquire their full heads of steam around midnight

—or later. Since the Métro stops running at 1am, be prepared to use taxis and to sleep in the next morning.

SPECTACLES

Leading off is an array without which no Paris roll call would be complete. While decidedly expensive, they give you your money's worth by providing some of the most lavishly spectacular floor shows to be seen anywhere.

Lido Cabaret Normandie, 116 bis av. des Champs-Elysées, 8e (tel. 45-63-11-61), is housed in a panoramic room with 1,200 seats, having excellent visibility. This palatial nitery puts on an avalanche of glamour and talent, combined with enough showmanship to make the late Mr. Barnum look like an amateur. The permanent attraction is the Bluebell Girls, a fabulous precision ensemble of long-legged international beauties. The rest of the program changes.

The dinner dance at 8:30pm ranges in price from 570F ($86.05) to 695F ($104.95), including half a bottle of champagne. However, you can go solely for La Revue (at either 10:15pm or 12:30am) and pay a minimum of 395F ($59.65), including half a bottle of champagne. Service and taxes are included in the prices quoted. Go at least once in a lifetime. Métro: George-V.

According to legend, the first GI to reach Paris at the Liberation in 1944 asked for directions to the **Folies Bergère,** 32 rue Richer, 9e (tel. 42-46-77-11). His son and grandson do the same today. Even the old man comes back for a second look.

A roving-eyed Frenchman would have to be in his second century to remember when the Folies began. Apparently, it's here to stay, like Sacré-Coeur and the Eiffel Tower. The affection of Parisians for it has long turned into indifference (but try to get a seat on a July night). Some, however, recall it with sentimentality. Take, for example, the night the "toast of Paris," Josephine Baker, descended the celebrated staircase, tossing bananas into the audience.

Opened in 1886, since the turn of the century the Folies Bergère has stood as the symbol of unadorned female anatomy. Fresh off the boat, Victorians and Edwardians—starved for a glimpse of even an ankle—flocked to the Folies to get a look at much more. Yet the Folies also dresses its girls (at least 1,600 costumes at the last revue I saw) in those fabulous showgirl outfits you associate with Hollywood musicals of the 1930s.

The big musical revue begins nightly, except Monday, at 8:45pm. You can go to the box office anytime between 11am and 6:30pm for tickets. Prices range from about 100F ($15.10) to 361F ($54.50), with seats ranging from the *galerie* (usually the least expensive) to a *loge* in the orchestra or balcony. A scale model at the box office shows locations of the various seats. Métro: rue Montmartre or Cadet.

The **Moulin-Rouge,** place Blanche, Montmartre, 18e (tel. 46-06-00-19). Toulouse-Lautrec, who put this establishment on the map about a century ago, probably wouldn't recognize it today. The windmill is still there and so is the cancan. But the rest has become a super-slick, gimmick-loaded variety show with the accent heavy on the undraped female form. You'll see underwater ballets in an immense glass tank, a magnificent cascade, young women in swings and on trick stairs, all interspersed with animal acts, comic jugglers, and song trios. These are just a smattering of the acts usually found on the daily bill of fare. This multicolored candy-floss stuff is expertly staged, but any connection with the old Moulin-Rouge is purely coincidental.

If you go around 8pm for dinner, you can stay and see the revue at 10pm at a cost of 530F ($80.05). Attending the revue only costs 365F ($55.10), including the obligatory champagne. There's no minimum if you sit at the bar, where the average drink costs 190F ($28.70). Of course, the view is nothing like what you get at the tables. Open nightly. Métro: Place Blanche.

Le Paradis Latin, 28 rue Cardinal-Lemoine, 5e (tel. 43-25-28-28), is in a building built by Gustave Eiffel as his only venture into theater architecture, using the same metallic skeleton format he used for the Eiffel Tower. That theater takes credit for formalizing the introduction of vaudeville and musical theater to Paris. This monument's darkest days came in 1903, when the premises became a warehouse. In the 1970s, it was transformed, glossier than ever, into one of the most successful cabarets in Paris. Paradis Latin presents a dinner spectacle at 8pm that costs 570F ($86.10), and a revue at 10pm that costs 395F ($59.65) for entrance plus a half bottle of champagne. The patter of the master of ceremonies is in French, but the shows are lively enough to be understood by non-French-speaking audiences. The revue ends at midnight. Open Wednesday through Monday. Métro: Jussieu or Cardinal-Lemoine.

Alcazar, 62 rue Mazarine, 6e (tel. 43-29-02-20), offers a mixture of entertainment based on the mystique of Paris. It ranges from music hall to cabaret intimacy, all very French and sometimes very tongue-in-cheek. You'll hear live singers performing the classics of Maurice Chevalier and Edith Piaf, as well as impressions by live singers of musical stars from the fifties to the nineties. For dinner and a show starting at 8pm, the price is 510F ($77) per person. The 10pm show (without dinner) costs 350F ($52.85) per person. A half bottle of champagne or two drinks is included in the price. The cost is less if you watch the show from one of the bars. Open nightly. Métro: Odéon.

The **Milliardaire,** 68 rue Pierre-Charron (off Champs-Elysées), 8e (tel. 47-23-25-17). Smaller and less spectacular, but more stylishly elegant, this velvety night-nest is reached through a backyard that contrasts intriguingly with the plush interior. The program doesn't dwell exclusively on dishabille, but includes comics, jugglers, and first-rate dance interludes. You can watch the show for 320F ($48.30) per person, which includes two drinks at your table, or 125F ($18.90) at the bar. Two different spectacles are staged nightly —the first from 10:30pm, the second at 12:30am. Métro: F. D. Roosevelt.

SONGS AND SENTIMENT

I had to find a special label for the next group because the spots wouldn't fit under any other. A cross between familiar American folk cellars and modified French boîtes, they have an appeal depending entirely on your digging their brand of tunes. Chances are you will—mightily.

The He and She Mystery

Madame Arthur, 75 bis rue des Martyrs, 18e (tel. 42-64-48-27). One of the leading female impersonator cabarets of Europe, this place Pigalle showplace is directed by Madame Arthur, who is no lady. Your first drink costs 165F ($24.90). A dinner show is priced at 250F ($37.75). The establishment opens at 10pm, with the first show starting at 11pm. The cabaret is open nightly until 3am. Métro: Abbesses.

Au Caveau de la Bolée, 25 rue de Hirondelle, 6e (tel. 43-54-62-20). You descend into the catacombs of the early-14th-century Abbey of Saint-André, once a famous literary café, drawing such personages as Verlaine and Oscar Wilde, who downed (or drowned in) glass after glass of absinthe here. The French songs are good and bawdy and just what the young students, who form a large part of the audience, like. Occasionally the audience sings along.

The fixed-price dinner, which costs about 250F ($37.75), is served Monday through Saturday at 9pm and is followed by a cabaret show. However, you won't understand the jokes and references made in the show unless your French is extremely good. The cabaret starts at 10:30pm and if you've already had dinner, you can order a drink for 100F ($15.10). On Sunday, a jazz show begins at 10pm.

You'll find this establishment, which seats only 24 people, on a tiny street leading into the western edge of the place St-Michel. The beginning of the street is down a short flight of steps under a giant archway beneath one of the square's grandiose buildings. Métro: St-Michel.

Au Lapin Agile is perched near the top of Montmartre, at 22 rue des Saules, 18e (tel. 46-06-85-87). This tiny rustic cottage was once a celebrated haunt of writers, impressionist painters, and their models. Some of their spell still lingers. You sit at carved-up wooden tables in a low, dimly lit room, the walls covered with Bohemian memorabilia, and listen to your hosts sing, play, and recite.

They sing—singly or in groups—old French folk tunes, love ballads, army songs, sea chanties, and music-hall ditties. They sing so simply, so naturally, with so much esprit and talent, that you desperately want to join in, even if you can't speak a word of French. And before you know it you're belting out the "oui, oui, oui—non, non, non" refrains of "Les Chevaliers de la Table Ronde," and humming along with "Larilette" and "Madelon." And while these merry and sad and incredibly catchy songs last, you feel as one with the nation that produced them.

It's at its best out of the tourist season and on a weeknight. The admission and the price of each drink is 90F ($13.60). Evening performances are Tuesday through Sunday at 9:15pm, ending at 2am. Métro: Lamarck.

Caveau des Oubliettes. It's hard to say which is more interesting in this place—the program or the environment. At 11 rue St-Julien-le-Pauvre, 5e (tel. 43-54-94-97), in the Latin Quarter and just across the river from Notre-Dame, this nightspot is housed in a genuine 12th-century prison—complete with dungeons, spine-crawling passages, and scattered skulls. The word *oubliette* means a dungeon with a trap door at the top as its only opening, but some victims were pushed through portholes into the Seine to drown. The caveau is beneath the subterranean vaults that communicated many centuries ago with the fortress prison of the Petit Châtelet.

Performers in medieval costumes sing French folk songs and tavern choruses—sentimental, comic, and bawdy—to exclusively tourist audiences. It's rather artificial and stagey, but with charm. There's nothing artificial, however, about the adjoining museum, which displays a working guillotine, chastity belts, and instruments of torture. The place is open Monday through Saturday from 9pm to 2am. The 100F ($15.10) to 125F ($18.90) entrance fee includes your first drink. Métro: St-Michel.

AN ELEGANT STRIP JOINT

Crazy Horse Saloon, 12 av. George-V, 8e (tel. 47-23-32-32). Texans in ten-gallon hats are fond of "Le Crazy," which is considered by many to be the leading nude dancing joint in the world. Alain Bernardin parodies the American West in the décor, but only purists claim that Cheyenne was never like this.

Two dozen performers do their acts entirely nude. Sandwiched between the more sultry scenes are three international variety acts. The first show, lasting less than two hours, is staged nightly at 9pm, with the second act going on at 11:30pm. At the bar, one drink costs 190F ($28.70), although you'll pay as much as 480F ($72.50) at a table, including service. Métro: George-V.

A SUPPER CLUB

Villa d'Este, 4 rue Arsène-Houssaye, 8e (tel. 43-59-78-44). When Amalia Rodrigues, Portugal's leading fadista and an international star, is in Paris, she's likely to appear at this supper club. Its owners book top talent from both Europe and America. A short stroll from the Champs-Elysées, the Villa d'Este has been around for a long time, and the quality of its offerings remains high. If you go for dinner, at 8:30pm, expect to pay at least 300F ($45.30). However, at 10pm you can see the show and order a drink for 101F ($15.25). A show is presented every night, and reservations are necessary on Friday and Saturday. Closed in August. Métro: Charles de Gaulle (Etoile).

DANCE HALLS AND DISCOS

Although Paris is supposedly the birthplace of the discothèque, nobody here seems to know anymore what, precisely, constitutes one. Originally the discos were small, intimate dives where patrons danced to records—hence the term. Now, however, the tag is applied to anything from playground-size ballrooms with full orchestras to tiny bars with taped tunes—where they don't let you dance at all.

The samples below are a few of the hundreds of spots where people go chiefly to dance—as distinct from others where the main attraction is the music.

Le Palace, 8 rue de Faubourg-Montmartre, 9e (tel. 42-46-10-87). Shades of the Coconut Grove in Los Angeles and the old Garden of Allah in Hollywood. One of the leading nightclubs of Paris, Le Palace re-creates the old glamour of Hollywood in the 1940s. At any minute you expect a sultry Lana Turner to emerge. The dance floor was redesigned into a lookalike of the Aztec pyramids, and now there's a private bar on the uppermost terrace, connected to the rest of the club by a series of catwalks not unlike the tendrils of a spider's web. The terraces are covered with seasonally selected plants, evoking the Babylonian gardens a Hollywood studio might have crafted. There are also visual references to Grauman's Chinese Theater, and one salon is in the shape of an Egyptian pyramid.

Dinner, costing from 150F ($22.65), begins in the restaurant at 8:30pm, but the actual nightclub doesn't open until 11pm, the action continuing until dawn. Every night a different theme is in vogue, everything from a fiesta party to the "French touch." An entrance and the first drink costs 120F ($18.10). Métro: Montmartre.

This entire region opposite and around the church of St-Germain-des-Prés is so honeycombed with dance dives of one sort or another, and they are so ephemeral (some have the life spans of sickly butterflies), that it's almost impossible to keep track of their coming and closing. What's hopping at the time of writing might be a hardware store by the time you get there. But chances are there'll be two new joints in the same block.

La Coupole, 102 bd. Montparnasse, 14e (tel. 43-20-14-21), is reviewed below as a historical landmark café (see "Cafés and Bars,"). One of the big Montparnasse cafés and a former stronghold of bohemia, it is a throwback to the days when locals waltzed and tangoed to the strains of a live orchestra. If you caught *Last Tango in Paris* on the late show, it would help as a prelude to a visit here. In addition to its upstairs café, La Coupole has a large basement ballroom reserved for dancing. Charging 100F ($15.10) for admission, it is open Friday from 9pm to 3am, Saturday from 3 to 7pm and 9pm to 3am, and on Sunday from 3 to 7pm. Métro: Vavin.

Club Zed, 2 rue des Anglais, 5e (tel. 43-54-93-78), one of the most frequented after-dark haunts in Paris, offers . . . well, you name it. Just show up and be surprised by, say, samba music straight out of Rio, nostalgic tunes from the 1960s, a jazz beat, and "le rock" on Sunday afternoon or Wednesday night. The club is open Wednesday and Thursday from 10:30pm to 3:30am, Friday from 10:30pm to 4:30pm, and Sunday from 4 to 8pm; closed August. Your first drink costs 100F ($15.10). If a live band is appearing, you might also be assessed a 50F ($7.55) cover charge: Métro: Maubert-Mutualité.

Le Balajo, 9 rue de Lappe, 11e (tel. 47-00-07-79). Remember the "little sparrow," Edith Piaf? This famous French chanteuse is still dearly remembered by the people of Paris, even the young ones who never saw her live but still listen to her recorded music. Le Balajo is the club—practically a national shrine—where Piaf used to appear frequently during her tortured lifetime. The place is still popular, drawing a medley of the young and the "Oh, to be young again" crowd. Filled with nostalgia, it's open Thursday through Monday from 10pm to 5am. A cover, including your first drink, is 100F ($15.10). After performances at l'Opéra Bastille are over, you can continue the night here. Métro: Bastille.

MAINLY MUSIC

At a few spots, despite the fact that some of them title themselves "discothèques," you sit and listen.

L'Escale, 15 rue Monsieur-le-Prince, 6e (tel. 43-54-63-47), is one of the true charmers of St-Germain-des-Prés. It's not exactly cheap, but worth every cent in terms of atmosphere and artistry. The bar is semidark and very intimate. The Mexican mural on the wall is almost invisible in the dim light. This is the oldest salsa and Latin music nightclub of Paris, set in a 17th-century building. Musicians play Latin American songs, not the diluted stuff you usually hear, but the really melancholy and wild gaucho airs, with the smoldering fire that is their special idiom. The first drink, which you can nurse as long as you like, costs 65F ($9.80). The club also has a *cave* where you can dance to a Latin combo. It's open daily from 10:30pm to 3 or 4am. Métro: Odéon.

JAZZ AND ROCK

You can probably listen and dance to more jazz in Paris than in any U.S. city, with the possible exception of San Francisco. The great jazz revival that long ago swept America is still going full swing in Paris, with Dixieland or Chicago rhythms being pounded out in dozens of jazz cellars, mostly called "caveaux."

This is one city where you don't have to worry about being a self-conscious dancer. The locals, even young people, are not particularly good. The best dancers on any floor are usually American. And although Parisians take to rock with enthusiasm, their skill does not match their zest.

The majority of the jazz/rock establishments are crowded into the Left Bank near the Seine between rue Bonaparte and rue St-Jacques, which makes things easy for syncopation-seekers. Herewith are a few sample spots out of perhaps a dozen similar ones.

Club St-Germain/Le Bilboquet, 13 rue St-Benoît, 6e (tel. 45-48-81-84), enjoyed great fame during its existentialist heyday. It's still around, offering some of the best jazz in Paris. The film *Paris Blues* was shot here. Right in the heart of throbbing St-Germain-des-Prés, it offers both a "jazz restaurant" and a disco. The basement level is reached via a mirrored stairwell. There, you'll find a sunken rather small dance floor with pink spotlights, red walls, and black leather banquettes. Open from midnight till dawn seven days a week, this is the disco part. Called the Club St-Germain, both it and the jazz club charge 90F ($13.60) for a drink.

On the upper level is Le Bilboquet, where you hear "all that jazz." A copper ceiling and wooden wall panels surround a sunken bar with brass trim, forgiving lighting, Victorian candelabra, and comfortable seats. On an encircling raised tier, as well as an elevated balcony, you'll find linens covering the dinnertables. The menu is limited but classic French, specializing in dishes such as carré d'agneau (rack of lamb), fish, and beef, which might be preceded by a large choice of appetizers, including smoked salmon and terrines. Count on spending 200F ($30.20) and up. The restaurant is open nightly from 8pm to 12:30am, and the bar serves from 8pm to 3am. The music usually begins at 10:30pm, ending at 3am. Métro: St-Germain-des-Prés.

Trois Mailletz, 56 rue Galande, 5e (tel. 43-54-00-79), used to be the medieval cellar that housed the masons who constructed Notre-Dame. Many of them carved their initials into the walls. Today it's a haven for jazz aficionados of all nationalities, and one of the few places in the district where students don't predominate. Musical celebrities appearing here have included Memphis Slim, Bill Coleman, and Nina Simone.

A piano bar on the upper floor is open every day from 8pm to 5am and requires no cover charge. The jazz club is on the lower level, and it's open from 10:30 or 11pm till "very, very late" every day except Monday and Tuesday. The entrance fee is from 65F ($9.80), depending on the artists. Alcoholic drinks cost 65F ($9.80) Métro: Maubert-Mutualité.

Caveau de la Huchette, 5 rue de la Huchette, 5e (tel. 43-26-65-05), is a celebrated jazz *cave,* drawing a young crowd, mostly students, who listen and dance rapturously to the hot stuff poured out by well-known jazz combos. This is a cellar hideaway, reached by a winding staircase. In pre-jazz days, it was frequented by Robespierre and Marat. The entrance fee is 45F ($6.80) Sunday to Thursday, 55F ($8.30) on Friday and Saturday. However, female students pay only 40F ($6.05); drinks for everyone begin at 15F ($2.25). The caveau is open daily, with the fun starting at 9:30pm, lasting until 3am. On Friday and Saturday, the club remains open until 4am. Métro: St-Michel.

A quick sweep over the rest of the jazz field would include the **Slow Club,** 130 rue de Rivoli, 1er (tel. 42-33-84-30), a stylish and smart stronghold of New Orleans fare featuring the well-known French jazz band of Claude Luter, who played for ten years with the late Sidney Bechet. This is one of the most famous jazz cellars in Europe. The regular entrance price is 50F ($7.55), 62F ($9.35) on Friday, Saturday, and holiday eves. The club is open Tuesday through Thursday from 9:30pm till 3am, on Friday till 2am and on Saturday and holidays till 4am. Drinks begin at 14F ($2.10). Métro: Châtelet.

New Morning, 7-9 rue des Petites-Ecuries, 10e (tel. 45-23-51-41), was named for Bob Dylan's 1970 album. The premises were once occupied by a daily newspaper and designed in 1981 to become a jazz club. The high-ceilinged loft allows jazz-maniacs to dance, talk, flirt, and drink elbow-to-elbow at the stand-up bar. The appropriate dress code is jeans or whatever, and concerts and musical soirées might include a range of practically everything except disco. The only rule here seems to be that there are few rules. It might be open at 9:30pm or closed just any night, but when it's in business, closing (except on salsa nights) is at 1:30 or 2am. If Stan Getz or Dizzy Gillespie can be booked on a Sunday, the place is open on Sunday. A phone call will let you know what's going on on the night of your visit. The entrance cost is 100F ($15.10) to 120F ($18.10). No food is served. Métro: Château d'Eau.

Jazz Club Lionel Hampton, Hôtel Meridien, 81 bd. Gouvion-St-Cyr, 17e (tel. 40-68-34-34), near the Champs-Elysées and the Arc de Triomphe, offers jazz great Lionel Hampton. Performances are daily from 10pm to 2am in the hotel's central courtyard. Admission of 130F ($19.65) includes a welcoming drink. Métro: Porte Maillot.

---

3. Cafés and Bars

Contrary to general belief, the coffeehouse is not a French invention. It began in 17th-century Vienna and flourished in London long before taking root in France. But when the Parisians adopted it, they infused it with such Gallic flair and local flavor that it became an accepted symbol of their inimitable brand of joie de vivre.

It's almost impossible to venture a guess at the number of cafés in Paris. A single block in the central arrondissements may house three or four. They thin out a little in the farther suburbs, but still remain far more numerous than, for instance, hamburger stands in the United States. And somehow each gets its quota of customers.

It's nearly as difficult to define their precise function. They aren't restaurants, although the larger ones may serve complete and excellent meals. They aren't bars, although they offer an infinite variety of alcoholic potions. And they aren't coffee shops in the Anglo-American meaning, because they'll serve you a bottle of champagne just as readily as an iced chocolate.

Parisians use them as combination club-tavern-snackbars, almost as extensions of their living rooms. They are spots where you can read your newspaper or meet a friend, do your homework or write your memoirs, nibble at a hard-boiled egg or drink yourself into oblivion. At cafés you meet your dates to go on to a show or to stay and talk. Above all, cafés are for sitting and people-watching.

Perhaps their single common denominator is the way they let you sit. Regardless of whether you have one small coffee or the most expensive cognac in the house—nobody badgers, pressures, or hurries you. If you wish to sit there until the place closes, *eh bien,* that's your affair. For the café is one of the few truly democratic institutions—a solitary soda buys you the same view and sedentary pleasure as an oyster dinner.

All cafés sport an outdoor portion. Some, merely a few tables on the pavement; others, immense terraces, glassed in and heated in winter. Both categories, however, fulfill the same purpose: they offer a vantage point from which to view the passing parade.

Coffee, of course, is the chief potion. It comes black in a small cup, unless you specifically order it *au lait* (with milk). Tea *(thé,* pronounced "tay") is also fairly popular, but not on the same level of quality.

The famous apéritifs, French versions of the before-dinner drink, are the aniseed-flavored, mild-tasting Pernod, Ricard, and Pastis, all mixed with ice and water. Also there are St. Raphael and Byrrh, tasting rather like port wine, and the slightly less sweet Dubonnet.

If you prefer beer, I advise you to pay a bit more for the imported German, Dutch, or Danish brands, incomparably better than the local brew. If you insist on the French variety, at least order it *à pression* (draft), which is superior. A great local favorite as an apéritif is the Italian Campari, drunk with soda and ice, very bitter and refreshing. Try it at least once.

In the teetotal bracket, you get a vast variety of fruit drinks, as well as Coca-Cola and the specifically French syrups, like Grenadine. They're about on the same level as the stuff you get at home. But French drinking-chocolate—either hot or iced—is absolutely superb and on a par with the finest Dutch brands. It's made from ground chocolate, not a chemical compound.

Cafés keep delightfully flexible hours, depending on the season, the traffic, and the part of town they're in. Nearly all of them stay open till one in the morning, some till two, a few all night.

Now just a few words on café etiquette. You don't pay when getting your order, but only when you intend to leave. Payment indicates that you've had all you want. *Service compris* means the tip is included in your bill, so it isn't really necessary to tip extra; still, feel free to leave an extra franc or so if service has been attentive.

You'll hear the locals call the "garçon," but as a foreigner it would be more polite to use "monsieur." *All* waitresses, on the other hand, are addressed as "mademoiselle," regardless of age and marital status.

In the smaller establishments, you may have to share your table. In that case, even if you haven't exchanged one word with them, you bid your table companions good-bye with a perfunctory "messieurs et dames," on leaving.

FAMOUS CAFES

Café de la Paix, place de l'Opéra, 9e (tel. 42-68-12-13). This hub of the tourist world virtually commands the place de l'Opéra, and the legend goes that if you sit there long enough, you'll see someone you know passing by. Huge, grandiose, and frighteningly fashionable, it harbors not only Parisians, but, at some time or another, every visiting American, a tradition that dates from the end of World War I. Once Emile Zola and Oscar Wilde sat on the terrace; later, Hemingway and F. Scott Fitzgerald frequented it. You pay 39F ($5.90) to 50F ($7.55) for a whisky, 22F ($3.30) for a Coca-Cola, and 15F ($2.25) for a café espresso, service included. It's open daily from 10am to 1:30am. Métro: Opéra.

The two following cafés are next to each other and so alike in fame and clientele that I'll treat them as twins. They are the **Deux Magots** (tel. 45-48-55-25) and the **Flore** (tel. 45-48-55-26), at

170 and 172 bd. St-Germain, 6e, right in the legendary St-Germain-des-Prés. Both made history as the haunt and hatching place of the Existentialists and have hosted nearly all of the French intellectuals who shaped the world's philosophical innovations during the post-war years.

Sartre, Camus, de Beauvoir, and Juliette Greco have vanished from the scene, but their shadows still linger. The crowd is still on the highbrow side, richly sprinkled with devastating damsels and the more sophisticated Anglo-American visitors. Both places get fearfully packed in the evening and the best time to enjoy their charms is around 10 o'clock in the morning.

Neither is what you'll call economical. Expect to pay 18F ($2.70) for coffee, the same for a small domestic beer. Hours are daily from 8am to 2am. Métro: St-Germain-des-Prés.

Across the street is the world-famous **Brasserie Lipp,** 151 bd. St-Germain, 6e (tel. 45-48-53-91). On the day of Paris's liberation in 1944, former owner Roger Cazes (now deceased) spotted Hemingway, the first man to drop in for a drink. But famous men—then and now—customarily drop into the Lipp for its beer, wine, and conversation. Food is secondary, of course, yet quite good, providing you can get a seat (an hour and a half waiting time is customary on many occasions if you're not a "friend of the management"). The specialty is sauerkraut garni. Each day the Lipp features about four plats du jour, ranging in price from 95F ($14.35) to 150F ($22.65). You can perch on a banquette, admiring your face reflected—along with that of, say, Françoise Sagan—in the "hall of mirrors." The Lipp was opened in 1870–1871, following the Franco-Prussian War, when its founder, Monsieur Lippman, fled German-occupied territory for Paris. It's been a Parisian tradition ever since. Even if you don't drop inside for a drink, you can sit at a sidewalk café table, enjoying a cognac and people-watching. It's open daily from 8am to 2am; closed eight days for Christmas and mid-July to mid-August. Métro: St-Germain-des-Prés.

Le Dôme, 108 bd. du Montparnasse, 14e (tel. 43-35-25-81). After an unsuccessful attempt as a drugstore, Le Dôme, the most famous of the Montparnasse cafés, is back in business but elegantly modernized in an art deco format. All that remains of Le Dôme of times past are recollections of the café in its heyday. The memories of Hemingway linger here, and some of the most celebrated names in the world of art sat on the terrace in the years between 1920 and 1925.

Many guests come here for only a coffee, costing 12F ($1.80). However, it's possible to order a full meal, beginning at about 350F ($52.85). Fresh oysters are sold right on the sidewalk. At a table, you might select such specialties as pot-au-feu or turbot with fresh morels, perhaps bourride provençale, served only for two persons. Hours are Tuesday through Sunday from 10am to 2am. Métro: Vavin.

La Coupole, 102 bd. du Montparnasse, 14e (tel. 43-20-14-20), was once a leading center of Parisian artist life and is now a bastion of traditionalism in Montparnasse in the grand Paris brasserie style. This big and attractive café has, however, grown more fashionable with the years, attracting fewer locals—such as Jean-Paul Sartre and Simone de Beauvoir in the old days—and rarely a struggling artist. But some of the city's most interesting foreigners show up. In days of yore patrons included Josephine Baker, Henry Miller, Dali, Calder, Hemingway, Dos Passos, Fitzgerald, and Picasso. Today you might see Belmondo with Catherine Deneuve. The sweeping outdoor terrace is among the finest to be found in Paris. At one of its sidewalk tables, you can sit and watch the passing scene, ordering a coffee or a cognac VSOP. The food is quite good, despite the fact that the dining room resembles a railway station. Try, for example, such main dishes as sole meunière, curry d'agneau (lamb), or cassoulet. The fresh oysters and shellfish are especially popular. Meals begin at 250F ($37.75). A petit déjeuner is served on a buffet from 7:30 to 10:30am. Open daily from noon to 2am. Métro: Raspail.

Fouquet's, 99 av. des Champs-Elysées, 8e (tel. 47-23-70-60), has been collecting anecdotes and a patina since it was founded at the turn of the century. A celebrity favorite, it has attracted Chaplin, Chevalier, Dietrich, Mistinguett, even Churchill and Roosevelt. The premier sidewalk café on the Champs-Elysées, it sits behind a barricade of potted flowers at the edge of the sidewalk. You can select a table outdoors in the sunshine or retreat to the glassed-in elegance of the leather banquettes and the rattan furniture of the street-level grill room. There, meals cost from 220F ($33.20). Most visitors, however, simply stop in for a glass of wine at 35F ($5.30) or a sandwich for 50F ($7.55). The café and grill room are open all year long. On the upper level, the restaurant and private banqueting rooms are closed Saturday, Sunday, and from mid-July to late August. Open Monday through Friday from 8am to midnight. Métro: George-V.

La Rotonde, 105 bd. du Montparnasse, 6e (tel. 43-26-68-84), was once patronized by Hemingway. The original Rotonde faded into history but it still is a memory, drawn from the pages of *The Sun Also Rises.* Papa wrote, "No matter what café in Montparnasse you ask a taxi driver to bring you to from the right bank of the river, they always take you to the Rotonde." Lavishly upgraded, the reincarnation of La Rotonde has an art deco paneled elegance, sharing the once-hallowed site with a motion-picture theater. Full meals cost from 200F ($30.20), or else you can order a glass of wine for 17F ($2.55). If you stand at the bar, prices are lower. Hours are daily from 7:30am to 2am (until 3am on Friday and Saturday). Métro: Vavin.

Le Sélect, 99 bd. du Montparnasse, 6e (tel. 42-22-65-27), may be down the social ladder from the other glittering cafés of Montparnasse, but I find it the liveliest and friendliest. It opened in 1923, and really hasn't changed all that much. At one time it was the favorite hangout of Jean Cocteau. They have 40 different whiskies and 20 different cocktails, some rather exotic. Coffee costs 9F ($1.40) to 12F ($1.80), depending on the hour of the day or night, and hard drinks range from 43F ($6.50). Hours Sunday through Thursday are 8am to 2am, until 3:30am on Friday and Saturday. Métro: Vavin.

Café de Cluny, 20 bd. St-Michel or 102 bd. St-Germain, 5e (tel. 43-26-68-24), is placed strategically at the intersection of these two famous avenues, overlooking the hub of the Left Bank and the Museé de Cluny. This large, bustling oasis is one of the main meeting places for visitors and locals alike. Local beer goes for 15F ($2.25), a cup of coffee 11F ($1.65). The café also serves meals. For example, a plate of sauerkraut garni costs 48F ($7.25). The place is open from 7am to 2am daily. Métro: St-Michel.

Le Mandarin, 148 bis bd. St-Germain, 6e (tel. 46-33-98-35), is an elegantly decorated corner café thronged with young people of the Left Bank or visitors soaking up the atmosphere of St-Germain-des-Prés. At the brass bar you can order fine wines, certainly a coffee. Decorated with lace-covered hanging lamps, brass trim, and lots of exposed wood, the establishment serves good food, including crêpes for 19F ($1.40) to 42F ($6.35) or onion soup at 40F ($6.05). Coffee ranges from 10F ($1.50) to 13F ($1.95). The café is open daily from 8am to 2am. Métro: Odéon or Mabillon.

WINE BARS

Many Parisians now prefer to patronize wine bars instead of their traditional café or bistro. The food is often better, and the ambience more inviting. Wine bars come in a wide range of styles, from old traditional places to modern gathering centers.

Willi's Wine Bar, 13 rue des Petits-Champs, 1er (tel. 42-61-05-09). Journalists and stock brokers alike are attracted to this increasingly popular wine bar in the center of the financial district, close to the Bourse. Surprisingly, it is run by two Englishmen, Mark Williamson and Tim Johnston. They offer about 250 different kinds of wine, and each week about a dozen "specials" are featured.

Very crowded at lunchtime, it often settles down to a lower decibel count in the evening, when you can better admire the 16th-century beams and the warm, friendly ambience. A blackboard menu informs you of the daily specials, which are likely to include brochette of lamb flavored with cumin or lyonnaise sausage in a truffled vinaigrette with pistachios, and a spectacular dessert, the chocolate terrine. The plat du jour will most likely cost 40F ($6.05) to 95F ($14.35), and you can enjoy wines by the glass. The bar is open Monday through Saturday from noon to 2:30pm and 7 to 11pm. Métro: Bourse or Louvre.

Au Sauvignon, 80 rue des Saints-Pères, 7e (tel. 45-48-49-02), is considered the best-known wine bar in Paris. It is minuscule, although it overflows onto a covered terrace. Still, it has a very chic reputation. The owner is from Auvergne, and when he's not polishing his zinc countertop or preparing a plate of charcuterie for a client, he will sell you Beaujolais. Beaujolais is the cheapest wine at 15F ($2.25) per glass at the bar. Puligny Montrachet is the most expensive wine, costing 36F ($5.45) at the bar. All wines cost an additional 2F (30¢) if consumed at a table. Auvergne-derived specialties, including goat cheese and terrines, are served if you'd like to have a snack with your wine. The fresh Poilâne bread is ideal with the Auvergne ham, the country pâté, or the Crottin de Chavignol goat cheese. The place has a décor of old ceramic tiles and frescoes done by Left Bank artists.

It is closed on Sunday, on major religious holidays, and for three weeks in August, but open otherwise from 9:30am to 10:30pm. Métro: Sèvres-Babylone.

Wild Boar Pâté at the Pont Neuf

Taverne Henri-IV, 13 place du Pont-Neuf, 1er (tel. 43-54-27-90), is quite different from my other recommendations. This one is called both a *taverne* and *bistro à vin*. The location couldn't be more magnificent—in a 17th-century building at the Pont Neuf, on the Ile de la Cité. The host, Monsieur Cointepas, does his own bottling, or at least some of it. His prize wines are listed on a blackboard menu. You might order a special Beaujolais or perhaps a glass of Chinon, the latter "tasting more of the earth." If you sit at a table (drinks are cheaper at the bar), you can order a big glass costing 16F ($2.40) to 25F ($3.80), service included. Snacks, including wild-boar pâté, range from 18F ($2.70) to 22F ($3.30). As the owner puts it, the price depends on what you spread on your slice of bread. Eight farmer's lunches are offered at 55F ($8.30) each, with service included. The place is closed Sunday and in August, but open otherwise from 11:30am to 9:30pm. Métro: Pont-Neuf.

La Tartine, 24 rue de Rivoli, 4e (tel. 42-72-76-85), is Old Paris. It's like a movie set. Inset mirrors, brass decorative details, a zinc bar, and frosted globe chandeliers form the door. At any moment you expect to see Tito, Trotsky, or Lenin walk in the door (each was a former patron). At least 50 wines are offered at reasonable prices, and all categories of wine are served by the glass. A plate of charcuterie will cost from 34F ($5.15), and you can order sandwiches for 15F ($2.25). At least seven kinds of Beaujolas are offered, along with a large selection of Bordeaux. The light wine Sancerre is more favored than ever. Wine by the glass costs from 5.50F (85¢). With your wine, why not taste some young goat cheese from the Loire Valley?

Hours are Thursday through Monday from 8am to 10pm, Wednesday from noon to 10pm. It is also closed for two weeks in August. Métro: St-Paul.

Les Domaines, 56 rue François ler, 8e (tel. 42-56-15-87). Music and show-business types often have a rendezvous over a glass of wine at this stylish wine-bar restaurants. Vintage wines can be ordered by the glass. The establishment also serves full meals, including breakfast.

The décor of designer Philippe Starck includes high-tech combinations of chrome tubing, mottled granite, and space-age simplicity. At lunch or dinner, a fixed-price classic French menu costs 130F ($19.65) per person. À la carte meals, costing from 220F ($33.20), might include scallops with Noilly sauce, grilled quail with a pepper-and-tomato sauce, breast of duckling in the style of the Vendeene, sea trout with sage, and the establishment's trademark specialty of crème brulée. Open Monday through Saturday from 8am to 11pm. Métro: George-V.

Blue Fox Bar, 25 rue Royale (Cité Berryer), 8e (tel. 42-65-10-72), adjoins Moulin du Village (see Chapter V, "Paris Dining"). This successful wine bar is supplied by the highly regarded Caves de la Madeleine, one of Paris's leading wine dealers. A large selection of wines by the glass is sold, along with "charcuterie," salads, cheeses, and plats du jour. It's an unpretentious place, but frequented by some of the chicest people of Paris. It's on two levels, with lace curtains and lots of country-style wood. At lunch it tends to be overcrowded, as it fills quickly with the people who staff the shops around the place de la Madeleine and along rue Royale. The entrance is on a little alleyway around the corner from Maxim's. A meal and a glass of wine here will cost from 200F ($30.20). The bar is open Monday through Friday from noon to 10pm. Métro: Concorde or Madeleine.

Au Franc Pinot, 1 quai de Bourbon, 4e (tel. 43-29-46-98). At the foot of Pont Marie, this is the oldest wine bistro in Paris. Its double tier of vaulted cellars dates from the early 17th century. The establishment was renovated in 1980 by Bernard and Michelle Meyruey, who added an inventory of about two dozen wines that are sold by the glass. These you can consume while standing at the large wooden bar (which is crowned by a large metal rooster), or seated on one of the bentwood chairs in the warm glow of the stained-glass windows.

If you descend into one of the deepest cellars of Paris, you will find a cozily intimate restaurant. A set menu goes for 190F ($28.70), although à la carte dinners average 300F ($45.30). This might include such specialties as lamb with crayfish in a tarragon cream sauce, or terrine of foie gras with fresh duckling from Landes, and a small selection of other classic French dishes. The last glass of red Sancerre, Beaujolais, or riesling is consumed at the bar at 11:30pm, but you can go as early as 6pm for food. It is closed every Sunday and Monday. Métro: Pont-Marie.

Ma Bourgogne, 19 place des Vosges, 4e (tel. 42-78-44-64), is a fine brasserie with a good selection of wines in an area that has had a facelift and is lit up both day and night. You can go here to sit and contemplate this dreamy square, following in the footsteps of Victor Hugo. Under the arcades you can enjoy coffee at 8F ($1.20), or for 14F (60¢) you can order a glass of Beaujolais. Monsieur Aimé, the owner, selects all the wines himself. There are rattan sidewalk tables for summer sitting and a cozy room within with a beamed ceiling. Madame Aimé offers a wide choice of country dishes. Customers come from all over the city to eat her famous tartar steak. A meal costs 150F ($22.65). The brasserie is open daily from 8am to 1am; closed February. Métro: St-Paul or Chemin Vert.

BARS AND PUBS

These are Anglo-American imports to France and—with few notable exceptions—strike an alien chord. They're about equally divided between those trying to imitate Stateside cocktail bars and those pretending to be British pubs. Some go to amazing lengths in the process.

Bar-hopping is fashionable with Paris's smart set, as distinct from café-sitting, which is practiced by the entire populace. Bar prices, therefore, are generally a fraction higher, a biggish fraction if the place boasts a well-known bartender.

A Drink with Your Renault

If you like to combine your hamburgers with shopping for a Renault, you'll be at the right place if you drop in at **Pub Renault,** 53 av. des Champs-Elysées, 8e (tel. 42-25-28-17). At first you'll think you've come to an automobile showroom . . . and you have. But proceed to the rear, where a bar of "horseless carriages" is waiting. Here you can either order a set menu for only 66F ($9.95) or an à la carte meal for 120F ($18.10). You can also visit just for a drink, with a whisky costing from 35F ($5.30) at the bar. The pub is open daily from 11am to 1:30am. Métro: F. D. Roosevelt.

Harry's New York Bar, 5 rue Daunou, 5e (tel. 42-61-71-14). "Sank roo doe Noo," as the ads tell you to instruct your cab driver, is the most famous bar in Europe—quite possibly in the world. Opened on Thanksgiving Day in 1911, it's sacred to Hemingway disciples as the spot where Ernest did most of his Parisian imbibing. To others it's hallowed as the site where white lady and sidecar cocktails were invented in, respectively, 1919 and 1931. Also, it is the birthplace of the Bloody Mary and French '75, as well as headquarters of the International Bar Flies (IBF).

The upstairs bar is excessively hearty and masculine, but it gets smoother down below under the influence of an excellent pianist performing from 10pm to 2am. The bars are always crammed with Anglo-Americans and their Gallic admirers.

A dry martini costs 40F ($6.05) and whiskies range from 46F ($6.95) to 165F ($24.90), the latter price for a 1965 MacAllan single-malt scotch. The downstairs room has been redecorated and fitted with its own wet bar. Harry's is open daily from 10:30am to 4:30am; closed Christmas. Métro: Opéra or Pyramides.

Rosebud, 11 bis rue Delambre, 14e (tel. 43-35-38-56), is a name taken from Orson Welles's greatest film, *Citizen Kane.* Rosebud is just around the corner from the famous cafés of Montparnasse. It once attracted such devotees as the late Jean-Paul Sartre, Simone de Beauvoir, Eugène Ionesco, and Marguerite Duras. Drop in at night for a glass of wine or perhaps something to eat, maybe a hamburger or chili con carne. Light meals cost 120F

($18.10) to 150F ($22.65), not including drinks. Hours are daily from 7pm to 2am. Métro: Vavin.

Sir Winston Churchill, 5 rue de Presbourg, 16e (tel. 45-00-75-35), on a fashionable Right Bank street, is the most authentic-appearing pub in Paris. It uses English advertising posters and serves real ale and imported British tea—along with roast beef and Yorkshire pudding. All the elements of an Edwardian décor are here: cut-glass mirrors, plush banquettes, highly polished dark wood. Complete meals are served, with menus costing 200F ($30.20) to 250F ($37.75). An Irish whiskey costs 32F ($4.85) to 48F ($7.25), depending on whether it's served during the day or at night, when a pair of enthusiastic musicians plays guitar and piano. Hours are daily from 9am to 2am. Métro: Place Charles de Gaulle (Etoile).

Pub Saint-Germain-des-Prés, 17 rue de l'Ancienne-Co-médie, 6e (tel. 43-29-38-70), is the only one in the country to offer 24 draft beers and 450 international beers. Leather niches render drinking discreet. The décor consists of gilded mirrors on the walls, hanging gas lamps, and a stuffed parrot in a gilded cage. Also, leather-cushioned handrails are provided for some mysterious purpose—guidance perhaps? You'll need it. There are nine different rooms and 500 seats, which makes the pub the largest in France. The atmosphere is quiet, relaxed, and rather posh, and it's open day and night nonstop. Genuine Whitbread beer is sold, and Pimm's No. 1 is featured. You can also order snacks or complete meals here. Drinks start at 17F ($2.55), menus begin at 85F ($12.85). In the evening, there is entertainment by a band, both rock and variety. Open daily from 10:30am to 4am. Métro: Odéon.

A Student Hangout

Le Bar. That's the actual name of this small and intimate hangout at 10 rue de l'Odéon, 6e (tel. 43-26-66-83), right off the place de l'Odéon on the Left Bank. This place is permanently thronged with swarms of noisy, friendly, amorous, and argumen-tative university students and is an ideal spot to make contact with them—if that's what you desire. Plastered with posters, both an-tique and pop, it reverberates to the strains of an overworked jukebox. Drinks range in price from 17F ($2.55). Hours are daily from 5:30pm to 2am. Métro: Odéon.

GRAND HOTEL BARS

If you want to re-create the elegance of the salons of 18th-century France in a late-20th-century setting, try one of the bars of the grand hotels of Paris. Dress up, talk softly, and be prepared to spend a lot for a drink. You're not paying for the drink but for an ambience unmatched in most other places.

The **George V Bar,** 31 av. George-V, 8e (tel. 47-23-54-00), is a divinely elegant combination of modern and classical design. All of it is arranged in an attractively symmetrical format of black accents over beige and maroon marble in a design that looks almost like a stage set. Most prominent is the massive crystal lighting fixture whose edges pleasingly correspond to the dimensions of the rectangular room. Of course, if there's someone you're trying to avoid, you can always sit among the upholstered couches and Regency antiques of the nearby salon. Hard drinks cost from 70F ($10.55). Hours are daily from 11am to 2am. Métro: George-V.

Hôtel de Crillon, 10 place de la Concorde, 8e (tel. 42-65-24-24). This world-famous watering hole inside this world-famous hotel used to attract some of the most eminent members of the Lost Generation, including Hemingway and Scott and Zelda Fitzgerald. Do you recall that Hemingway's fictional heroine, Brett Ashley, broke her promise to rendezvous there with Jake Barnes in *The Sun Also Rises?* Over the years it has also attracted most of the Kennedys, along with Noël Coward and practically every upper-level staff member of the American Embassy. Classified as a historic monument, the hotel was recently refurbished under the watchful eye of fashion designer Sonia Rykiel. The décor of the bar no longer basks in its 1950s glow, but has undergone a covering of wood paneling. Drinks cost from 75F ($11.35). It is open daily from noon to 2am. Métro: Concorde.

Bar Anglais, Hôtel Plaza Athénée, 25 av. Montaigne, 8e (tel. 47-23-78-33). On your way through this deluxe citadel, you'll pass a chattering telex machine, which carries recent quotes from the world's leading stock exchanges, in case you want to check on your investment portfolio. In the rarefied atmosphere of this elegant bar, it seems appropriate to do so. As its name would imply, the bar has a décor that is vintage Anglo-Saxon, although the service is definitely French and the drinks, beginning at 75F ($11.35), are international. On the lower level of the hotel, the bar is open daily from 10am to 1am. Métro: Alma-Marceau.

Hôtel Bristol Bar, 112 rue du Faubourg St-Honoré, 8e (tel. 42-66-91-45). Looking over a central courtyard covered with latticework and dotted with greenery, you can sit in wicker chairs between pink marble columns and thick Oriental rugs. Some distance away (one thing about the Bristol is that it has lots of space), a raised platform has a better view of the Regency-style bar. Specialties are usually mixed by the chief barman, Michel Le Regent, who has developed such prize-winning combinations as a "crazy horse cocktail" (strawberries, bananas, scotch, and champagne), a nanny's cocktail (lemon and pineapple juice, blue curaçao, banana liqueur, and vodka), or a Pluton (orange juice, pineapple juice, Pernod, vodka, and strawberries). A pianist adds to the pleasure nightly between 7:30pm and midnight. The bar is open from 11am to 1:30am. Drinks cost from 75F ($11.35). Métro: Miromesnil.

LES DRUG STORES

Le Drug Store, 149 bd. St-Germain-des-Prés, 6e (tel. 42-22-92-05), is an upbeat totally Parisian version of that old corner drugstore and soda fountain back home . . . but vive la différence!

Unlike its American cousin, this establishment is sophisticated and stylish. It still sells shampoo and toothpaste, and has an ice-cream soda fountain, but that's only the beginning. Behind the rather staid façade is a carnival of activity with lots of little boutiques selling everything from baby powder to costume jewelry. The décor is centered around a series of bronze molds of the lips of Moreau, Dietrich, Monroe, Bardot, Greco, and Sagan. At the soda fountain, you can order a banana split or a Coca-Cola float, but champagne and caviar are also available. The most popular item is a hamburger on a toasted bun at 56F ($8.45). There's also a cocktail lounge, a coffeehouse, and a snackbar. Métro: St-Germain-des-Prés or Odéon.

You'll find several other Les Drug Stores, all quite similar to the one at St-Germain, throughout Paris. All are open daily from 10am till 2am, even on Sunday.

TEA ROOMS

The *salon de thé* or tea room has had a surprising revival in Paris. London no longer enjoys a monopoly.

Ladurée, 16 rue Royale, 8e (tel. 42-60-21-79). Here, more than at any other salon de thé in Paris, the men look important, the ladies affluent, and the desmoiselles self-consciously casual. The croissants have been described as superb by battalions of French gastronomes who have watched this establishment flourish during world wars and multiple changes of government. In turn-of-the-century grandeur, you can sip tea or coffee at tables barely big enough to hold a napkin. Matronly waitresses in frilly aprons take orders for light lunches and an array of just-baked pastries, as clients talk quietly beneath the ceiling frescoes of the main salon. There, pink clouds support chubby cherubs as they bake pastries in the heat of the powerful sun. Coffee costs 13.80F ($2.10), tea 16F ($2.40). Hours are Monday through Saturday from 8am to 7pm. Métro: Concorde.

Fanny Tea, 20 place Dauphine, 1er (tel. 43-25-83-67). The tea it serves is so flavorful that it's featured as the leading tea room of Paris in Japanese-language guidebooks. The view from its windows encompasses the orderly rows of trees on one of the most idyllic and historic squares of Paris. Inside, the verdigris wall coverings, the incense, and the well-oiled wooden surfaces give a touch of Victoriana to the minuscule room that is the perfect place to wind down after a tour of the Ile de la Cité. The charming French owner, half descended from Scots, derived the name of her establishment from "theophany" (manifestation of God), corrupting the word into "Fanny Tea." The handwritten menu lists 13 kinds of tea but only one kind of coffee, priced at from 27F ($4.10) each. Homemade pastries, lemon mousse, and toast with smoked salmon cost from 50F ($7.55) each. The tea room is open Saturday and Sunday from 3:30 to 8pm, Tuesday through Friday from 1 to 7:30pm; closed mid-July to the end of August. Métro. Pont-Neuf or Cité.

4. Movies

I don't know what you're doing going to the movies when there's all Paris out there to walk through at night. But if that's your wish (and you know it's a hard habit to break, even on a trip), you'll find English-language films listed in *Pariscope* and in the papers, where the letters "V.O." stand for "Version Originale" and mean that the soundtrack is in the original language and the film is subtitled, not dubbed, in French. Movies run from 2pm to midnight daily, not always continuously, and you often have to stand in line at the theater even during midweek. Many of the major first-run movie palaces are along the Champs-Elysées.

Of special interest is the **Cinémathèque Française,** Musée de Palais de Chaillot, av. President Wilson, 16e (tel. 47-04-24-24). French film aficionados flock to this government-backed theater in droves. Foreign films (which are often shown here) are in their original language with French subtitles. On some days, nearly half a dozen films are shown; on other days, half that. Call for a schedule of what classic or would-be classic is playing. The screen is black on Monday. Métro: Trocadéro.

The largest cinema in Paris (a virtual attraction itself) is **Le Grand Rex,** 1 bd. Poissonière, 2e (tel. 42-36-83-93), seating 2,800 viewers. First-run films in their original versions are the feature here. Métro: Bonne-Nouvelle.

ONE-DAY EXCURSIONS

Paris—the city that grew from an island—is itself the center of a curious landlocked island known as the Ile de France.

Shaped roughly like a saucer, it lies encircled by a thin ribbon of rivers: the Epte, Aisne, Marne, and Yonne. Fringing these rivers are mighty forests with famous names—Rambouillet, St-Germain, Compiègne, and Fontainebleau. These forests are said to be responsible for Paris's clear, gentle air, and the unusual length of its spring and fall. This may be a debatable point, but there's no argument that they provide the capital with a chain of excursion spots, all within easy reach.

The forests were once the possessions of kings and the ruling aristocracy, and they're still sprinkled with the magnificent châteaux or palaces of their former masters. Together with ancient hamlets, glorious cathedrals, and little country inns, they turn the Ile de France into a traveler's paradise. Because of Paris's comparatively small size, it's almost at your doorstep.

The difficult question is: where to go? What I'm offering in this chapter is merely a handful of suggestions out of the dozens of possibilities for one-day jaunts.

1. Versailles

The town of Versailles, about 15 miles from Paris, is a stodgily formal place, but the palace is the sight of a lifetime, unbelievably vast and as ornately artificial as a jewel box.

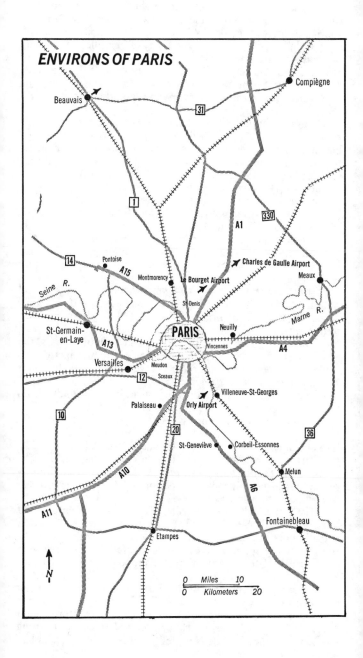

The kings of France built a whole glittering private world for themselves, far from the grime and noise and bustle of Paris. For viewing purposes, the palace is divided up into sections, one including the Hall of Mirrors (where the Treaty of Versailles was signed), the museum, and the Grand Apartments. The other contains the apartments of Madame de Pompadour, the queen's private suites, and the salons. Seeing all of it would take up an entire morning and leave you pretty exhausted. Perhaps you should skip some of the rooms to save energy for the park.

This is the ultimate in French landscaping—every tree, shrub, flower, and hedge disciplined into a frozen ballet pattern and blended with soaring fountains, sparkling little lakes, grandiose stairways, and hundreds of marble statues. More like a colossal stage setting than a park—even the view of the blue horizon seems embroidered on—it's a Garden of Eden for puppet people, a place where you expect the birds to sing coloratura soprano.

The **Grand Apartments,** the **Royal Chapel,** and the **Hall of Mirrors** can be visited without a guide Tuesday through Sunday between 9:45am and 5pm; closed holidays. Admission is 23F ($3.45). Other sections of the château may be visited only at specific hours or on special days. Some of the sections are closed temporarily as they undergo restoration.

Try to save time to visit the **Grand Trianon,** which is a good walk across the park. In pink-and-white marble, it was designed by Hardouin-Mansart for Louis XIV in 1687. The Trianon is furnished mostly with Empire pieces.

You can also visit the **Petit Trianon,** which was built by Gabriel in 1768. This was the favorite residence of Marie Antoinette, who could escape the rigors of court here. Once it was a retreat for Louis XV and his mistress, Madame du Barry.

The Grand Trianon is open Tuesday through Sunday from 9:45am to noon and 2 to 5pm. Entrance costs 15F ($2.25). The Petit Trianon is open the same days from 2 to 5pm; admission is 10F ($1.50). A combination ticket to both Trianons is 18F ($2.70).

On Sunday, reduced rates are available to all visitors: 12F ($1.80) for the château, 8F ($1.20) for the Grand Trianon, 5F (75¢) for the Petit Trianon. The same reduced rates are offered Tuesday through Saturday to people ages 18 through 25 and over 60. For more information, call 39-50-58-32.

The **tourist office** in Versailles (7 rue des Réservoirs, 78000 Versailles; tel. 39-50-36-22) offers a program of evening fireworks and illuminated fountains on several occasions throughout the summer. These spectacles are announced a full season in advance. Dates usually fall on Saturday night, although schedules change from year to year. Spectators sit on bleachers clustered at the boulevard de la Reine entrance to the Basin of Neptune. The most desirable frontal view seats cost 150F ($22.65); seats with a side view go for 75F ($11.35); and standing room on the promenoir sells for 45F ($6.80), free for children under 10. Gates admitting you to the Grande Fête de Nuit de Versailles open one and a half hours before showtime.

Tickets can be purchased in advance at the tourist office in Versailles, or in Paris at Agence Perrossier, 6 place de la Madeleine, 8e (tel. 42-60-58-31), and Agence des Théâtres, 78 av. des Champs-Elysées, 8e (tel. 43-59-24-60). If you've just arrived in Versailles from Paris, you can always take your chances and purchase tickets an hour ahead of showtime at boulevard de la Reine. The show lasts for one and a half hours.

From the beginning of May until the end of September, a less elaborate spectacle is staged each Sunday. Called Grandes Eaux Musicales, it is a display of fountains in the park. Classical music is also played.

GETTING THERE

Versailles lies only 13 miles southwest of Paris. If you're driving down (Rte. N10), you can park your car on the place des Armes in front of the palace. To reach Versailles without a car, it's not necessary to take a guided tour. Instead, take the Métro to the Pont de Sèvres exit and switch onto bus 171. The trip takes 15 minutes. To get there from Paris, it's cheaper if you pay with three Métro tickets from your carnet packet. You'll be let off near the gates of the palace. It's also possible to travel to Versailles on one of the commuter trains leaving every 15 minutes from Paris. The station is connected to the Invalides Métro stop. Go all the way to the Versailles–Rive Gauche station, turning right when you come out. Eurailpass holders travel free.

WHERE TO DINE

For lunch, you can dine in regal style at the **Trianon Palace Hôtel,** 1 bd. de la Reine (tel. 39-50-34-12). Set in a five-acre garden, the hotel became world famous in 1919 when it was the headquarters for the signers of the Treaty of Versailles. It still retains its old-world splendor, its dining room decorated with crystal chandeliers, fluted columns, and cane-backed Louis XVI–style chairs. You can order from an extensive menu that might begin with cold salmon with a green sauce, followed by coquilles St-Jacques provençale (scallops in garlic sauce), plus a selection of vegetables and salads, then a choice from the cheese board, and finally, a rich-tasting dessert, such as meringue glacée Chantilly.

A set menu is offered at 235F ($35.50), including tax and service. You can also select the traditional dishes on the à la carte menu.

Les Trois Marches, 3 rue Colbert (tel. 39-50-13-21). Gérard Vie is, it is conceded, the most talented and creative chef feeding visitors to Versailles these days. He has brought a remarkable culinary experience to his restaurant and, because of that, he attracts a discerning clientele who don't mind paying the high prices. If you order à la carte, it is likely to cost from 650F ($98.15). Fixed-price meals, however, go for 325F ($49.10) to 450F ($67.95), including service.

The cuisine moderne is subtle, often daringly inventive and

conceived, the service smooth. In summer you can dine in a garden partially shaded from the sun by a tent. The main building is a former private house from the 18th century, filled with sumptuous curtains and fine paneling.

Specialties are likely to include roast pigeon in a garlic-cream sauce (bound with its own blood), a celery terrine with duck liver, and veal with sea urchins, along with ravioli stuffed with lobster, truffles, and spinach. The restaurant is open Tuesday through Saturday from noon to 2pm and 8 to 9:30pm. Reservations are essential.

Le Rescatore, 27 av. St-Cloud (tel. 39-50-23-60), in the center of town, is devoted entirely to seafood. The décor is classic and conservative, within a pink-hued, high-ceilinged room whose tall French doors overlook ornate wrought-iron balconies and the busy avenue below. The chef de cuisine, Jacques Bagot, creates an illusion of living near the sea with his cassoulet of fish, his perfectly prepared turbot sweetened with mild garlic, and his pot-au-feu of seafood. Occasionally he offers a selection of grilled exotic fish.

A superb fixed-price menu is offered for 225F ($34), but it's available only at lunch Monday to Friday. The same menu is served to diners who pay 350F ($52.85) at night. Open Monday through Friday from 12:30 to 2pm and 7:30 to 10pm, Saturday from 7:30 to 10pm.

Le Potager du Roy, 1 rue du Maréchal Joffre (tel. 39-50-35-34). Philippe Le Tourneur used to work for another Versailles chef, Gérard Vié, before setting up his own attractive restaurant on a busy streetcorner in a commercial part of town. Set behind a maroon façade, in a modern décor of several warmly decorated rooms, he offers a menu for 150F ($22.65). You can also dine à la carte for around the same price. You might begin with a lamb terrine with raisins and pistachio nuts, then follow with calf's head in a ravigote sauce or steamed filet of sole with summer vegetables. You might also try roast lamb en papillote. Open Tuesday through Saturday from noon to 2pm and 7:30 to 10pm.

2. Fontainebleau

South of Paris on the main route to Lyons, around one hour by frequent train from the Gare de Lyons, is yet another royal palace. This one is surrounded by a superb forest of 50,000 acres, the hunting preserve of monarchs from François I to Napoléon.

Fontainebleau Palace is smaller and more intimate than Versailles. It's a product of the French 16th-century Renaissance, built before styles went rococo. Napoléon later added most of the furnishings you'll see.

The surrounding forest is a magical retreat of ravines, wild gorges, Martian rock formations, and dark ponds. A beautiful area for hikes and picnics, it used to lure some of the greatest 19th-century painters—among them Millet and Rousseau—who turned the nearby village of **Barbizon** into an artists' colony.

The apartments at the château (tel. 64-22-27-40) are open Wednesday through Monday from 9:30am to 12:30pm and 2 to 5pm. The last ticket is sold 45 minutes before closing. Admission to the Grands Apartments is 25F ($3.80); to the Petits Apartments, 14F ($2.10).

GETTING THERE

Fontainebleau is reached by frequent train service from the Gare de Lyons in Paris, a 37-mile journey. Depending on which train you take, the trip lasts from 35 minutes to one hour. The train station of Fontainebleau is just outside the town in Avon, a suburb of Paris. For the two-mile trip to the château, you can take the town bus, which makes a round trip every 10 to 15 minutes Monday through Saturday, every 30 minutes on Sunday.

WHERE TO DINE

One of the leading restaurants is **Le Beauharnais** at the Hôtel de l'Aigle Noir (Black Eagle Hotel), 27 place Napoléon-Bonaparte (tel. 64-22-32-65). Although it's been completely renovated, it has retained its old charm. Opposite the château, the building was once the home of the cardinal of Retz. It dates from the 16th century, but was converted into a hotel in 1720. The restaurant, the most beautiful in town, was installed in a former courtyard. The interior is filled with Empire furniture and potted palms.

Specialties include roast duckling in the style of Rouen, sweetbreads with foie gras served pot-au-feu, and grilled pigeon with pistachio nuts. There is a changing array of other dishes, depending on seasonal produce. Open daily from 12:30 to 2:30pm and 7:30 to 9:30pm. Set menus range from 200F ($30.20) to 280F ($42.30), with à la carte dinners averaging 400F ($60.40).

The hotel has 57 bedrooms and suites, all with private baths and such modern conveniences as color TVs, radios, minibars, direct-dial phones, double windows, and electric heating. Each is individually decorated, often with antiques and pleasantly tasteful colors. Singles range in price from 790F ($119.30); doubles, from 950F ($143.45).

Le Dauphin, 24-26 Grande-Rue (tel. 64-22-27-04), offers one of the best and most inexpensive meals in town. In the inner city, it is near the tourist office, a short walk from the château. The décor is that of a country tavern, with walls upholstered in flowery fabrics. Specialties include endive in roquefort dressing, steak au poivre flambé in cognac, and confit de canard (duck) from Landes with flap mushrooms. Dessert could be a tarte tatin or a pear sorbet. Fixed-price menus cost 72F ($10.85) Monday to Saturday, going up to 135F ($20.40) on Sunday. A la carte dinners could run as high as 180F ($27.20). The restaurant serves Tuesday from noon to 2pm, Thursday through Monday from noon to 2pm and 7 to 9:30pm; closed February and one week in September.

Le Filet de Sole, 5-7 rue du Coq-Gris (tel. 64-22-25-05), is an honored little restaurant, just a few minutes' walk from the château. Its neo-Norman façade is difficult to spot on a narrow street deep in the heart of town, but it's well worth the search. You might begin with a lobster or fish soup, followed by your main dish, perhaps the namesake of the restaurant: filets de sole with a lobster sauce or else veal kidneys. Mouthwatering crêpes suzette is the preferred dessert, for two people. During the week, the only fixed-price menu served costs 110F ($16.60) for three courses. However, on Sunday, a four-course midday menu goes for only 150F ($22.65), with à la carte dinners averaging around 250F ($37.75). The restaurant is open Thursday through Monday from noon to 2pm and 7 to 9pm; closed July. It's run by Mr. and Mrs. René Vachet. He is the chef; his wife usually greets you at the door.

---

3. Chantilly

This elegant little town 30 miles north of Paris boasts the finest racecourse as well as the most enchanting château in France. It's just an hour by train from the Gare du Nord, but take my tip and *don't* go during the racing season (first two weeks of June and September) unless you like getting stomped by turf fanatics.

The famed Chantilly racing stables—almost as delightful as the palace—are decorated with carvings and sculptures that could grace any mansion. But the actual château, once the seat of the dukes of Condé, is a fairy-tale creation.

Château de Chantilly and **Musée Condé** are idyllically situated on an artificial lake, lying about one and a half miles from the station. You approach it through a shady forest glade. Suddenly, it lies before you—dazzling white with blue roofs, reflected in the blue waters of the garden lakes, surrounded by lawns like green velvet. It's all turrets and towers and gables that seem to have been manufactured for a Hollywood epic. Inside are some of the country's greatest art treasures, including pictures by Holbein, Raphael, and Giotto. The château and museum (tel. 44-57-08-00) are open April through October, Wednesday to Monday from 10am to 6pm; November through March, Wednesday to Monday from 10:30am to 5pm. Admission is 30F ($4.55). Trains leave Gare du Nord station in Paris, the trip taking about an hour.

WHERE TO DINE

A favorite restaurant in town is **Tipperary,** 6 av. du Maréchal Joffre (tel. 44-57-00-48). Monsieur and Madame Greffe will welcome you to their traditional establishment on the main floor of a town house. Café tables are placed outdoors, and in fair weather you can enjoy an apéritif here. To begin your repast, try the chef's specialty, ravioli stuffed with shrimp and snails. Other specialties include marinated salmon and sea bass with a crêpe and fresh cream and herbs, scallops, roast duck with apples, and soufflés. Expect to spend at least 180F ($27.20) for a really good meal. Open daily from noon to 2:30pm and 7 to 10:30pm.

Les Quatre Saisons de Chantilly, 9 av. du Général Leclerc (tel. 44-57-04-65), is a winning Franco-Scandinavian combination on a major artery on the outskirts of town. Meals are served in a flowered terrace. However, if you decide to eat inside, the décor there is almost like a garden too. Menu items are divided into equal parts of Nordic, Burgundian, and moderne. The marinated herring might be the best way to begin your meal, which could then include several kinds of salmon dishes (one in smoked blini), plus a wide range of Danish beers or French wines. The restaurant is enormously popular and is connected with the famed Flora Danica in Paris. Fixed-price meals cost from 150F ($22.65). A la carte dinners go for 300F ($45.30). Meals are served daily from noon to 2:30pm and 7 to 10:30pm; closed Sunday from November through March; closed January 2 to 16.

---

4. Chartres

This medieval city 60 miles southwest of Paris houses one of the world's greatest Gothic cathedrals. Chartres is a one-hour ride by train from the Gare Montparnasse.

Even if you're tired of church architecture, Chartres is unforgettable. The cathedral was completed in 1220 and features all the painstaking artistry to which the craftsmen of the Middle Ages devoted their lives. The Portail Royal, on the west side, is a piece of carving unmatched anywhere, while the vaulted interior is transformed into a stone fantasy by the light streaming in through the superlative stained-glass windows. The whole structure seems to change its form as the light varies during the day.

The city matches the cathedral—a huddle of gabled houses, some of them dating back seven or more centuries, sprinkled with equally ancient inns dishing up a memorable French provincial cuisine.

WHERE TO DINE

The finest of the lot is **Henri IV,** 31 rue Soleil-d'Or (tel. 37-36-01-55). For years, the "brigade" taught by the late Monsieur Maurice Cazalis, one of the master chefs, has been welcoming gourmet-minded Parisians and foreigners who journey south to the cathedral city. Specialties remain the grand tradition of French cuisine, but the sauces are lighter today. Specialties include turbot with pistachio butter, filet of sole in orange sauce, duck liver with apples, and homemade pastries. I recommend the small meringue cakes with nuts, named in honor of George Sand. On the ground floor, simpler and less expensive courses are offered. On the second floor of a tiny house, a few minutes' walk from Chartres cathedral, the restaurant has paneled walls and beams overhead, not enough décor, really, to distract from the grande cuisine.

The cost-conscious will stick to the standard menu of 180F ($27.20). Others can order à la carte at 300F ($45.30). Incidentally, the restaurant has one of the best *cartes des vins* in France. Don't just take my word for that. It's officially recognized as such. Open Monday from 11:45am to 2:15pm, Wednesday through Sunday from 11:45am to 2:15pm and 6:30 to 9pm; closed for part of February.

Another old-style inn is **Normand,** 24 place des Epars (tel. 37-21-04-38). Even farther from the cathedral, but still within walking distance, this restaurant offers the personalized cuisine of Madame Normand. Plaster walls with timbers, lamps of wrought iron, even stained-glass windows from the backdrop for this cozy restaurant. Specialties on Madame's à la carte menu include coq au vin, escalope normande, and Normandy chicken. You can always get a good grilled steak. The chef prepares excellent pastries as well. Count on spending from 100F ($15.10) to 200F ($30.20) for a complete meal. The restaurant is open Tuesday through Sunday from noon to 2:15pm and 6:45 to 9pm; closed holidays.

5. Rouen

The capital of Normandy lies beyond the Ile de France, but so close that it makes my one-day excursion list. It's just 70 minutes by train from St-Lazare station.

Known as the "hundred-spired city," Rouen is a living museum of a town, showing every type of building erected in France, from 4th-century walls to 1980s office blocks. The modern impact is a result of the bomb damage suffered by Rouen during the Allied invasion of Normandy in 1944, but standing intact is **place du Vieux-Marché,** the gabled marketplace where Joan of Arc was burned at the stake on May 30, 1431. A mosaic marks the spot.

An even more important site is **Rouen Cathedral,** whose spirit was captured in a series of paintings by Monet. It, too, was heavily bombed, but has been restored. The cathedral was originally consecrated in 1063, and it has seen many building crews over the centuries. It's distinguished by two soaring towers, one called the Tour de Beurre (Tower of Butter). The devout, willing to pay for the privilege of eating butter during Lent, financed its construction. It was built in the flamboyant Gothic style. Inside, the Chapelle de la Vierge is graced with the tombs of the cardinals d'Amboise in the Renaissance style. Also, Jean Goujon designed a tomb for Louis de Brézé, the husband of Diane de Poitiers. Richard the Lion-Hearted, incidentally, gave his "heart" to the people of Rouen as a token of affection.

The **Church of Saint-Maclou,** in back of the cathedral, is built in the florid Gothic style. It contains handsome cloisters plus a step-gabled porch. This church is known for its panels of doors, dating from the 16th century. Rebuilt in 1436, Saint-Maclou was consecrated in 1521. The lantern tower, however, is from the 19th century.

The **Church of Saint-Ouen** is reached by walking down rue de la République to the place du Général de Gaulle. Originally a 7th-century Benedictine abbey, it is now a Gothic church, one of the best known in France, with an octagonal lantern tower called "the ducal crown of Normandy." The stained glass inside is remarkable.

Three museums are important. The **Musée des Beaux-Arts,** place Verdrel (tel. 35-71-28-40), is considered one of the finest provincial museums of art in the country. It includes works by Ingres, Delacroix, Caravaggio, Velázquez, and various impressionists, including a version of *Rouen Cathedral* by Monet.

Even more fascinating to some is the unique **Le Secq des Tournelles,** a museum of wrought iron (entrance on rue Jacques-Villon). The museum (tel. 35-07-31-74) is sheltered in the Church of Saint-Laurent, which dates from the 15th century. More than 12,000 pieces of wrought iron, including everything from Roman keys to sophisticated jewelry, are to be found here.

Musée de la Céramique, 1 rue Faucon (tel. 35-07-31-74), is in a 17th-century house. One of the greatest treasures is the Rouen faïence, which pioneered a special red glaze in 1670. Porcelain by two masters, Abaquesne and Poterat, is exhibited, and an exceptional showcase is devoted to chinoiseries dating from 1699 to 1745.

Admission to each museum is 11F ($1.65). They are all open Wednesday from 2 to 6pm, Thursday through Monday from 10am to noon and 2 to 6pm.

WHERE TO DINE

Rouen is famous for its duck. The best place to sample it is at **La Couronne,** 31 place du Vieux Marché (tel. 35-71-40-90). A half-timbered building on the square where Joan of Arc met her death, this is the oldest restaurant in the city, dating from 1345. In fact, it claims to be the oldest auberge in all of France. Dining is on several crooked floors. The dish everybody orders here is caneton (duckling) à la rouennaise for two persons. The duck's neck is wrung so as not to lose any blood. It is then roasted, the breast slices flamed in Calvados. Then it is covered in a blood sauce. The drumsticks are grilled until crisp. Other specialties are filets of sole cardinal (with lobster and lobster sauce), sautéed duck liver with Pommeau, a liqueur from Normandy, and soufflé Norman with Calvados.

Set menus are offered for 195F ($29.45) and 250F ($37.75), plus wine. If you order à la carte, dinner will cost around 350F ($52.85). The restaurant is open daily from noon to 2:30pm and 7:30 to 10:30pm.

Maison Dufour, 67 rue St-Nicolas (tel. 35-71-90-62), is also good. A 17th-century inn, it is a five-story corner building in the typical style of plaster and timbers. Under mellowed beams, you have your choice of several dining rooms. An always reliable opener is a kettle of black mussels in a creamy sauce. You might also enjoy chicken from the Auge Valley or brains in a black butter sauce. Lamb in a garlic-cream sauce is another enticing main dish. Set menus range from 140F ($21.15) to 220F ($33.20), with à la carte dinners averaging 240F ($36.25). The restaurant is open Sunday from 12:15 to 1:45pm, Tuesday through Saturday from 12:15 to 1:45pm and 7:15 to 9:30pm; closed in August.

BEYOND PARIS

After Paris, where? This question poses the knottiest problem of the entire book. The answer entails not just an embarrassment of riches, but an inundation.

Covering 212,741 square miles, France is slightly smaller than Texas. But no other patch on the globe concentrates such a fabulous diversity of sights and scenery in so compact an area.

Within its borders, France houses each of the natural characteristics that make up Europe: the flat, fertile north, the rolling green hills of the central Loire country, the snow-capped alpine ranges of the east, the starkly towering Pyrenees in the south, and the lushly semitropical Mediterranean coast of the southeast.

Name your taste and France has a spot for you. The château country around Orléans for castles and vineyards. Normandy and Brittany for rugged seashores and apple orchards. The Mont Blanc area for mountain-climbing and skiing. The Champagne for sun-warmed valleys and the greatest of all wines. Languedoc for Spanish flavor, olive groves, and Provençal cooking. The Riviera for golden sands, palm-fringed beaches, and bodies beautiful.

Because the country is—by American standards—not very large, all these contrasts beckon within easy traveling range. By train from Paris, it's just four hours to **Alsace,** five hours to the **Alps,** seven hours to the **Pyrenees,** and eight hours to the **Côte d'Azur.**

France's National Railroads (SNCF) operate one of the finest services in the world. Most of the lines are electrified, the trains impeccably punctual, clean, and comfortable, the food excellent but expensive. They're also impressively fast to and from Paris, but more inclined to crawl on the routes unconnected with the capital.

The French National Railroads is also the major promoter of the remarkable **Eurailpass,** allowing you unlimited rail transportation in Western Europe, which can be purchased only in North America before you leave on your trip. Be sure to consult your travel agent about a Eurailpass if you plan to visit several European cities or countries.

There are some 44,000 miles of roadway at your disposal, most in good condition for fast, long-distance driving. But take a tip and don't stick to the autoroute network all the time. Nearly all the scenic splendors lie alongside the secondary roads, and what you'll lose in mileage you'll more than make up for in enjoyment.

But this still leaves you with the question—where to?

The answer depends entirely on your time, whim, and inclination. Here I'll give you merely a few sample tidbits, each from a contrasting area, to nudge your private decision computer. However, in a larger companion guide to this book, I document all the major provinces of France. It's jam-packed with information and is called *Frommer's France.*

THE LOIRE VALLEY

About 120 miles southwest of Paris stretches the "green heart of France," the breathtakingly beautiful region of the Loire Valley. The towns of this area have magic names, but they also read like Joan of Arc's battle register—Orléans, Blois, Tours, Chinon. Every hilltop has a castle or palace, there are vineyards as far as your eye can see, the Loire winds through like a silver ribbon, and the walled cities cluster around medieval churches.

Unless you're driving, I advise you to take one of the organized tours of this region, since you couldn't see more than a fraction of its charms otherwise. **Cityrama** runs a two-day jaunt of the area, operated April through mid-November. The trip includes a visit to Chartres, Châteaudun, Tours, Langeais, Azay-le-Rideau, Vouvray, and a historical "Sound and Light" spectacle at Amboise. However, the best way to tour the château country is in your own rented car.

It is estimated that the average American spends only three nights in the Loire Valley. A week would be better. Even then, you will have only skimmed the surface. If you're severely hampered by lack of time, then try at least to see the following châteaux: Chenonceaux, Amboise, Azay-le-Rideau, Chambord, Chaumont, and Blois.

MONT-ST-MICHEL

Massive walls, more than half a mile in circumference, enclose what is considered one of the greatest sightseeing attractions in Europe. At the border between Normandy and Brittany, the citadel crowns a rocky islet. Seen for miles around, the rock rises 260 feet high.

The tides around Mont-St-Michel are notorious, having claimed lives. They are reputedly the highest on the continent of Europe. At particular times of the year they rise upward to 50 feet. It is dangerous to wander across the sands around the mount. Many have been trapped in quicksands.

A causeway links the granite hilltop to the mainland. A Benedictine monastery was founded on this spot in 966 by Richard I, Duke of Normandy. It was destroyed by fire in 1203, but subsequently rebuilt. One of the most important Gothic masterpieces in Europe, the Merveille (Marvel), is enclosed by ramparts. The abbey church dates from the 11th century, and is noted for its flamboyant Gothic choir, as well as a Romanesque nave and transept.

The abbey stays open year round, and you must take a guided tour to see it. However, tours leave every 15 minutes and last less than an hour.

Those journeying here from Paris by train have to get off at Pontorson. This is the nearest station to "The Mont," although it is six miles away. Bus connections take you to the abbey.

While in Mont-St-Michel, it's customary to order one of the legendary omelets at **La Mère Poulard,** which you'll see on your right as you begin your long climb to the abbey.

REIMS AND VERDUN

This means a journey to the memory of two world wars. Reims, 100 miles northeast of Paris, has one of mankind's greatest Gothic cathedrals. Dating from the 13th century, it was almost reduced to rubble by shellfire in 1914–1918, then painstakingly rebuilt with funds from a Rockefeller grant. It also contains the schoolhouse in which the Germans surrendered on May 7, 1945.

Nearby Verdun marks France's bloodiest battle epic. The old fortress town created the motto "They shall not pass!" They didn't . . . but the price was terrible, and the relics of that 1916 stand make somber viewing.

But the country all around is the champagne region, where you can sample the most splendid of all wines right at the source.

DINARD AND ST-MALO

These enchanting resort towns in Brittany, on the northwest coast, face each other across an estuary. St-Malo, an ancient pirates' stronghold and walled fishing village, is the more colorful; Dinard, with a gambling casino, sheltered beach, golf courses, and tennis courts, the more playful. Since they're only a boat hop apart, you can enjoy both in one trip. The scenery all around is superb.

Brittany is fascinatingly "alien," the native Breton a Celtic language more akin to Gaelic than to French. The entire peninsula has 600 miles of coast, with chains of beaches, rustic fishing ports, and some of the greatest seafood you'll ever taste.

LANGUEDOC AND PROVENCE

The Rhône River forms the dividing line between Languedoc in the west and Provence in the east. Both portions are equally drenched in sunshine, sprinkled with vineyards and olive groves, and dotted with fascinating towns. The main difference is that Languedoc has an intriguing Spanish air and is somewhat less fashionable, and thus less expensive, than Provence.

Two of its most charming cities are **Nîmes** and **Montpellier,** only 31 miles apart. Nîmes contains the most impressive Roman ruins in France, including an Arena and the Temple of Diana. Montpellier is the center of southern wine production and lies in a scenic setting of unsurpassed beauty.

Provence, on the east side of the Rhône River, can be divided into two units from the vacation viewpoint. The portion closer to the Rhône is studded with fascinating towns—large and tiny— each of which provides a holiday setting.

There's **Avignon,** surrounded by ancient ramparts and the seat of the popes during the 14th century. **Arles** cast a spell over Van Gogh and inspired some of his greatest paintings. **Marseille,** the second-largest city in France, is one of the world's major seaports and among the most colorful, turbulent, sometimes dangerous, and exotic places in the country.

THE FRENCH RIVIERA

Now we come to France's sunny south, the holiday region par excellence. Known to the world as the **Côte d'Azur,** this is a short stretch of curving coastline near the Italian border. Much to the delight of vacationers from all parts of the globe, it's a land drenched in sunshine, sprinkled with vineyards and olive groves, and dotted with some of the world's most fascinating tourist meccas.

The season doesn't start till June and lasts only till September, although many shrewd travelers prefer the months of May and October. During those out-of-favor periods, the crowds often drop by more than 70%, the prices by about 20%. The Riviera can give you then exactly what the travel posters promise.

In winter, although it's too cold for swimming, the temperature is higher here than in the rest of France, mainly because of the alpine chain that protects the Côte d'Azur from those cold continental winds. Towns such as Menton have long enjoyed a thriving colony of expatriate visitors, drawn to such rich Mediterranean vegetation as the mimosa, the rose-laurel, jasmine, carnation, rose, the creeping and crawling bougainvillea, the eucalyptus fluttering in the sea breezes, and the orange and lemon trees studding the hillsides. Nice boasts only three days of frost per year, with an average January temperature hovering around 48°F. In October the average temperature at Nice is about 77°F.

Perhaps the most compelling endorsement of the Riviera has been the number of artists drawn to its shores and hillside villas. At Cagnes, Renoir praised the "light effects" of the region. Bonnard stayed at Le Cannet. Nice was selected by Matisse as the spot in which to spend the final years of his life (you can visit his remarkable Chapel of Saint Dominique at Vence). For the fishermen of Villefranche, Cocteau decorated a chapel. Picasso left an art legacy from one end of the Riviera to the other. Even on one of the rainy days that occasionally occur, you can enjoy an "art-hopping" tour, seeing some of the most interesting contemporary work in Europe, such as the Léger Museum at Biot.

A trio of roads or corniches connects Nice with the Italian frontier, over a distance of 20 miles. The Middle Corniche, finished at the outbreak of World War II, was created specifically for tourists, although they didn't see fit to use it extensively until many years had passed. Motorists taking this route, even rushed motorists, should stop off at the "eagle's nest" village of **Eze,** resting on a peak more than 1,312 feet above sea level. Originally, Napoléon ordered the construction of the Grand Corniche to replace the old Roman Aurelian Way. The Shoreline Corniche is in many ways the most interesting. You don't get the lofty spectacular views afforded by the two other motor roads, but you do receive a firsthand preview of the string of resorts dotting the coastline, including Saint-Jean-Cap-Ferrat, where W. Somerset Maugham lived for so many years.

Selecting your resort might be your most difficult decision, as there are at least 26 of them, spread out along a distance of 70 miles from Menton to Saint-Raphaël, their joie de vivre varying widely. Nearly all of them have one thing in common—an excellent range of hotel facilities. The Côte d'Azur is one of the most heavily built-up hotel districts in the world. From the most elegantly furnished "palace" to the more modest converted once-private villa that now receives paying guests, you'll nearly always find an accommodation to fit your tastes and your pocketbook.

Of course, one of the reasons visitors come to the Riviera is to dine. Do try some of the specialties, especially the salade niçoise, which can mean different things to different chefs but essentially includes fresh vine-ripened tomatoes, small radishes—either red or black—green peppers, and often potatoes and green beans. The thick, saffron-flavored fish soup of the Mediterranean, the bouillabaisse, is eagerly ordered by diners all over the Riviera, as is the ratatouille (a mixture of small eggplants, tomatoes, miniature squash, and red peppers simmered in olive oil).

CHAMONIX–MONT BLANC

At an altitude of 3,422 feet, Chamonix, opening onto Mont Blanc, is the historic capital of alpine skiing. Chamonix lies huddled in a valley, almost at the junction of France, Italy, and Switzerland. Dedicated skiers all over the world know of its ten-mile Vallée Blanche run, considered one of the most rugged in Europe, certainly the longest. Daredevils also flock here for the mountain climbing and the hang-gliding.

A charming, old-fashioned mountain town, Chamonix has a most thrilling backdrop—Mont Blanc, Europe's highest mountain, rising to a peak of 15,771 feet.

With the opening of the seven-mile miracle, the Mont Blanc Tunnel, Chamonix became a major stage on one of the busiest highways in Europe. The tunnel provides the easiest way to go through the mountains to Italy, by literally going under those mountains. Motorists now stop at Chamonix even if they aren't interested in winter skiing or summer mountain climbing.

Because of its exceptional equipment, Chamonix is one of the major resorts of Europe, attracting an international crowd. The Casino de Chamonix is the hub of its nightlife activity.

STRASBOURG

Capital of Alsace, Strasbourg is one of France's greatest cities. It is also the capital of pâté de foie gras. It was in Strasbourg that Rouget de Lisle first sang the "Marseillaise." In June of every year, the artistic life of Strasbourg reaches its zenith at the **International Music Festival** held at the Château des Rohan and at the cathedral.

Strasbourg is not only a great university city, the seat of the Council of Europe, but one of France's most important ports, lying two miles west of the Rhine. Visits by motor launch and a number of Rhine excursions are offered from there. Go to the tourist office at the place Gutenberg for the most up-to-date data on these excursions, whose schedules vary, depending on the season and the number of passengers interested.

Despite war damage, much remains of **Old Strasbourg.** It still has covered bridges and the old towers of its former fortifications, and many 15th- and 17th-century dwellings with painted wooden fronts and carved beams.

The **Strasbourg Cathedral,** which inspired the poetry of Goethe, was built on the site of a Romanesque church of 1015. Today it stands proudly, one of the largest churches of Christianity, and one of the most outstanding examples of German Gothic, representing a harmonious transition from the Romanesque. Construction on it began in 1176.

INDEX

GENERAL INFORMATION

SIGHTS AND ATTRACTIONS

ACCOMMODATIONS

Paris

Key to Abbreviations: *B* = Budget ("Great Value"); *M* = Moderate; *VE* = Very Expensive, Deluxe, and First Class

RESTAURANTS

Paris

Key to Abbreviations: *B* = Budget; *E* = Expensive; *M* = Moderately Priced; *VE* = Very Expensive ("Great")

Outside Paris

NOW, SAVE MONEY ON ALL
YOUR TRAVELS!
Join Frommer's™ Dollarwise® Travel Club

Saving money while traveling is never a simple matter, which is why the **Dollarwise Travel Club** was formed 31 years ago. Developed in response to requests from Frommer's Travel Guide readers, the Club provides cost-cutting travel strategies, up-to-date travel information, and a sense of community for value-conscious travelers from all over the world.

In keeping with the money-saving concept, the annual membership fee is low—$18 for U.S. residents or $20 for residents of Canada, Mexico, and other countries—and is immediately exceeded by the value of your benefits, which include:

1. Any TWO books listed on the following pages.
2. Plus any ONE Frommer's City Guide.
3. A subscription to our quarterly newspaper, *The Dollarwise Traveler*.
4. A membership card that entitles you to purchase through the Club all Frommer's publications for 33% to 50% off their retail price.

The eight-page **Dollarwise Traveler** tells you about the latest developments in good-value travel worldwide and includes the following columns: **Hospitality Exchange** (for those offering and seeking hospitality in cities all over the world); **Share-a-Trip** (for those looking for travel companions to share costs); and **Readers Ask . . . Readers Reply** (for those with travel questions that other members can answer).

Aside from the Frommer's Guides and the Gault Millau Guides, you can also choose from our Special Editions. These include such titles as *California with Kids* (a compendium of the best of California's accommodations, restaurants, and sightseeing attractions appropriate for those traveling with toddlers through teens); *Candy Apple: New York with Kids* (a spirited guide to the Big Apple by a savvy New York grandmother that's perfect for both visitors and residents); *Caribbean Hideaways* (the 100 most romantic places to stay in the Islands, all rated on ambience, food, sports opportunities, and price); *Honeymoon Destinations* (a guide to planning and choosing just the right destination from hundreds of possibilities in the U.S., Mexico, and the Caribbean); *Marilyn Wood's Wonderful Weekends* (a selection of the best mini-vacations within a 200-mile radius of New York City, including descriptions of country inns and other accommodations, restaurants, picnic spots, sights, and activities); and *Paris Rendez-Vous* (a delightful guide to the best places to meet in Paris whether for power breakfasts or dancing till dawn).

To join this Club, simply send the appropriate membership fee with your name and address to: Frommer's Dollarwise Travel Club, 15 Columbus Circle, New York, NY 10023. Remember to specify which single city guide and which two other guides you wish to receive in your initial package of member's benefits. Or tear out the next page, check off your choices, and send the page to us with your membership fee.

FROMMER BOOKS
PRENTICE HALL PRESS
15 COLUMBUS CIRCLE
NEW YORK, NY 10023
212/373-8125

Date_____

Friends:

Please send me the books checked below.

FROMMER'S™ GUIDES

(Guides to sightseeing and tourist accommodations and facilities from budget to deluxe, with emphasis on the medium-priced.)

☐ Alaska. $14.95		☐ Germany $14.95
☐ Australia $14.95		☐ Italy $14.95
☐ Austria & Hungary $14.95		☐ Japan & Hong Kong. $14.95
☐ Belgium, Holland & Lux-		☐ Mid-Atlantic States $14.95
embourg $14.95		☐ New England $14.95
☐ Bermuda & The Bahamas $14.95		☐ New York State. $14.95
☐ Brazil $14.95		☐ Northwest. $14.95
☐ Canada. $14.95		☐ Portugal, Madeira & the Azores. $14.95
☐ Caribbean $14.95		☐ Skiing Europe $14.95
☐ Cruises (incl. Alaska, Carib, Mex, Ha-		☐ South Pacific $14.95
waii, Panama, Canada & US). .$14.95		☐ Southeast Asia $14.95
☐ California & Las Vegas. $14.95		☐ Southern Atlantic States $14.95
☐ Egypt $14.95		☐ Southwest. $14.95
☐ England & Scotland. $14.95		☐ Switzerland & Liechtenstein. $14.95
☐ Florida $14.95		☐ USA $15.95
☐ France. $14.95		

FROMMER'S $-A-DAY® GUIDES

(In-depth guides to sightseeing and low-cost tourist accommodations and facilities.)

☐ Europe on $40 a Day $15.95		☐ New York on $60 a Day $13.95
☐ Australia on $40 a Day $13.95		☐ New Zealand on $45 a Day. $13.95
☐ Eastern Europe on $25 a Day .$13.95		☐ Scandinavia on $60 a Day. $13.95
☐ England on $50 a Day $13.95		☐ Scotland & Wales on $40 a Day. $13.95
☐ Greece on $35 a Day $13.95		☐ South America on $35 a Day. $13.95
☐ Hawaii on $60 a Day $13.95		☐ Spain & Morocco on $40 a Day $13.95
☐ India on $25 a Day $12.95		☐ Turkey on $30 a Day $13.95
☐ Ireland on $35 a Day $13.95		☐ Washington, D.C. & Historic Va. on
☐ Israel on $40 a Day $13.95		$40 a Day $13.95
☐ Mexico on $35 a Day. $13.95		

FROMMER'S TOURING GUIDES

(Color illustrated guides that include walking tours, cultural and historic sites, and other vital travel information.)

☐ Amsterdam $10.95		☐ New York. . . . . : $10.95
☐ Australia. $9.95		☐ Paris. $8.95
☐ Brazil $10.95		☐ Rome $10.95
☐ Egypt $8.95		☐ Scotland $9.95
☐ Florence $8.95		☐ Thailand $9.95
☐ Hong Kong $10.95		☐ Turkey. $10.95
☐ London. $8.95		☐ Venice. $8.95

TURN PAGE FOR ADDITONAL BOOKS AND ORDER FORM

0690